AGRICULTURE AND TRADE IN CHINA AND INDIA

AGRICULTURE AND TRADE IN CHINA AND INDIA
POLICIES AND PERFORMANCE SINCE 1950

T. N. Srinivasan
with contributions from
Justin Yifu Lin and Yun-Wing Sung

An International Center for Economic Growth Publication

ICS Press
San Francisco, California

The authors would like to acknowledge the assistance of Louise Dani-shevsky and Heidi Fritschel in the publication of this book.

© **1994 Institute for Contemporary Studies**

Publication of this book was funded by the United States Agency for International Development (AID), the Pew Charitable Trusts, and the Starr Foundation.

Publication signifies that the International Center for Economic Growth believes a work to be a competent treatment worthy of public consider-ation. The findings, interpretations, and conclusions of a work are en-tirely those of the author and should not be attributed to ICEG, its affil-iated organizations, its Board of Overseers, or organizations that support ICEG.

Inquiries, book orders, and catalog requests should be addressed to ICS Press, 720 Market Street, San Francisco, California, 94102. Telephone: (415) 981-5353; fax: (415) 986-4878. For book orders and catalog requests, call toll free in the continental United States: **(800) 326-0263.**

Editing by Heidi Fritschel
Index by Shirley Kessel
Cover design by Irene Imfeld

Library of Congress Cataloging-in-Publication Data

Srinivasan, T. N., 1933–
    Agriculture and trade in China and India : policies and performance since 1950 / T.N. Srinivasan, with contributions from Justin Yifu Lin and Yun-Wing Sung.
      p.   cm.
    "An International Center for Economic Growth publication."
    Includes bibliographical references and index.
    ISBN 1-55815-281-4
    1. Produce trade—Government policy—China.   2. Produce trade—Government policy—India.   3. Agriculture and state—China.
    4. Agriculture and State—India.   5. China—Commercial policy.
    6. India—Commercial policy.   7. China—Economic policy—1949–
    8. India—Economic policy—1947–   I. Lin, Justin Yifu.   II. Sung, Yun-Wing.   III. Title.
    HD9016.C62S65   1994
    338.1′851—dc20   93-32010
                                                    CIP

CONTENTS

LIST OF TABLES

LIST OF FIGURES

PREFACE

The world's two most populous countries, China and India, are currently engaged in an attempt to liberalize and revitalize their economies after decades of state control. Although the two nations adopted different political systems in the 1940s—communism in China and democracy in India—they followed similar development strategies from the early 1950s through the 1980s. In both countries, the state was the engine of development, and planning guided economic decisions. Now each is faced with undoing decades of government control, regulation, and ownership of economic enterprises.

China began its economic reforms in 1978 under Deng Xiaoping. Since then it has gradually allowed for greater individual initiative by farmers and businesspeople and has conducted a number of experiments in liberalization in various regions of the country. Productivity in the country has risen dramatically.

India did not begin reforms until 1991, and then only in response to economic crisis. Facing high debt, high inflation, increased oil prices, and the possibility of default on foreign loans, the government made far-reaching changes to the system of foreign trade and payments.

The authors of *Agriculture and Trade in India and China* look carefully at the economic history of these two countries since 1950 to determine how the vital sectors of agriculture and trade influenced development. In both countries agriculture accounted for most of the employment and output in 1950 and gradually gave way to industry. Now China and India are discovering, as are many developing countries, that trade offers great promise for growth if they can harness its potential by competing successfully in world markets. As yet both countries are still struggling to make their export products competitive, and T. N. Srinivasan, Justin Yifu Lin, and Yun-Wing Sung assess the future prospects for the two countries. If they succeed in liberalizing their economies and reaping the benefits of trade, they will serve as important examples to the many other countries, such as those in the former Soviet bloc, who are embarking on this same path. More important, China and India can, together, improve the lives of nearly half the world's population.

The International Center for Economic Growth is pleased to publish this important work, which offers valuable insights for scholars and policy makers around the world.

Nicolás Ardito-Barletta
General Director
International Center for Economic Growth

Panama City, Panama
December 1993

1

Overview

T. N. Srinivasan

Four decades ago Wilfred Malenbaum opened an article comparing and contrasting China and India as they began their quest for economic development by saying: "Few economic events during the coming decade will be of more importance than the comparative economic development of India and China" (Malenbaum 1956: 1). He concluded that

> on the whole, therefore, the early accounts of comparative progress should show advantages for the Indian effort. Moreover, even if the Chinese program were to gain momentum relative to India's—by its fourth or fifth year, say—the longer-run outcome would probably be a very much greater relative increase in Chinese total output than in her standards of consumption (p. 24).

Just three years later the same Malenbaum wrote that "the present analysis thus indicates economic developments overwhelmingly favourable to Chinese effort, both with respect to actual performance and to potential for further growth"! He cautioned, however, that the Chinese economy performed better not because "totalitarian methods serve better than those concerned and implemented under democracy"

I have drawn extensively on the subsequent four chapters of this volume by Justin Yifu Lin (on China's agriculture), Yun-Wing Sung (on China's foreign trade), and myself (on India's agriculture and foreign trade). I thank Anne Krueger, Justin Yifu Lin, and Yun-Wing Sung for their comments on an earlier draft.

but because the Chinese government was better than the Indian government at defining the tasks of growth realistically and implementing them faithfully (Malenbaum 1959: 298, 308).

Two decades later, the American Economic Association (AEA) devoted a session to a comparison of China and India at its annual conference in December 1974. The authors of the two papers presented at the session agreed that China had outperformed India until then. Richman concluded that "China has done considerably better than India in the last twenty five years or so with regard to most indicators of development" and that "unfortunately, the outlook for India's future development does not look nearly so bright at this time" (Richman 1975: 345, 354). Interestingly, he argued that "if China does evolve into a truly advanced economy, it would seem that some of the more important aspects of pure Maoist-Marxist-Leninist ideology would have to be compromised considerably in the process" (p. 354). This statement only apparently anticipates the Deng Xiaoping "deviation" that has occurred since 1978. Unlike Deng, who views the deviation as a necessary condition for China's becoming a truly advanced economy, Richman views it as a concomitant of China's evolution into an advanced economy. Weisskopf concluded,

> In sum, neither the Chinese nor the Indian approach to development can be considered optimal with respect to the achievement of rapid economic growth. Yet the Chinese approach appears to have been significantly more conducive to growth as well as to equity and to self-reliance than the Indian approach (Weisskopf 1975: 362).

One of the discussants of the two papers, Desai, rightly criticized the two authors for their inadequate methodology and for their eagerness to draw conclusions based on flimsy evidence. She asked, "When facts are scarce and scholarly analysis and scrutiny are rare because infeasible [*sic*], how does one arrive at the critical judgments that are necessary to evaluate and compare the Chinese society and economy with the Indian?" (Desai 1975: 367). She then listed six issues on which critical judgments were necessary but impossible to reach because of lack of information. The other discussant, Gurley, dismissed the analyses of both authors, asserting that their "explanations" were a bit superficial, "for they suggest that 'India' and 'China' each sat down, like Rodin's thinker, to work out the best thing to do. China, with more brains, a firmer resolve, and wider options, won out." While complimenting Weisskopf for getting to the heart of the matter when he ascribed China's wider options to the fact that the Chinese leadership has achieved a true redistribution of power, Gurley nevertheless concluded that this insight "should only be the beginning and, not ending, of an analysis" (Gurley 1975: 370–71).

Malenbaum wrote fairly early in the development of the two countries, and the AEA discussion in 1974 preceded the death of Mao Zedong, a full revelation of the horrors of the Cultural Revolution, and Deng's initiation of reforms in 1978. Besides, as Desai pointed out, the information (particularly with respect to China) on which comparisons were based left much to be desired. Nonetheless, Malenbaum was right about the importance of a comparative analysis of the development strategy, policies, and performance of China and India. After all, China and India, the two most populous and poorest countries of the world, have attempted to develop economically and alleviate poverty through similar development strategies but under vastly different political frameworks, namely, a communist dictatorship in China and a representative democracy in India. Both have undertaken major economic reforms, China beginning in 1978 and India in a piecemeal fashion in the 1980s and comprehensively since 1991. An analysis of their successes and failures is of great relevance to the developing world.

In the two decades since the AEA session, much more information on and critical analysis of the Chinese economy have become available. This study is an attempt to compare, and contrast where appropriate, the Chinese and Indian policies and performance with respect to agriculture and foreign trade. In both economies agriculture provided employment to over 60 percent of the labor force as recently as 1990 and is a significant source of raw materials for processing industries and exports as well. Policies with respect to foreign trade, particularly the pursuit of import substitution, have been central to the industrial development of both economies. While concentrating on these two important sectors, the study touches also on other aspects of development of the two societies, including in particular the social sector.

It is worthwhile to begin with a brief description of the two economies as they initiated their development efforts in the late 1940s, their politico-economic-social frameworks, and their achievement as of the early 1990s in terms of important socioeconomic indicators.

India and China are among the poorest and most populous countries of the world, with an estimated population of 850 million and 1.13 billion respectively in 1990. The Chinese Communist party took the reins of government of a unified country in 1949 after a protracted civil war and foreign invasion. British colonial rule in India ended in 1947 with the establishment of the two independent countries of India and Pakistan into which the states previously under the control of princes subordinate to the British crown were also integrated. The governments of both China and India turned to planning for national development soon thereafter: China's First Five-Year Plan covered the period 1952–1957, while India's covered 1951–1956. China's Eighth Five-Year Plan is for the period 1991–1995 while India's is for 1990–1994. China is still a dictatorship, while India is a representative democracy with regular elections to the national parliament and the state legislatures. Until the death of Mao Zedong in 1976, China was a command economy in which private producers and markets played insignificant roles in resource allocation and factor accumulation. India is a mixed economy with a large private sector and functioning markets. China began moving away from the command system in 1978 with the introduction of the household responsibility system in agriculture and the development of export-oriented special economic zones in coastal areas. The large industrial state enterprise system, however, has yet to be reformed significantly, although smaller rural and township enterprises have grown rapidly. India also began liberalizing its economy, hesitantly and to a limited extent, in the early 1980s. In 1991 the government of Prime Minister P. V. Narasimha Rao embarked on a bolder, coherent, and mutually consistent set of reforms in several sectors of the economy.

Compared with data on India, data on the Chinese economy have always been, and continue to be, relatively sparse for the period before 1978. They are of uncertain reliability, and their internal consistency has not been subject to rigorous examination. China has undertaken four population censuses since 1949, in 1953, 1964, 1982, and 1990. The World Bank points out, however, that the first of these was a modest effort that canvassed individuals only about their age, sex, nationality, and relationship to the head of household (World Bank 1983: 231). The second census added questions on the education, class status, and occupation of individuals. Only the last two were comparable to censuses elsewhere in the world. India has had regular censuses each decade since 1881. In China's command economy the relative prices of goods and services could hardly be deemed to represent the marginal rates of substitution of commodities in their use or the marginal rates of transformation in their supply. This means that gross national product (GNP) at domestic Chinese prices is not a good indicator of China's production capacity or of the welfare of Chinese citizens. The World Bank (1992: 218) reports China's per capita GNP in 1990 as US$370 and India's as US$350. It also reports that the average annual rates of growth of GNP per capita between 1965 and 1990 in China and India were 5.8 percent and 1.9 percent respectively. If the data for 1990 GNP and the growth rate estimates for 1965–1990 are both correct, then China's GNP per capita in 1965 must have been only 41 percent of India's! No knowledgeable analyst of the two countries would subscribe to this relative value of China's GNP per capita in 1965. A plausible explanation for these paradoxical figures is that the figure of US$370 as China's 1990 per capita GNP reflects the consideration that a more realistic figure might soon make China ineligible for loans from International Development Association, the soft loan affiliate of the World Bank. In fact Ma and Gaurnaut (1992) suggest that only if China's per capita income were three to four times the income reported by the World Bank would the consumption pattern of China be comparable, as one would expect, to those of Taiwan and Hong Kong.

In its first detailed report on the Chinese economy, the World Bank (1983) also came to the conclusion that the Indian and Chinese economies enjoyed roughly similar per capita incomes in the range of US$50–60 (in 1952 dollars) in the early 1950s. China's population was a little over 1.5 times that of India's 360 million in 1951. On the one hand, India had a more diversified industrial structure and a more extensive network of transport and communications than China even in 1979 (India had three times the route kilometers of railways and more than 3.5 times the route kilometers of highways per square kilometer of land area). On the other hand, China's average yield per hectare of rice was twice that of India, and its yield of wheat was more than 1.5 times that of India. Crude birth rates were about the same (about thirty-seven to thirty-eight per thousand), while China's crude death rate, at about seventeen per thousand, was significantly lower than India's twenty-four per thousand (again in the early 1950s), perhaps reflecting the better nutritional status enjoyed by the Chinese population because of higher foodgrain output per head.

Rawski recently reworked the estimates of output in China for the period 1914–1949 and concluded that "with the exception of the war period 1937–49, China's economy has now experienced seven decades of rising aggregate and per capita output stretching back to 1914, if not earlier" (Rawski 1989: 347–48). A careful examination of Rawski's reworking of scanty Chinese data and a comparison with more plentiful and reliable Indian data for the period 1914–1949, however, led Kumar to conclude that "the safest view is still that the overall growth story was not very different in the two countries—a slow growth of population, and slow or no growth in per capita income, in marked contrast to the post 1950 experience in both countries. The per capita income of both India and China was very low in 1949 and given the margin of error, it is not worth arguing about which country was the poorer. The demographic data suggest that the physical quality of life was higher in China, but this is based on unreliable data" (Kumar 1992: 30).

The available data thus do not seem to support any stronger conclusion than that India and China had roughly the same level of per capita income in the early 1950s and had experienced similar growth in the previous fifty years. If World Bank figures of per capita GNP of the two countries in 1990 are taken at their face value, then their growth in the forty years following 1950 could not have been dissimilar either! On the other hand, Maddison's estimates of per capita real gross domestic product (GDP, in 1980 dollars adjusted for purchasing-power parity) for China and India respectively were US$370 and US$350 in 1830 and 1870; US$415 and US$399 in 1913, US$338 and US$359 in 1950, US$774 and US$513 in 1973, and US$1,748 and US$662 in 1987 (Maddison 1991: 39). Given the problems with the primary data and the procedures for adjusting for price differences, there is likely to be a wide margin of error surrounding each of Maddison's estimates, but at least they are consistent with the widely held belief that real GNP per capita grew much faster in China than in India after 1950.

Whether or not China's per capita income was roughly the same as India's in 1950 and 1990, the World Bank data suggest that China was far ahead of India in 1990 in social indicators such as life expectancy (seventy years in China compared with fifty years in India), infant mortality (twenty-nine per thousand live births compared with ninety-two), and adult literacy (73 percent compared with 48 percent). In the 1980s overall economic growth, as well as the growth of exports, was much faster in China than in India. With the initiation of reforms in 1978, China's real GDP rose by 2.5 times and exports by more than 3 times between 1980 and 1990, while in India the corresponding figures were 1.8 times for both GDP and exports. The apparently superior performance in terms of social indicators and the greater success of reforms in China compared with India call for an examination of their development strategies and the thrust, content, and implementation of their economic reforms in the 1980s.

This chapter will offer an overview of the development strategies of the two countries, which gave primary importance to industrialization in general and to the development of heavy industry in particular. The continuing importance of the agricultural sector as a source of employment for an overwhelming majority of the labor force in the two countries is in part a reflection of the failure of the development strategy of both countries to generate productive employment opportunities outside of agriculture. Drawing on chapters 2–5, I will then compare the agricultural policies and performance of China and India and the foreign trade and exchange control regimes employed by the two countries in support of their import-substituting, capital-intensive industrialization strategies.

DEVELOPMENT STRATEGIES

Not only were India and China at a similar stage of development when they began planning for national development in the early 1950s, but they also adopted similar development strategies. Not surprisingly, the Communist leadership of China was heavily influenced by the then-perceived success of the Soviet Union in rapidly industrializing a largely rural economy in the relatively short span of four decades without significant external assistance. China received aid from the Soviet Union until 1960, when relations between the two Communist giants were broken off. In the case of India, the future prime minister, Jawaharlal Nehru, had visited the Soviet Union in the late 1920s and come away deeply impressed with its planning. He was the chairman of the National Planning Committee established in 1938 by the dominant political party that led the struggle for India's independence from the British. This committee, which completed most of its work before Nehru's arrest by the colonial government in 1940, articulated a development strategy whose main elements were incorporated into postindependence planning. Besides this committee, other groups (of, for example, business-men, labor unions, and followers of Gandhi) published their own ideas for India's development in the postindependence era. Indeed, many of the ideas and debates about development strategy in the post–World War II literature were clearly anticipated in these prewar Indian development plans and debates (Srinivasan 1993). From the mid-1950s until its collapse in 1991, the Soviet Union provided India with technological and defense-related aid as well as political support.

Professor P. C. Mahalanobis, the author of India's Second Five-Year Plan (1956–1961), which formally articulated the development strategy that was pursued over the next thirty-five years, had also visited the Soviet Union and was familiar with the major features of the Soviet planning system. Indeed, the Mahalanobis two-sector model of development, which provided the analytical foundation for the plan, had been formulated in the Soviet Union by Grigorii Alexandrovich Feldman in the 1920s, though Mahalanobis apparently arrived at it independently. The model postulated a closed economy with two production sectors, a consumer goods sector and a capital goods sector, each with its own capital-output ratio. With capital as the only factor of production, the share of investment devoted to augmenting the stock of capital in the equipment-producing sector determined the long-run rate of growth of the economy. The larger this share, the greater the growth rate. Devoting a large share of investment to expanding capital goods–producing heavy industry was therefore supposed to accelerate long-run growth. This rationale led both China and India to adopt a Soviet-style, inward-oriented development strategy that emphasized heavy industry, producing intermediate and capital goods. As they gained experience over time both countries made some changes in emphasis in the strategy.

In the early 1950s neither China nor India had any capital goods–

producing industry to speak of. Most of the equipment needed for investment therefore had to be imported, at least until enough capacity had been built in heavy industry. Heavy industry was capital-intensive as well. Thus the emphasis on heavy industry made substantial demands on foreign exchange and investment flows. To generate and allocate resources for heavy industrial development, both countries relied on administrative mechanisms such as investment licenses and import quotas rather than a price mechanism working through markets. Clearly the operation of these discretionary administrative mechanisms created rents (for example, import premia), with the inevitable diversion of resources from production to seeking rents and administrative corruption. Until China's reforms of 1978, however, the rents (as well as resources directed to rent seeking) in that country were modest. The scope for consuming rents was limited because the goods available for consumption were few in number and poor in quality. Accumulating rents was not attractive either since private wealth was difficult to hide and conspicuous consumption was politically risky. This is not to deny that party functionaries engaged in "collective" rent seeking and conspicuous consumption in heavily protected party "guest houses," but only to suggest that the diversion of resources to such activities was limited. In postreform China, with wealth accumulation no longer frowned upon and with the phenomenal increase in the supply of consumer goods (particularly imported durables), the diversion of resources for rent seeking has increased substantially. Chinese policy makers, however, have attempted to eliminate any potential rents quickly, as indicated by the difference in the black market and official prices of foreign exchange and raw materials. Yet given the still rudimentary and segmented markets in China and the fact that *guanxi* (or "connections") is still important in getting ahead, it is unlikely that rents have been eliminated. In India corruption and rent seeking have been significant all along. Further, with a legal ban on corporate contributions to political parties, politicians have been unable to resist opportunities to create rents through the administrative mechanisms and to extract part of the rent for use in Indian electoral campaigns. The economic, social, and political costs of the administrative allocation system have been substantial.

Both countries shifted relatively rapidly away from agriculture. The share of GDP originating in agriculture fell from over 50 percent in the early 1950s to about 27 percent in China and 30 percent in India in 1991. In India, however, the share of manufacturing industry in GDP rose slowly, from about 15 percent in the early 1950s to about 20 percent in 1991, while in China this share rose to nearly 40 percent in 1991 from less than 20 percent in the 1950s. In both countries the capital-intensive nature of investment in industry meant that the share of agriculture in total employment remained high, as much as 60 percent in China and nearly two-thirds in India in 1991. Thus agriculture continues to be the major employer in both countries.

It was noted earlier that both China and India implemented their industrialization programs through controls on investment and foreign trade, although the mechanisms of control were somewhat different. In India's mixed economy with a large private sector, the control mechanism had to ensure that industrial development in the private sector conformed to the national plans by preventing diversion of investible resources and foreign exchange to privately profitable but socially undesirable activities. The World Bank (1983) reports that in the three decades between 1950 and 1980 real growth in China's foreign trade was about the same as that in GNP so that the share of trade in GNP hardly changed. In the 1980s, however, China's trade expanded phenomenally, raising its share in GDP from about 13 percent in 1980 to a high of 37 percent in 1991. In India the share of trade in GDP fluctuated; until the early 1960s it averaged over 12 percent, only to decline to a low of less than 10 percent in the early 1970s and to slowly rise thereafter to about 16 percent in 1979/80. Since then the share has moved within a narrow range of 18 to 20 percent. While India's share in world exports declined from over 2 percent in the early 1950s and stabilized around 0.5 percent in the 1980s, China doubled its share from 1 percent to 2 percent between 1980 and 1991, the share having fallen from about 1.25 percent in 1952–1955 to 0.75 percent in 1978.

AGRICULTURAL POLICIES AND PERFORMANCE

When the People's Republic was established in 1949, China was an overwhelmingly rural agrarian economy. For millennia the traditional farming institution had been the small, independent family farm with a few large landlords owning a significant proportion of the cultivated area (around 40 percent in 1950). The socialist regime that took power in 1949 confiscated land from landlords and rich peasants without compensation and redistributed it to poor and landless households that were gradually collectivized. Until 1955 the collectives were largely small "mutual aid" teams of 4 or 5 neighboring households that pooled their farm tools and animals and exchanged labor while retaining the ownership of land and the claim to its produce. The next stage was the elementary cooperative, in which 20 to 30 neighboring households pooled their farm implements, animals, and land under a unified management. The net income was divided into one payment for the use of tools, animals, and land owned by each household and another payment for labor. The third stage was the advanced cooperative, in which all means of production, including land, were collectively owned with the remuneration of each member depending solely on the amount of work he or she contributed. Thus the income of a family depended on the number of "work points" earned by its members, and the average value of a work point was determined by the net income of the cooperative. Starting from about 30 households, advanced cooperatives evolved to include all 150 to 200 households in each village. By 1957, 750,000 advanced cooperatives with 119 million member households had been established.

Collectivization encountered no serious resistance from the peasantry initially. What is more, it succeeded in raising the real gross value of agricultural output by 28 percent and the value of grain by 22 percent between 1952 and 1958. This apparent success emboldened the leadership to proceed to a further stage in collectivization, the establishment of "people's communes," with tragic consequences. In a short span of three months between August and November of 1958, the then 753,000 collective farms with 120 million member households (99 percent of the rural population) were forcibly transformed into 24,000 communes. The average size of the commune was around 5,000 households with 10,000 workers and 10,000 acres of land. Worker compensation arrangements were radically changed, and the subsistence needs of households, rather than the work contributed by them, became the dominant consideration. Household members were no longer allowed to work on private plots.

By significantly reducing the incentives for work and encouraging free riding, the coercive measures and new compensation system quickly and unsurprisingly led to a profound agricultural crisis. The gross value of agricultural output fell by 14 percent in 1959, 12 percent in 1960, and a further 2.5 percent in 1961. Grain output dropped by 15 percent in 1959 and 16 percent in 1960. The steep decline in grain output culminated in a famine in which 30 million people (in excess of normal mortality) died from starvation and malnutrition. Although both China and India had experienced periodic famines in their long history before World War II, India has had no famines since independence. In totalitarian China, unlike in democratic India, there was no free press to clamor for remedial action through grain imports from better-endowed regions and the rest of the world to prevent the fall in output from resulting in a famine. It has been claimed that China attempted to import grain during the famine but did not succeed (except for imports from Australia) because of a trade embargo orchestrated by the United States. This argument is not wholly convincing. First of all, the United States did not succeed when it tried a similar embargo against the Soviet Union much later, and second, an open admission by the Chinese leaders of the severity of famine would have resulted in worldwide sympathy for China and a demand for the lifting of the embargo. That the leadership let the famine occur is enough to indict the Chinese regime, whatever might be its achievements in the social sectors. Even the death of 30 million, however, did not lead the regime to abandon communes but only to delegate management tasks in each commune to much smaller units called "production teams," consisting of about twenty to thirty households. Land was nonetheless still jointly owned by the commune, brigade, and production team. More important, the income of each household was based on the work points contributed by its members to the production team. While several improvements in the valuation of work points were made after 1962, the production team remained the basic farming institution until the reforms of 1978 introduced the house-hold responsibility system.

In India, before independence, land ownership was extremely con-centrated, and layers of intermediaries between the tiller and the state laid claim to the produce of land. An agrarian reform committee estab-lished by the government soon after independence concluded that land must belong to the tiller and that all intermediary rights ought to be abolished. It recommended that subletting of land be prohibited, that tenants be given the right to purchase the land they were then leasing at a reasonable price, and that occupancy rights be conferred on those who had been cultivating land continuously for a period of six years or more. Based on the committee's recommendations, the Indian Parlia-ment enacted laws changing the terms and security of tenure, abolish-ing the so-called zamindari farming rights conferred in perpetuity by the British in certain parts of India, and setting ceilings on the size of individual landholdings. In India's constitutional democracy, the courts declared some of these laws unconstitutional. In response, the government amended the constitution within a year of its adoption to place land reform legislation out of the purview of the judiciary.

The land reform laws other than those abolishing zamindari rights and stipulating tenancy rights proved to be ineffective. The laws setting ceilings on landholdings were largely evaded. Yet the very process of evasion through division of large holdings among extended family members appears to have resulted in a reduction in the concentration of the distribution of land *owned* as well as land *operated* (that is, land owned plus land leased in minus land leased out).

The organization of agricultural production, as distinct from reform of ownership rights, also attracted the attention of policy makers. At the time of the formulation of the First Five-Year Plan in 1951, the govern-ment proposed that each village community manage all the land (cultivated and uncultivated) in the village as if it were a single farm, but with actual cultivation undertaken by households with their own holdings in cooperation with other households. Whatever its economic merits, this idea turned out to be politically infeasible.

Twenty-five years later the National Commission on Agriculture asserted that the organization of production in small peasant farms run with household labor supplemented with labor exchanged with other households and occasional hired labor was most appropriate under Indian conditions. This conclusion simply recognized a long-standing reality: India, as the Royal Commission on Agriculture had stated in its report of 1928, was "predominantly the land of small holders and the typical agriculturist is still the man who possesses a pair of bullocks and who cultivates a few acres with the assistance of his family and occasional hired labour" (as quoted in India, Ministry of Agriculture 1976: 126–27).

The green revolution, which introduced high-yielding dwarf varieties of rice and wheat and hybrids for other cereal crops in the mid-1960s made middle peasants far more prosperous than small and large operators. Although the green revolution technology was mostly neutral with regard to scale, middle peasants had the greatest access to inputs needed to derive the full benefits of the technology, such as irrigation water, fertilizers, and credit for working capital, because of the way public policies operated. Available data suggest that the cultivated area under tenancy steadily declined from about a fifth in the early 1950s to less than a tenth in the early 1980s, though a rise since then cannot be ruled out.

Both China and India operated an urban public distribution system for the supply of limited rations of foodgrains and other necessities. In 1953 China instituted a restrictive rationing system, which remained essentially unchanged until the post-Mao reforms of the late 1970s. To secure food for urban rationing, the country established a compulsory procurement system under which peasants were required to sell specified quantities of grains, edible oils, cotton, and other crops at government-set prices. In India as well, the government purchased foodgrains (primarily rice and wheat) at specified procurement prices, which until recently were below the ruling open-market prices. The process of setting procurement prices, however, became politicized over time. The procurement prices at which only the limited quantity needed to maintain the public distribution system was to be bought became support prices at which the government was required to buy all that was offered. Over time, therefore, the implicit taxation of producers, based on purchasing their goods at below-market prices, disappeared. Since the government sold the foodgrains to urban consumers in ration shops at prices below the cost of procurement, transportation, and storage, subsidies for the public distribution system became substantial. In addition, government subsidies offset the relatively high cost of fertilizers produced domestically under the import-substituting industrialization strategy. Electricity and irrigation water used by farmers were subsidized as well. Food, fertilizer, electricity, and irrigation subsidies together accounted for 3 to 4 percent of GDP in 1990/91.

The fact that the land reform legislation in India did not result in a major redistribution of land, whereas in China land ownership was collectivized and access to land through the collectives was relatively egalitarian would lead to the expectation that income distribution in rural areas would be more unequal in India than in China. In fact, unequal distribution of rural incomes was not significantly higher in India. Based on available data, the World Bank concluded that the poorest 40 percent of people received 20 percent of rural income in 1979 in China (World Bank 1983). The richest 20 percent received 39 percent of rural income. Likewise, in India the poorest 40 percent received 20 percent of rural income in 1975/76, while the richest 20 percent received 42 percent. The Gini coefficient was 0.31 in China in 1979 and 0.34 in India in the 1973–1976 period. Although the World Bank reports a somewhat higher inequality in urban income distribution in India in 1975/76 than in China in 1979, the large weight of rural areas in both countries means that overall income distribution was roughly similar in the two countries. Since income distribution data are problematic in both countries, however, these figures have to be used with caution.

China and India each cover a large and agroclimatically diverse geographical area, and substantial regional income disparities might be expected in both. It has been suggested that regional disparities are greater, and intraregional inequalities smaller, in China than in India even though the overall inequalities are about the same in the two countries. If individuals and households are likely to be more concerned about their incomes relative to those of their neighbors within a region than relative to those of households in distant regions, then intraregional inequality would be of more serious concern than interregional inequalities. But there is no evidence that households behave in this fashion. In India the government imposed few policy barriers to the movement of labor and capital across state lines, although in practice sociocultural differences, including language differences, restricted labor mobility. In China public policy prohibited labor migration. Moreover, in the prereform era the Chinese government encouraged the economic self-sufficiency of the provinces for security reasons. Because the various regions developed differently in the prereform era, their ability to respond to reforms also differed, with the more-developed regions having the most success. Some evidence suggests that because of these differences regional disparities have widened and continue to widen in the postreform period in China.

Both China and India emphasized agricultural research, establishing agricultural research institutes and universities. China developed a high-yielding dwarf variety of rice in 1964, two years before the release of the well-known dwarf variety IR-8 by the International Rice Research Institute in the Philippines. In 1976 China became the first, and as yet the only, country to develop and commercialize the production of hybrid rice. Some of the Indian agricultural research institutions date to the preindependence era. Starting from imported germ plasm in the mid-1960s Indian plant breeders quickly developed a number of high-yielding dwarf varieties of rice and wheat suited to varying local agroclimatic conditions and tastes. Chinese researchers, in spite of their isolation from the international research community, performed as well as or better than the international community in plant breeding. Although Indian researchers were not isolated in principle, in practice constraints on resources limited their interchanges with the international community.

Although institutional changes, such as changes in land tenure, evolved differently in the two countries and there were differences as well as similarities in their agricultural policies, their overall performances did not differ greatly. Between 1952 and 1978, before the introduction of the household responsibility system, the average annual growth rate of agricultural output in China was about 2.9 percent (in real value terms). In India the average annual growth rate of the output of all crops from 1949/50 to 1989/90 was 2.66 percent. The corresponding figures for grain output were 2.69 percent in China and 2.67 percent in India [Ministry of Agriculture 1992: 258]. The rate of growth of agriculture in India and China is modest and less rapid than that in some other low-income countries. For example, the World Bank (1992: 220) reports that gross value added by agriculture grew at an average annual rate of 5 percent in Kenya, 4.3 percent in Indonesia, and 3.3 percent in Pakistan between 1965 and 1980, compared with China's 2.8 percent and India's 2.5 percent.

FOREIGN TRADE AND PAYMENTS REGIMES

Until the reforms of 1978, Chinese foreign trade was monopolized by nine national foreign trade corporations. The profits and losses of these corporations were absorbed by the Treasury. Neither the producers nor the corporations had an incentive to be cost-conscious and efficient. In India, since foreign trade was largely in the hands of the private sector, the government established an elaborate system for controlling and allocating foreign exchange to ensure that the foreign exchange earned by exporters was used to import only those commodities that conformed to the priorities set in the five-year plans. The complexity of the system led to a wide range of implicit exchange rates across the spectrum of imports and exports and associated efficiency losses.

Before 1978, foreign trade policy in China shifted with the ideological winds. The country did not exploit foreign trade to achieve efficient development based on its dynamic comparative advantage. Three broad periods can be distinguished before 1978: 1949–1958, the period before the Great Leap Forward; 1958–1970, the period from the Great Leap Forward until the dust from the Cultural Revolution settled; and 1970–1978, the period of recovery from the aftermath of the Cultural Revolution until the overthrow of the Gang of Four.

Chinese industrial output grew rapidly between 1952 and 1957, resulting in massive imports of plant and equipment. Exports at constant world prices grew at the rate of 9.7 percent a year from 1950 to 1960 and imports at 10.7 percent. Over 70 percent of the value of exports from 1952 to 1959 consisted of food and raw materials including cotton.

Soviet aid to China ceased in 1960. The failures of the Great Leap Forward turned China from a modest net exporter of grain into a net importer. The share of food in exports dropped dramatically and that of manufactures rose to around 50 percent, where it remained on average for more than two decades beginning in 1959. Imports of machinery had to be cut sharply. During the period 1963–1965, the economy recovered from the ravages of the Great Leap and the famine that had killed 30 million people. By 1966 the nominal value of trade regained its 1959 value. But Chairman Mao unleashed the Cultural Revolution and the Red Guards the same year, bringing disaster on the economy and society. According to Liu Guoguang et al. (1987), in 1966–1976, the decade of the Cultural Revolution,

> The production developed at a lower speed than before, with the result that a decrease was registered in agriculture, industry and the national income; the already serious imbalance between industry and agriculture and between heavy and light industries worsened; the economic results deteriorated with quite a few norms falling below those of the First Five-Year Plan period; the real wages of workers and staff members fell, the income of peasants rose only nominally, and the people as a whole were leading a hard life (p. 21).

The period 1970–1979 saw the revival of foreign trade, with the share of exports in GDP rising from 2.55 percent in 1970 to 5.30 percent in 1979. Foreign trade was no longer viewed as a necessary evil, but as an essential ingredient in modernizing the economy. Although the open door policy and a modernization program initiated by Mao's successor, Hua Guofeng, were poorly conceived and largely failures, they led to reforms that were much more carefully thought out. These reforms included the creation of new agencies to promote exports, attract foreign investment, and introduce foreign technology. Also, foreign trade reforms were coordinated with domestic economic reform. The country took, however, "two steps forward and one step backward." In each reform drive China opened up several geographic areas and gave them autonomy in their foreign trade and investment decisions. Each opening led to an investment and import boom, resulting in inflation and balance of payments problems. In response to these problems the government paused in its reform drive but soon opened up more areas and so on. There were three such drives between 1979 and 1988.

Although the open door policy was by no means free of controls on exports, imports, and foreign exchange transactions, it nevertheless led to rapidly rising exports, particularly of manufactures. As mentioned earlier, exports of all goods and services grew rapidly in the 1980s, rising from US$18 billion in 1980 to US$71 billion (at constant 1987 prices) in 1991. Manufactured exports rose from US$11 billion in 1980 to US$49 billion in 1991. Imports of goods and services grew from US$23 billion in 1980 to US$56 billion in 1991 (World Bank 1992: Tables 3.5, 3.8, and 4.3).

It is virtually impossible to evaluate the resource cost of this impressive performance. The Chinese domestic price structure remains distorted, and the net effect of various incentives and disincentives on exports and imports is difficult to quantify. Substantial investment has gone into developing the infrastructure, consisting of highways, railway lines, housing, water supply, telephone systems, and luxury hotels, in coastal areas, particularly in special economic zones near Hong Kong and Macao. A hard-headed cost-benefit analysis using appropriate prices and discount rates is needed to judge whether the return from this investment was as high as that from other forgone investment opportunities.

India's development strategy has three broad objectives: economic growth, self-reliance, and social justice. It assigned the state a dominant role in development and made key industries such as railways, telecommunications, and electricity generation the exclusive responsibility of the public sector. The massive rise in investment and high level of imports during the second plan created the expectation that foreign exchange would become scarce and precipitated a severe balance of payments crisis in 1957. Ever since, Indian planning has been driven by the perceived need to conserve foreign exchange expenditures. The broad features of the foreign exchange and investment licensing system instituted in the late 1950s remained essentially unchanged, though its severity waxed and waned, until the reforms of 1991.

The licensing mechanism was designed to approve (sometimes with modifications) or deny an application for a license. Since the criteria for evaluating applications were broad, licensing authorities had significant room for discretion. At best the licensing mechanism placed bureaucrats under constant pressure from interested parties, and at worst it led to their corruption and to the politicization of their decisions. An information system to keep track of the licenses granted and their implementation did not exist. In the final analysis, the procedure for granting licenses followed rules of thumb rather than any economic rationale. It degenerated into an exercise in dispensing political and other forms of patronage and a source of rents for personal or political use.

The following periods can be distinguished between 1957 and 1991: 1957–1966, which began with a foreign exchange crisis and ended with the devaluation of the rupee; 1966–1968, covering an abortive attempt at economic liberalization; 1968–1975, when the government reverted to a restrictive regime; 1975–1985, a decade of selective relaxation of controls in response to an exogenous improvement in foreign exchange availability; and finally, 1985–1991, a period of somewhat more systematic liberalization (Bhagwati and Srinivasan 1975; Srinivasan 1992).

The system of quantitative restrictions (QRs) on foreign trade, instituted by the colonial government during World War II, was vastly expanded after the 1957 foreign exchange crisis. It was also used to provide automatic and custom-made protection to any domestic activity that substituted imports. By 1962 policy makers realized that the QR regime was penalizing exports and introduced a plethora of export subsidization schemes. A severe drought in 1965 and the suspension of foreign aid following the Indo-Pakistani war of late 1965 caused import premiums to rise to unprecedented levels by early 1966. Donors made the resumption of large-scale aid and access to IMF credit conditional on the liberalization of the economy, the first step of which was the devaluation of the rupee. In June 1966 the government devalued the rupee, eliminated export subsidies, and reduced import duties.

The drought of 1965 was followed by another disastrous drought in 1966, resulting in price increases, decreases in traditional exports, and an industrial recession induced by a shortage of agro-based raw materials. Devaluation was seen as capitulation to external pressure, not only by the opposition but also by some within the ruling Congress party, whose power was eroded in the 1967 general elections. Further, the promised external aid did not materialize. The hesitant steps toward liberalization introduced with devaluation were largely abandoned by 1968. With the abandonment of liberalization, import premiums returned to high levels. Export subsidies were reinstated and augmented. Industrial licensing reverted to its severely restrictive mode. Import allocation criteria became increasingly complex.

The restrictive regime continued until the mid-1970s, when foreign exchange availability improved dramatically, fueled in part by remittances from the increasing number of Indians working in West Asia. With the spread of the green revolution, foodgrain imports ceased. The net result of these changes was a relaxation in the severity of the QR regime. Import allocation rules were made simpler, and allocation of foreign exchange for essential imports not competing with domestic production was increased.

The next stage in liberalization came in April 1985 when the government announced an import and export policy that was to cover a period of three years, rather than six months or a year as it had in the past. This innovation was meant to bring some stability to the policy. But in practice no such stability was achieved. Thus the 1988–1991 policy statement candidly recognized that changes would have to be announced within the three-year period and stated, "It is proposed to issue a revised version of the import and export policy at the beginning of each year."

The import control regime has confined imports to essential consumer goods, raw materials, and investment goods needed for domestic production and exports. The composition of India's exports has shifted moderately away from primary products to manufactured goods. The share of manufacturers rose from about 50 percent in 1950/51 to about 80 percent in 1990/91. Yet, the professed objective of planners, a diversified and dynamic export sector, has not emerged: among manufactured products, just four items (leather, gems, garments, and textiles) account for 56 percent of the growth between 1980–1985 and 1986–1990. Of course, considerations of dynamic comparative advantage do not necessarily imply that all countries should diversify the commodities in their export basket. Given India's diversified resource base and the pattern of industrial development, however, it is not unreasonable to presume that a diversification of exports would have been consistent with India's comparative advantage.

The prereform development strategies of India and China had restricted foreign trade even beyond the limited role that it is expected to play in economies with large domestic markets. Whether, given India's poverty and slow growth in per capita income, it would be considered large in this sense is an open question. The policy instruments used to implement this strategy created avoidable efficiency losses, including those arising from diversion of productive resources to rent seeking.

Both economies have succeeded in building a diversified industrial structure. Both produce a far greater variety of industrial goods, including capital goods, than most developing countries. They depend to a much lesser extent on imported equipment. Their scientific and technological capability is evident in their success in ventures ranging from putting satellites into orbit to designing and operating nuclear power plants. Both have so far avoided accumulating a heavy foreign debt, although India is close to joining the ranks of the heavily indebted. China has succeeded in eliminating abject poverty and improved the education, health, and nutritional status of its population, as shown by its high literacy rate for males and females and high life expectancy at birth, although regional inequalities in income remain and may even be increasing since the reforms. Although India's achievements are less impressive, they are nonetheless significant.

These achievements have been obtained at a high cost. The diversified industrial structure is in most, if not all, cases not internationally competitive in cost and quality of output, certainly in India and perhaps in China. The Indian industrial and import licensing system encouraged the creation of small-scale, high-cost plants in many industries and sheltered them from internal and external competition. Most of the industries in the public sector have yielded negligible returns. It is doubtful whether the protected capital goods industries in the two countries have accumulated the dynamic learning experience to bring about significant technical improvements in the equipment they produce. There is ample evidence showing that total factor productivity in India's manufacturing industry did not rise and possibly declined until the early 1980s and some evidence of a rise thereafter (Ahluwalia 1985, 1991).

A comparison with South Korea will illustrate the extent of the failure of the two giants. In 1965 exports of manufactured goods from India and China were valued respectively at US$607 million and US$554 million. These were about eight times as much as manufactured exports of Korea at US$72 million (Yeats 1991). By 1990 Korea was exporting nearly US$41 billion of manufactured goods to countries of the Organization for Economic Cooperation and Development (OECD), compared with India's US$9 billion and China's US$34 billion. The size of Korea's manufacturing sector as measured by value added was less than US$2 billion (at purchaser's prices) in 1970 compared with India's US$8 billion (at producer's prices) and China's US$28 billion (at purchaser's prices). By 1989 the figure for Korea was

US$66 billion against India's US$44 billion and China's US$146 billion (World Bank 1992: 228). Korea's total external debt at the end of 1990 was US$34 billion compared with India's US$70 billion and China's US$53 billion. Because of its high GNP and export growth, Korea is not viewed as a potential problem debtor, while India might become one.

The contrast between the achievements of China and India with respect to poverty alleviation and in the social sectors is significant. The World Bank (1983), in its very first report on China, concluded:

> China's most remarkable achievement during the past three decades has been to make low-income groups far better off in terms of basic needs than their counterparts in most other poor countries. They all have work; their food supply is guaranteed through a mixture of state rationing and collective self-insurance; most of their children are not only at school, but being comparatively well taught; and the great majority have access to basic health care and family planning services. Life expectancy—whose dependence on many other economic and social variables makes it probably the best single indicator of the extent of real poverty in a country—is (at 64 years) outstandingly high for a country at China's per capita income level (p. 11).

Yet a comparison with Sri Lanka is instructive. Sri Lanka was a peaceful democracy until deadly ethnic conflict broke out in the 1980s, and its per capita income was not much higher than that of India or China. Its superior achievements in social sectors suggest that neither higher incomes nor a totalitarian regime such as China's (or Cuba's) are needed to promote social development. In any case, China's achievements in social sectors were by and large accomplished by the early 1960s. For example, the crude death rate had fallen from about twenty-eight per thousand in 1945–1949 to ten per thousand in 1965, and life expectancy at birth had risen from about thirty-six years to sixty years during the same period. Adult illiteracy had been halved by 1965 from about 80 percent in 1945–1949. As such, it is difficult to excuse continued totalitarianism in China, even if one were to believe it was needed to bring about significant improvements in social indicators.

REFERENCES

Ahluwalia, I. J. 1985. *Industrial Growth in India: Stagnation since the Mid-Sixties.* New Delhi: Oxford University Press.

_____. 1991. *Growth and Productivity in Manufacturing.* New Delhi: Oxford University Press.

Bhagwati, J. N., and T. N. Srinivasan. 1975. *Foreign Trade Regimes and Economic Development: India.* New York: Columbia University Press.

Desai, P. 1975. "Discussion." *American Economic Review* 65, no. 2: 365–68.

Guogang, L., L. Wensen, T. Jianghas, and S. Liren. 1987. *China's Economy in 2000.* Beijing: New World Press.

Gurley, J. 1975. "Discussion." *American Economic Review* 65, no. 2: 368–71.

India, Ministry of Agriculture. 1976. *Report of the National Commission on Agriculture, Part I.* New Delhi: Government of India Press.

India, Ministry of Agriculture. 1992. *Area and Production of Principal Crops in India 1989–90.* New Delhi: Government of India Press.

Kumar, D. 1992. "The Chinese and India Economics from ca 1914–1949." CP No. 22, Research Programme on the Chinese Economy, STICERD. London: London School of Economics.

Ma, G. and R. Gaurnaut. 1992. "How Rich Is China: Evidence from the Food Economy." Working Paper, Department of Economics, Research School of Pacific Studies. Canberra: Australian National University.

Maddison, A. 1991. "Postwar Growth and Slowdown: A Global View." In G. Gahlen, H. Hesse, and H. G. Ramser, eds., *Wachstumstheorie und Wachstumpolitik.* Tübingen: J.C.B. Mohr (Paul Siebech).

Malenbaum, W. 1956. "India and China: Development Contrasts." *Journal of Political Economy* 64, no. 1: 1–24.

_____. 1959. "India and China: Contrasts in Development." *American Economic Review* 49, no. 3: 284–309.

Rawski, T. G. 1989. *Economic Growth in Prewar China.* Berkeley: University of California Press.

Richman, B. 1975. "Chinese and Indian Development: An Interdisciplinary Environmental Analysis." *American Economic Review* 65, no. 2: 345–55.

Srinivasan, T. N. 1992. "Planning and Foreign Trade Reconsidered." In S. Roy and W. E. James, eds., *Foundations of India's Political Economy.* New Delhi: Sage Publications.

_____. 1993. "Indian Economic Reforms: Background, Rationale and Next Steps." New Haven: Yale University, processed.

Weisskopf, T. 1975. "China and India: Contrasting Experiences in Economic Development." *American Economic Review* 65, no. 2: 356–64.

World Bank. 1983. *China: Socialistic Economic Development.* Vol. 1. Washington, D.C.: World Bank.

_____. 1992. *World Development Report 1992.* New York: Oxford University Press.

Yeats, A. 1991. "China's Foreign Trade and Comparative Advantage." Discussion Paper 141. Washington, D.C.: World Bank.

2

Chinese Agriculture: Institutional Changes and Performance

Justin Yifu Lin

China's socialist revolution of 1949 brought dramatic changes to the country's farming institutions. Traditional agriculture in China had been characterized by small, independent household farms with less than one hectare of fragmented landholding. As the socialists gained control over the country in the late 1940s, however, they effected a land reform program, which spread across the nation by 1952. Under this program, the government confiscated land from landlords and rich peasants without compensation and gave it to poor and landless peasants. Individual household farms were then collectivized under the provisions of the First Five-Year Plan in 1953. This collective farming system prevailed until the introduction of the household responsibility system in 1979.

Two achievements of the collective farming system are frequently mentioned: it fed an exploding population, and it supported a dramatic structural change in China's economy. When the socialist government was founded in 1949, the amount of cultivated land per capita was only 0.18 hectare. By 1978 this figure had dropped to 0.1 hectare as a result of rapid population growth.[1] Nevertheless, the collective system was

---

1. The cultivated land and population were 97.9 million hectares and 541.7

able to keep food production ahead of population growth. Meanwhile, the economy experienced a spectacular transformation, with industrial income expanding from 12.6 percent of total national income in 1949 to 46.8 percent in 1978.

An important issue that confronts most developing countries is how to develop agriculture rapidly in order to support urban industrialization and to meet the increased food demands brought on by explosive population growth. The small and fragmented holdings that characterize the landscapes in most developing countries are often regarded as obstacles to mechanization, irrigation, plant protection, and efficient allocation of inputs. Therefore, some economists suggested that collective farming in China provided a model of agricultural development for underdeveloped, densely populated economies (Robinson 1964). Recently released data, however, indicate that between 1952 and 1978 grain production grew at a rate of 2.4 percent per year, only 0.4 percent above the population growth rate for the same period. Per capita availability of grain, therefore, increased only 10 percent in more than a quarter of a century. The per capita income of the farm population increased only about 50 percent in the same period. Compared with the remarkable economic transitions in other East Asian economies—Taiwan, Hong Kong, Singapore, and Korea—China's economic performance in the 1960s and 1970s was disappointing.

Frustrated by their inability to improve the welfare of the Chinese population substantially after thirty years of socialist revolution, the veteran leaders who had been purged during the Cultural Revolution and regained power after the death of Mao Zedong in 1976 initiated a series of sweeping reforms in agriculture at the end of 1978. The reforms, including the replacement of the collective system with a new household-based farming system, resulted in remarkable growth during the first half of the 1980s. Between 1978 and 1984, the value of the agriculture sector as a whole grew at a rate of 7.4 percent annually, and grain output grew at 4.8 percent. Both of these rates are far above the 2.9 percent and 2.4 percent achieved during the previous twenty-six years. Meanwhile, the population growth rate dropped from an annual rate of 2 percent in 1952–1978 to 1.3 percent in 1978–1984. The availability of agricultural products and the overall living standards of both urban and rural populations improved substantially for the first time in about three decades.

The success of agricultural reforms in 1978–1984, especially the

---

million respectively in 1949, and 99.4 million hectares and 962.2 million in 1978.

remarkable growth of grain output, greatly encouraged China's political leaders. As a result, they undertook a series of more market-oriented reforms at the end of 1984 in both the urban and rural sectors. Agriculture as a whole still grew at a respectable average rate of 4.1 percent per year after 1984. Grain production, however, stagnated after reaching a peak of 407 million tons in 1984. Most political leaders in China give a high priority to the principle of grain self-sufficiency.[2] Therefore, the optimism that robust agricultural development generated during the first five years of rural reforms was swiftly replaced in the subsequent downturn by a pessimistic mood. Poor grain production from 1985 to 1988 gave some political leaders a strong reason to reemphasize more conservative, plan-oriented agricultural policies. Some leaders even called for re-collectivizing the individual household-based farming system with the ostensible goal of pursuing economies of scale in agricultural production. Although China's rural institutional reforms may have become irreversible, poor performance in grain production will always be a political issue in China.

In the rest of this chapter, I provide an analytical description of China's agricultural institutions and policies and their effects on agricultural performance and development. I will also examine issues related to sustained agricultural growth in China and discuss the reforms necessary to achieve this goal.

ECONOMIC DEVELOPMENT STRATEGY AND THE ROLE OF AGRICULTURE

To assess China's agricultural development after the socialist takeover in 1949, I will start with a description of the role of agriculture in the socialist government's overall economic development strategy. It will become clear in the following discussion that both the agricultural problems that preceded the 1979 reforms and those that followed the reforms stemmed from the development strategy that the Chinese government adopted in the early 1950s.

At the founding of the People's Republic in 1949, the Chinese government inherited a war-torn agrarian economy. More than 89 percent of the population resided in rural areas, and industry accounted for only 12.6 percent of national income. A developed heavy-industry sector was the symbol of a nation's power and economic achievement at

---

2. This political wisdom, shaped over millennia, is encapsuled in a motto—"*Wu nong bu wen*" (Without a strong agriculture, the society will not be stable)—often cited in agricultural policy debates in China.

**TABLE 2.1   SECTORAL COMPOSITION OF STATE INVESTMENT
IN CAPITAL CONSTRUCTION IN CHINA,
1953–1985 (PERCENTAGE)**

Five-year plan	Agriculture	Light industry	Heavy industry	Other
First (1953–1957)	7.1	6.4	36.2	50.3
Second (1958–1962)	11.3	6.4	54.0	28.3
1963–1965	17.6	3.9	45.9	32.6
Third (1966–1970)	10.7	4.4	51.1	33.8
Fourth (1971–1975)	9.8	5.8	49.6	34.8
Fifth (1976–1980)	10.5	6.7	45.9	36.9
Sixth (1981–1985)	5.1	6.9	38.5	49.5
1953–1985	8.9	6.2	45.0	39.9

Source: State Statistical Bureau, *Zhongguo guding zichan touzi tongji ziliao, 1950–1985* (China capital construction statistical data 1950–1985) (Beijing: China Statistics Press, 1987), p. 97.

that time. The new political leadership in China, like the leadership in India and many other newly independent developing countries, intended to accelerate the development of heavy industries. Moreover, after China's involvement in the Korean War and the resulting embargo and isolation from the Western camp, catching up with the industrial powers also became a necessity for national security reasons. In addition, the Soviet Union's outstanding record of nation building in the 1930s, contrasted with the Great Depression in the Western market economies, provided the Chinese leadership with both inspiration and experience for a development strategy oriented toward heavy industry. After its recovery from wartime destruction, therefore, the Chinese government adopted a Stalinist-type development strategy in 1953. The goal was to build the country's capacity to produce capital goods and military materials as rapidly as possible.

This development strategy was shaped in 1953 through a series of five-year plans.[3] Table 2.1 shows the sector shares in state investment in capital construction from the First Five-Year Plan (1953–1957) to the Sixth Five-Year Plan (1981–1985). Although more than three-quarters of China's population lived on agriculture, agriculture received less than 10 percent of the investment in 1953–1985, while 45 percent went to heavy industry. Moreover, heavy industry received most of the in-

---

3. The five-year plan was disrupted in 1963–1965, the period immediately after the agricultural crisis of 1959–1962, which will be discussed in detail in the next section. The First to the Seventh Five-Year Plans covered, respectively, the periods 1953–1957, 1958–1962, 1966–1970, 1971–1975, 1976–1980, 1981–1985, and 1986–1990.

TABLE 2.2   SECTORAL COMPOSITION OF NATIONAL
INCOME IN CHINA, 1949–1985 (PERCENTAGE,
IN CURRENT PRICES)

Year	Agriculture	Industry	Construction	Transportation	Commerce
1949	68.4	12.6	0.3	3.3	15.4
1952	57.7	19.5	3.6	4.3	14.9
1957	46.8	28.3	5.0	4.3	15.6
1962	48.0	32.8	3.5	4.1	11.6
1965	46.2	36.4	3.8	4.2	9.4
1970	41.3	40.1	4.1	3.8	10.7
1975	39.4	44.5	4.5	3.8	7.8
1980	39.1	45.8	5.0	3.4	6.7
1985	40.2	40.3	5.7	3.6	10.2

Source: State Statistical Bureau, *Guominshouru tongji ziliao huibian* (A compilation of national income statistical data) (Beijing: China Statistics Press, 1987), p. 9.

vestments under the heading "other," including workers' housing and infrastructure. At the same time, China prohibited most private initiative in economic activities. This pattern in government investment is the best indicator of the bias in the official development strategy. As a result of this development strategy, industry grew at an average rate of 11 percent between 1952 and 1980, and agriculture's share in national income declined. In 1952, the year before the heavy-industry strategy was implemented, agricultural income made up for 57.7 percent of the total national income. In the 1970s and 1980s agriculture's share dropped to about 40 percent. Meanwhile, the value of industrial output in national income grew from less than 20 percent in the 1950s to more than 40 percent in the 1970s and 1980s (see Table 2.2). Also, as a result of these investment priorities, fixed assets per industrial worker rose from 3,000 yuan per worker for 5.26 million industrial workers in 1952 to nearly 9,000 yuan per worker for 50.05 million industrial workers in the late 1970s. The rural work force of 294 million in the late 1970s had only 310 yuan of fixed assets per person (Perkins and Yusuf 1984: 16).

Heavy industry is a capital-intensive sector. The construction of a heavy-industry project has three characteristics: (1) it can take ten years or more to complete a project; (2) each project requires a large initial investment; and (3) most heavy equipment for the project must be imported from more advanced economies. The last characteristic is specific to a developing economy.[4] When the Chinese government initiated the heavy-industry development strategy in the early 1950s,

---

4. If a country produces its own heavy equipment, it is no longer a developing economy.

China was a poor, underdeveloped, capital-scarce, agrarian economy. Only limited credit was available in the market, and the interest rate was high.[5] Likewise, foreign exchange was scarce and expensive. The spontaneous development of capital-intensive industry in a capital-scarce economy is impossible.[6] Therefore, to implement a heavy-industry development strategy in a capital-scarce economy such as China's, a specific set of economic policies is required. To reduce the costs of interest and of importing equipment for the priority industry, China introduced a low interest rate policy and an overvalued exchange rate policy at the beginning of the First Five-Year Plan.[7] Meanwhile, for the purpose of securing enough funds for the industrial expansion, a policy of low wages for industrial workers evolved alongside the development strategy. Policy makers assumed that the state-owned enterprises would be able to create large profits through low costs and to reinvest the profits in infrastructure and capital construction. Therefore, although real GNP per capita tripled between 1952 and 1978, the real wage rate was kept almost constant, increasing only 10.3 percent during that period (State Statistical Bureau 1987c: 151).[8] The practice of establishing low prices for energy, transportation, and other raw materials, such as cotton, was instituted for the same reason.[9]

---

5. A rate of 3 percent per month, or 36 percent per year, was a normal interest rate in the informal financial markets before the revolution.

6. The spontaneous development of heavy industry in a capital-scarce economy is difficult for several reasons. First, it is difficult to mobilize enough funds for any large lump-sum investment. Second, the interest payment will make it impossible for any investment in a long-term construction project to be profitable. For example, if the interest rate is 30 percent per year (2.5 percent per month) and it takes ten years to complete the construction and beginning production, the principal and interest payment for each dollar's investment made in the first year of the project will be 13.8 dollars. Even if it only takes five years, the payment will be 3.7 dollars. It is obvious that no project that requires a long period of construction will be able to pay such a high interest rate. Since most equipment must be imported from industrial countries, the limited supply of foreign exchange also makes the construction of heavy industry expensive under the prevailing market rate.

7. For example, the interest rate of bank loans was officially set at about 5 percent per year. For a one-dollar investment at the beginning of a ten-year project, the principal and interest payment at the time the project was completed would be only 1.6 dollars.

8. The wage rate in the early 1950s probably was not underpriced, because of competition between the state enterprises and private enterprises. The private enterprises were soon nationalized, however, and the state became the sole employer and was able to depress the wage rate.

9. The low interest rate, overvalued exchange rate, low wage rates, and low prices for raw materials and living necessities constituted the basic policy

To make the policy of low wages possible, the government had to provide urban residents with inexpensive food and other necessities, including housing, medical care, and clothing. A restrictive rationing system was instituted in 1953 to distribute the low-priced food and other basic necessities, and this system remained in effect until the 1979 reforms.[10] At the same time, in order to secure a source of cheap supplies for urban rationing, a compulsory procurement policy was imposed in rural areas. The policy obliged peasants to sell to the state, at government-set prices, certain quantities of their produce, including grain, cotton, and edible oil. The state nearly monopolized the trades in grain and other major agricultural products. This monopoly completely insulates Chinese consumers from price fluctuations in domestic and international markets. Meanwhile, to prevent the rural population from

---

environment of the heavy-industry strategy. This policy environment created imbalances in the supply and demand of credit, foreign exchange, raw materials, grain, and other living necessities. In order to guarantee that the limited supply of credit, foreign exchange, and other resources were allocated to priority sectors, a system of administrative controls, including planning and rationing of credit, foreign reserves, labor, raw materials, and living necessities, was instituted. In the literature, many authors equate this set of policy environment and administrative controls with socialism. From the above discussion, however, we find that the rationale for the existence of these policies and controls is not "socialism." Rather, it is the adoption of a capital-intensive heavy-industry strategy in a capital-scarce economy. All the socialist economies had a similar set of policy environment and administrative controls because they all adopted the same development strategy, probably under the influence of Stalin. Nonsocialist developing economies, such as India, however, would also have a similar set of policy environment and administrative controls if they adopted the same development strategy. This policy environment and administrative control system made rapid expansion of heavy industry possible in a capital-scarce economy, but it also made resource allocation very inefficient. While the purpose of China's economic reforms was to improve the efficiency of the economy, so far most reforms only attempted to liberalize the administrative controls without altering this policy environment. Planning, rationing, and administrative controls are necessary because of the policy environment of the low interest rate, overvalued exchange rate, and low prices for raw materials and living necessities. Therefore, the liberalization of administrative controls without simultaneous reforms in the policy environment always results in unbearable chaos. For further discussions of the dilemmas involved in reforming administrative controls and maintaining the old policy environment, see Lin, Cai, and Shen (1989).

10. In addition to grain, edible oil, pork, sugar, cotton cloth, and other living necessities were also rationed. At the peak, the items of rationed goods for each urban residence numbered over 100. Since the reforms in 1979, the government has attempted to abolish the ration system. So far, the only remaining items are grain and edible oil. These last two items will also be eliminated in 1993.

TABLE 2.3   URBAN AND RURAL POPULATION IN
CHINA, 1949–1985

Year	Total population (millions)	Urban (%)	Rural (%)
1949	541.67	10.6	89.4
1952	574.82	12.5	87.5
1957	646.53	15.4	84.6
1962	672.95	17.3	82.7
1965	725.38	18.0	82.0
1970	829.92	17.4	82.6
1975	924.20	17.3	82.7
1980	987.05	19.4	80.6
1985	1,050.44	36.6	63.4

Source: State Statistical Bureau, *Zhongguo tongji nianjian 1989* (China statistical yearbook 1989) (Beijing: China Statistics Press, 1989), p. 87.

rushing to the cities to buy the low-priced rations, the government instituted a rigid urban household registration system, which virtually closed off rural-urban migration.[11] As a result, even though agriculture's share of the national income dropped from 57.7 percent to 39.1 percent owing to rapid industrialization from 1952 to 1980 (see Table 2.2), the rural population only dropped from 87.5 percent of total population to 80.6 percent in the same period (see Table 2.3).

In addition to providing cheap food for industrialization, agriculture was also the main source of foreign exchange, which, as mentioned earlier, was as important a constraint as capital for the heavy-industry strategy. In the early 1950s, most equipment and raw materials for heavy industry could not be produced in China at a reasonable cost because of the weak industrial base and needed to be imported from abroad. Agriculture remained the main source of scarce foreign exchange until the 1970s (see Table 2.4). In the 1950s, agricultural products alone made up over 40 percent of all exports. If processed agricultural products are also counted, agriculture contributed to more than 60 percent of China's foreign exchange earnings until the 1970s. And as Table 2.5 shows, except for the years during and immediately after the agricultural crisis of the early 1960s, most foreign exchange was used to import machinery, equipment, and raw materials for industrial uses.

---

11. The urban residents were entitled to numerous subsidies, estimated to be as high as 80 percent of their wage earnings, whereas the rural population had none of those benefits. The urban residents in effect became a new vested-interested class. They often became a barrier to market-oriented reforms in cities.

TABLE 2.4   COMPOSITION OF EXPORTS IN CHINA, 1953–1985

| Year | Total value (millions of US$) | Share in total exports (%) | | |
		Agricultural products	Processed agricultural products	Industrial and mineral products
1953	1,022	55.7	25.9	18.4
1957	1,597	40.1	31.5	28.4
1962	1,490	19.4	45.9	34.7
1965	2,228	33.1	36.0	30.9
1970	2,260	36.7	37.7	25.6
1975	7,264	29.6	31.1	39.3
1980	18,272	18.5	29.5	51.8
1985	25,915	17.5	26.9	55.6

Source: Editorial Board of the Almanac of China's Foreign Economic Relations and Trade, *Almanac of China's Foreign Economic Relations and Trade 1986* (Beijing: Zhongguo Zhanwang Press, 1986), p. 954.

TABLE 2.5   COMPOSITION OF IMPORTS FOR CHINA, 1953–1985

| Year | Value (millions of US$) | Share in total imports (%) | | | |
| | | Total machinery and equipment | Raw and intermediary materials | | Staple goods |
			For industrial use	For agricultural use	
1953	1,346	56.6	33.7	1.8	7.9
1957	1,506	52.5	34.6	4.9	8.0
1962	1,173	14.6	35.1	5.5	44.8
1965	2,017	17.6	40.1	8.8	33.5
1970	2,326	15.8	57.4	9.5	17.3
1975	7,487	32.1	45.7	7.6	14.6
1980	19,550	27.5	44.1	7.3	21.1
1985	34,331	31.9	46.6	4.3	17.2

Source: Editorial Board of the Almanac of China's Foreign Economic Relations and Trade, *Almanac of China's Foreign Economic Relations and Trade 1986* (Beijing: Zhongguo Zhanwang Press, 1986), p. 958.

The country's capacity to import capital goods for industrialization in the early stage of development clearly depended on agriculture's performance.

In short, agriculture played a supporting role in the heavy-industry development strategy in China. Although the majority of the population resides in rural areas, the state has invested only modestly in agriculture. Because of its meager initial state, however, agriculture's stagnation or poor performance would not only affect food supply, but also have an almost immediate and direct adverse effect on industrial expansion. Therefore, even though agriculture only assumes a support- ing role in the overall development strategy, the government can not ignore the importance of agriculture's growth. The unique feature of China's agricultural development, however, was the reliance on orga- nizational reforms as a means of achieving development goals. The following sections will examine the effectiveness of this agricultural development strategy.

RURAL INSTITUTIONAL CHANGES
AND DEVELOPMENT POLICIES

The major changes in Chinese agriculture after recovery from the war can be divided into two periods: (1) the collectivization period of 1952– 1978, and (2) the household-responsibility system reform period of 1979 to the present.

Collectivization and Agricultural
Development Policies

Although the top-priority sector in China's economic development strategy was heavy industry, the pace of industrialization was never- theless constrained by the performance of agriculture.[12] Agricultural development requires resources and investment as much as industrial development. The government, however, was reluctant to divert scarce resources and funds from industry to agriculture. Therefore, alongside the heavy-industry development strategy, the government adopted a new agricultural development strategy that would not compete for re- sources with industrial expansion. The core of this strategy involved the mass mobilization of rural labor to work on labor-intensive invest- ment projects, such as irrigation, flood control, and land reclamation, and to raise unit yields in agriculture through traditional methods and inputs, such as closer planting, more careful weeding, and the use of more organic fertilizer. Collectivization of agriculture was the institu- tion that the government believed would perform these functions.[13]

---

12. This subsection draws heavily on Lin (1992).
13. The government also viewed collectivization as a convenient vehicle for effecting the state's procurement program of grain and other agricultural prod- ucts. As an economist noted:

TABLE 2.6   CLASS STRUCTURE AND LANDHOLDING IN CHINA, 1950 AND 1954 (PERCENTAGE)

Status of peasants	1950		1954	
	Share of population	Share of land	Share of population	Share of land
Poor	52.37	14.28	52.2	47.1
Middle-income	33.13	30.94	39.9	44.3
Rich	4.66	13.66	5.3	6.4
Landlord	4.75	38.26	2.6	2.2
Other	5.09	2.86	0.0	0.0

Source: State Statistical Bureau, *Jianguo 30 nian chuanguo nongye tongji ziliao 1949–1979* (National agricultural statistics for the 30 years since the founding of the People's Republic of China 1949–1979) (Beijing: State Statistical Bureau, 1980), p. 19.

The independent family farm had been the traditional farming unit in rural China for thousands of years before the founding of the People's Republic. The typical farm was not only small, but also fragmented. In the wake of the socialist revolution, nearly 40 percent of the cultivated land in rural China was owned by landlords who leased land to peasant families (see Table 2.6). Rent was often as high as 50 percent of the value of the main crops. Starting in the 1940s, a land reform program was implemented in areas under the Communist party's control, under which land was confiscated without compensation from landlords and rich peasants and distributed free to poor and landless peasants. The land reform program was continued after the success of the revolution and completed nationwide in 1952. After the land reform, the distribution of land in rural China was quite equal, as Table 2.6 suggests.

Table 2.7 reveals that experiments with various forms of cooperatives began even before the completion of land reform. The first type of cooperative was the "mutual aid team" in which 4 or 5 neighboring households pooled their farm tools and draft animals and exchanged their labor on a temporary or permanent basis, with land and harvests belonging to each household. The mutual aid team was the predomi-

---

A still more fundamental reason for the collectivization of agriculture . . . was the fact that China had embarked on the construction of a planned socialist economy in 1953. For large-scale development of the national economy, it was imperative that changes be effected in the small peasant economy to enable it to provide the large quantities of grain, cotton, oil-bearing crops, sugar crops and other industrial raw materials needed by developing industry . . . the solution of which could only be found in the collectivization of agriculture (Luo 1985: 53).

TABLE 2.7   THE COLLECTIVIZATION MOVEMENT
IN CHINA, 1950–1958

	1950	1951	1952	1953	1954	1955	1956	1957	1958
Mutual aid teams: Number of teams (thousands)	2,724	4,675	8,026	7,450	9,931	7,147	850		
Households per team	4.2	4.5	5.7	6.1	6.9	8.4	12.2		
Elementary cooperatives: Number of coops (thousands)	0.018	0.129	4	15	114	633	216	36	
Households per coop	10.4	12.3	15.7	18.1	20	26.7	48.2	44.5	
Advanced cooperatives: Number of coops (thousands)	0.001	0.001	0.01	0.15	0.2	0.5	540	753	
Households per coop	32	30	184	137.3	58.6	75.8	198.9	158.6	
Communes: Number of communes									24,000
Households per commune									5,000

Blank cell indicates not applicable.
Source: Luo Hanxian, *Economic Changes in Rural China* (Beijing: New World Press, 1985), p. 59; Agricultural Cooperativization in China Editorial Office, "Chronicle of Events in Agricultural Cooperativization in Modern China II," *Zhongguo nongye hezuoshi ziliao* (Historical material of agricultural cooperativization in China), no. 3 (June 1987).

nant form of cooperative until 1955. The second type was the "elementary cooperative," in which about 20 to 30 neighboring households pooled farm tools, draft animals, and land under unified management. The net income of a cooperative was distributed in two categories: one payment for the land, draft animals, and farm tools owned by each household; and another for the work performed by each worker. The third type was the collective farm, or the "advanced cooperative," in which all means of production, including land, draft animals, and farm tools, were collectively owned. Remuneration in an advanced cooperative was based solely on the amount of work each member contributed. The income of a family in an advanced cooperative depended on the number of work points earned by family members and on the average value of a work point. The latter, in turn, depended on the net production of the collective farm. The size of an advanced cooperative was initially about 30 households and later evolved to include all 150–200 households in a village.

The official approach to collectivization was initially cautious and gradual. Peasants were encouraged to join the different forms of cooperative on a voluntary basis. In the summer of 1955, however, proponents of accelerating the pace of collectivization won the debate within the Party. There were only 500 advanced cooperatives in 1955. By the winter of 1957, 753,000 advanced cooperative farms, with 119 million member households, had been established on a nationwide basis (see Table 2.7).

Collectivization was surprisingly successful in its initial stage. It encountered no active resistance from the peasantry and was carried out relatively smoothly. The gross value of agriculture (measured at constant 1952 prices) increased 27.8 percent, and grain output increased 21.9 percent between 1952 and 1958 (Ministry of Agriculture 1989: 112, 143). This experience greatly encouraged the leadership within the Party and led them to take a bolder approach. The "people's commune," which consisted of about 30 collectives of 150 households each, was introduced in the fall of 1958. Within only three months, 753,000 collective farms were transformed into 24,000 communes, consisting of 120 million households, over 99 percent of total rural households in China in 1958. The average size of a commune was about 5,000 households, with 10,000 laborers and 10,000 acres of cultivated land. Payment in the commune was made partly according to subsistence needs and partly according to the work performed. Work on private plots, which existed in the other forms of cooperatives, was prohibited.

Although billions of man-days were mobilized, the commune movement ended in a profound agricultural crisis between 1959 and 1961. The gross value of agriculture, measured at 1952 prices, dropped 14 percent in 1959, 12 percent in 1960, and another 2.5 percent in 1961. Most important, grain output fell 15 percent in 1959 and another 16 percent in 1960. It remained at the same low level for another year and did not recover its 1952 level until 1962. This dramatic decline in grain output resulted in a widespread and severe famine. The evidence available now suggests that 30 million people died of starvation and malnutrition (Aston et al. 1984). This disaster was undoubtedly the worst catastrophe in human history.

Communes were not abolished after the great crisis. Starting in 1962, however, agricultural operation was divided and management was delegated to a much smaller unit, the "production team," which consisted of about twenty to thirty neighboring households. In this new system, land was jointly owned by the commune, the brigade, and the production team. The production team was treated as the basic operating and accounting unit, and income distribution, based on the number of work points earned by each member, was undertaken within the production team. This remuneration system was similar to that in the advanced cooperative. After 1962 many attempts to improve the grading of work points were made. The production team, however, remained the basic farming institution until the household responsibility system began in 1979.

China adopted a more realistic approach toward agricultural development after the 1959–1961 crisis. Although the mobilization of rural labor for public irrigation projects continued, greater emphasis was given to modern inputs. Irrigated acreage increased gradually from 30.55 million hectares (29.7 percent of total cultivated area) in 1962 to 44.97 million hectares (45.2 percent of total cultivated area) in 1978. As Table 2.8 shows, however, most of this increase resulted from the spread of powered irrigation rather than the construction of labor-intensive canals and dams. The use of chemical fertilizer was also accelerated. Starting from a modest 22.5 kilograms per hectare in 1962, usage per hectare increased to 291 kilograms in 1978. Equally impressive was the expansion in the use of electricity, which increased by a factor of 17.5 between 1962 and 1978.

As the use of chemical fertilizers and other modern inputs was increasing, the government also initiated a program to establish an agricultural research and promotion system for modern varieties. As a matter of fact, agricultural research is one of the few areas of which the Chinese government can be proud. In 1957 the Chinese Academy of Agricultural Sciences was founded in Beijing in 1957, and each of the twenty-nine provinces established its own academy of agricultural sciences as well. In the 1950s researchers focused on selecting and promoting the best local varieties. Their emphasis later shifted to the breeding of new, modern, high-yield varieties. A major breakthrough in rice breeding occurred in 1964, when China began full-scale distribution of fertilizer-responsive, lodging-resistant dwarf rice varieties with high-yield potential, two years earlier than the release of IR-8, the variety that launched the green revolution in other parts of Asia, by the International Rice Research Institute in the Philippines. At about the same time, hybrid corn and sorghum, improved cotton varieties, and new varieties of other crops were also released and promoted. Farmers rapidly adopted these high-yielding varieties. A second major breakthrough in rice breeding occurred in 1976, when China became the first, and until now the only, country to commercialize the production of hybrid rice. The innovation and commercial development of hybrid rice was heralded as the most important achievement in rice breeding

TABLE 2.8 USE OF IRRIGATION, TRACTORS, CHEMICAL FERTILIZER, AND ELECTRICITY IN CHINA, 1952–1988

| Year | Irrigation | | | Tractor-plowed area | | Chemical fertilizer | | Electricity |
	Total irrigated area (millions of hectares)	Irrigated area in total cultivated area (%)	Powered-irrigation in irrigated area (%)	Total area (millions of hectares)	Share in sown area (%)	Total amount (millions of tons)	Per hectare (kg/ha)	(millions of kilowatt-hours)
1952	19.96	18.5	1.6	0.14	0.1	0.08	2.25	50
1957	27.34	24.4	4.4	2.64	2.4	0.37	11.25	140
1962	30.55	29.7	19.9	8.28	8.1	0.63	22.50	1,610
1965	33.06	31.5	24.5	15.58	15.0	1.94	61.50	3,710
1978	44.97	45.2	55.4	40.67	40.9	8.84	291.00	25,310
1984	44.64	n.a.	56.4	34.92	n.a.	17.40	519.75	46,400
1988	44.37	n.a.	58.8	40.91	n.a.	21.42	616.49	71,200

n.a. = not available.
Source: State Statistical Bureau, Zhongguo tongji nianjian, 1989 (China statistical yearbook, 1989) (Beijing: China Statistics Press, 1989), p. 183; Ministry of Agriculture, Planning Bureau, Nongye jingji ziliao, 1949–1983 (Material of agricultural economics, 1949–1983 (Beijing, 1984), pp. 290–91; Ministry of Agriculture, Planning Bureau, Zhongguo nongcun jingji tongji ziliao daquan, 1949–1986 (A comprehensive book of China rural economic statistics, 1949–1986) (Beijing: Agriculture Press, 1989), pp. 340–41.

**TABLE 2.9   GRAIN OUTPUT, TRADE, AND AVAILABILITY IN
CHINA, 1952–1988**

Year	Population (millions)	Grain output (millions of tons) (2)	Grain trade[a] (millions of tons) (3)	Grain available per capita (kilograms) ((2 + 3)/1)
1952	547.8	163.9	−1.5	283
1957	646.5	195.1	−1.9	299
1962	673.0	160.0	3.9	244
1965	725.4	194.6	4.7	275
1978	962.6	304.8	5.7	322
1984	1,038.8	387.3	7.2	380
1988	1,096.1	394.1	8.2	367

[a]A positive figure indicates net imports, and a negative figure indicates net exports.
Source: State Statistical Bureau, *Zhongguo tongji nianjian, 1989* (China statistical yearbook, 1989) (Beijing: China Statistics Press, 1989), pp. 87, 198, 639, 642; Ministry of Agriculture, Planning Bureau, *Zhongguo nongcun jingji tongji ziliao daquan, 1949–1986* (A comprehensive book of China rural economic statistics, 1949–1986) (Beijing: Agriculture Press, 1989), pp. 520–22, 534–35.

in the 1970s (Barker and Herdt 1985: 61). By 1979 the percentage figures for area sown with high-yielding varieties were 80 percent for rice, 85 percent for wheat, 60 percent for soybeans, 75 percent for cotton, 70 percent for peanuts, and 45 percent for rape (Ministry of Agriculture, Planning Bureau, 1989: 348–49).

Despite the rapid increases in modern inputs and improvements in varieties in the 1960s and 1970s, the performance of agriculture remained poor. Although government leaders placed great emphasis on self-sufficiency, China changed from a net grain exporter in the 1950s to a sizable grain importer from the 1960s through the 1980s. The availability of grain per capita increased only 14 percent between 1952 and 1978 (see Table 2.9). This dismal picture prompted dramatic institutional reforms in 1979.

The Household Responsibility System

The discouraging record of Chinese agriculture changed abruptly in 1978 when China started a series of fundamental reforms in the rural sector.[14] Output growth accelerated to a rate several times the long-term average in the previous period. The annual growth rates for the three most important agricultural products—grain, cotton, and oil-bearing crops—averaged 4.8 percent, 17.7 percent, and 13.8 percent respec-

---

14. This subsection draws heavily on Lin (1992).

TABLE 2.10 AVERAGE ANNUAL GROWTH RATES OF AGRICULTURAL OUTPUT IN CHINA, 1952–1987 (PERCENTAGE)

Period	Agricultural output value	Crop output value	Grain output	Cotton output	Oil crops output	Population
1952–1978	2.9	2.5	2.4	2.0	0.8	2.0
1978–1984	7.4	5.9	4.8	17.7	13.8	1.3
1984–1987	4.1	1.4	−0.2	−12.9	8.3	1.3

Source: Ministry of Agriculture, Planning Bureau, *Zhongguo nongye tongji ziliao, 1987* (China agricultural statistical material, 1987) (Beijing: Agriculture Press, 1989), pp. 28, 34; Ministry of Agriculture, Planning Bureau, *Zhongguo nongcun jingji tongji ziliao daquan, 1949–1986* (A comprehensive book of China rural economic statistics, 1949–1986) (Beijing: Agriculture Press, 1989), pp. 112–15, 146–49, 189–92; State Statistical Bureau, *Zhongguo tongji nianjian, 1988* (China statistical yearbook, 1988) (Beijing: China Statistics Press, 1988), p. 97.

tively between 1978 and 1984, compared with the average rates of 2.4 percent, 1.0 percent, and 0.8 percent per year over the twenty-six years from 1952 to 1978. Average annual growth rates for the cropping sector and agriculture as a whole were equally impressive, rising from 2.5 percent and 2.9 percent to 5.9 percent and 7.4 percent (see Table 2.10). In 1985, China was once again a net grain exporter, the first time after a quarter of a century.[15]

This dramatic growth in output was a result of a package of reforms that reduced the function of ideology and planning and emphasized the roles of individual incentives and markets. Broad changes in rural policy began at the end of 1978, when policy makers recognized the importance of giving enough incentives to farmers to break the bottleneck of agricultural production. The original intention of the government, however, was to achieve this goal through raising the long-depressed government procurement prices for major crops, modifying management methods within the context of the collective system, and increasing budgetary expenditures on infrastructure, such as irrigation systems, for agricultural development.

Price reform.   The most important policy change envisioned by the government at the beginning of the reforms was the adjustment of pro-

---

15. In 1985 China exported 9.33 million tons of grain and imported 5.97 million tons (State Statistical Bureau, *China Statistical Yearbook,* 1986: 569, 572). The net export in 1986 was 1.69 million tons. Because of the decline in grain output in 1985 and stagnation afterward, however, China began to import grain again in 1987. The net grain imports for 1987 and 1988 were 8.81 million and 8.15 million tons, respectively (State Statistical Bureau, *China Statistical Yearbook,* 1989: 639, 642).

curement prices for major crops. Before the reform two distinct prices, quota prices and above-quota prices, existed in the state commercial system. Quota prices applied to crops sold in fulfillment of procurement obligations; above-quota prices to crops sold in excess of the obligation. Effective beginning in 1979, quota prices increased 20.9 percent for grain, 23.9 percent for oil crops, 17 percent for cotton, 21.9 percent for sugar crops, and 24.3 percent for pork. The average increase for quota prices was 17.1 percent (State Statistical Bureau 1984: 404–6). In addition, the premium paid for above-quota delivery of grain and oil crops was raised from 30 percent to 50 percent of the quota prices, and a 30 percent bonus was instituted for above-quota delivery of cotton.[16] The average increase for state procurement prices was 22.1 percent (State Statistical Bureau 1984: 401). If only the marginal prices, that is, the above-quota prices, are considered, the increase in the state prices was 40.7 percent (see Table 2.11).

Corresponding to the increase in procurement prices, retail prices rose 33 percent for pork, 32 percent for eggs, and 33 percent for fish in 1979. The retail prices for basic necessities such as grain and edible oils, however, were not changed. To compensate for the rise in retail prices of pork, eggs, and fish, each city dweller was given five to eight yuan a month,[17] thereby increasing the government's expenditure on public subsidies. The financial burden became especially unbearable when the unexpected output growth began to emerge in 1982. Price subsidies increased from 9.4 billion yuan (8.4 percent of the state budget) to 37 billion yuan (24.6 percent of the state budget) in 1984 (State Statistical Bureau, *China Statistical Yearbook,* 1988: 747, 763). In an effort to reduce the state's burden and to increase the role of markets, the mandatory procurement quotas were abolished, for cotton in 1984 and for grain in 1985, and replaced by procurement contracts that were to be negotiated between the government and farmers and agreed upon by both parties. The contract price was a weighted average of the basic quota price and above-quota price. This change resulted in a 9.2 percent decline in the price margin paid to farmers between 1984 and 1985 (see Table 2.11). Following the decline in grain and cotton production in 1985 and the stagnation thereafter, however, the contracts were made mandatory again in 1986 (Sicular 1988a).

---

16. For a detailed chronology of the price changes in 1979 and thereafter, see Sicular (1988a).

17. *Quanguo wujia gongzi huiyi jiyao* (Summary of National Conference on Wage and Price) in State Statistical Bureau, Urban Sampling Survey Team (1988: 8–14).

TABLE 2.11   PRICES, CROP PATTERNS, AND CROPPING
INTENSITY IN CHINA, 1965–1987

Year	Index of above-quota prices (1978 = 100)	Share of production teams using household responsibility system (%)	Crop patterns in sown areas			Multiple cropping index (%)
			Grain crops (%)	Cash crops (%)	Other (%)	
1965	84.1	0	83.5	8.5	8.0	138.3
1970	97.2	0	83.1	8.2	8.7	141.9
1971	98.4	0	83.1	8.2	8.7	144.7
1972	98.4	0	81.9	8.5	9.6	147.0
1973	98.1	0	81.6	8.6	9.8	148.2
1974	98.4	0	81.4	8.7	9.9	148.7
1975	98.7	0	81.0	9.0	10.0	150.0
1976	99.4	0	80.6	9.2	10.2	150.6
1977	100.0	0	80.6	9.1	10.3	150.5
1978	100.0	0	80.4	9.6	10.0	151.0
1979	140.7	1	80.3	10.0	9.7	149.2
1980	140.4	14	80.1	10.9	9.0	147.4
1981	145.1	45	79.2	12.1	8.7	146.6
1982	144.3	80	78.4	13.0	8.6	146.7
1983	144.9	98	79.2	12.3	8.5	146.4
1984	142.5	99	78.3	13.4	8.3	146.9
1985	129.4	99	75.8	15.6	8.6	148.4
1986	130.1	99	76.9	14.1	9.0	150.0
1987	130.2	99	76.8	14.3	8.9	151.3

Source: Justin Yifu Lin, "Rural Reforms and Agricultural Growth in China," *American Economic Reform* 82, no. 1 (March): p. 37.

Institutional reform.   Unlike the price reform, the change in the institutional structure of farming from the collective system to the household-based system, now known as the household responsibility system, was not intended by the government at the beginning of the reforms. Although the government had recognized in 1978 that solving managerial problems within the production team system was the key to improving low incentives, the official position at that time was still that the production team was to remain the basic unit of production management and accounting. Subdivision of collectively owned land and delegation of production management to individual households were considered violations of the socialist principle and thus prohibited. Nevertheless, toward the end of 1978 a small number of production teams, first secretly and later with the blessing of local authorities, began to try out the system of dividing a team's land and the obligatory procurement quotas among individual households in the team. A year later these teams were producing yields far larger than those of other teams. The central authorities later conceded to the existence of this new form of farming, but required that it be restricted to poor agricultural regions, mainly to hilly or mountainous areas and to poor teams in which people had lost confidence in the collective. This restriction, however, was ignored in most regions. Production performance improved after a team adopted the new system, whether it was a rich team or a poor team. Full official recognition of the household responsibility system as a universally acceptable farming institution was eventually given in late 1981, exactly two years after the initial price increases. By that time, 45 percent of the production teams in China had already instituted the household responsibility system. By the end of 1983, 98 percent of production teams in China had adopted this new system (see Table 2.11). It is worth emphasizing that the household responsibility system was created initially without the knowledge or approval of the central government. It was worked out by farmers themselves and spread to other areas because of its merits. In short, this institutional shift in Chinese agriculture was not brought about by any individual's will but evolved spontaneously in response to underlying economic forces. This change provides empirical evidence for the induced institutional innovation hypothesis.[18]

When the household responsibility system was originally introduced, a share of the collectively owned land was leased to each of the households in a team for one to three years. Along with the land lease was a contract between the household and the team specifying the household's obligations to fulfill state procurement quotas and to pay various forms of local taxes.[19] A household could, however, retain any product in excess of the stated obligations. In the distribution of land leases, egalitarianism was in general the guiding principle. Therefore, collective land in most cases was allotted strictly in proportion to the number of people in a household rather than the number of workers (Kojima 1988) and thus inhibiting efficient land use. Moreover, in the initial distribution, land was first classified into several different grades, and households were given portions of each grade. As a result, a household's holding was fragmented into an average of nine tracts, though the

---

18. For a chronology of the policy evolution, see Ash (1988). For a summary of the development from variants of the responsibility system to the household responsibility system, see Kueh (1984). For a discussion of some new issues related to the household responsibility system, see Kojima (1988). For a rigorous test of the induced institutional innovation hypothesis, see Lin (1987).
19. Crook (1985) provides a detailed analysis of a model contract.

total holding size was only about 1.2 acres. The one-to-three-year short contract was also found to have detrimental effects on incentives to invest in land improvement and soil conservation.[20] To remedy these problems, several new policies were introduced. First, in 1983 households were allowed to exchange labor with other households and to employ a limited amount of labor for farm work (Kueh 1985). Second, in 1984, to provide better incentives for soil conservation and investment, leases were allowed to be extended to fifteen years. Third, to make land consolidation possible and to prevent land from being left idle when the household engaged in nonfarm business, the subleasing of landholdings to other households with compensation was also sanctioned in 1984. These policy reforms may eventually revive labor and land markets in rural China. So far, however, transactions in land exist only marginally in China, and the hiring of labor for farm work is mainly confined to certain regions in the coastal provinces (Lin 1989).

National policy still stresses the importance of maintaining the institutional stability of the newly established household farming system. The doctrine of equating big tractors with advanced technology and large farm size with efficiency, however, is still deeply rooted in the minds of many scholars and prominent leaders (Ash 1988).[21] Because of increasing discontent with the stagnation of grain production since 1984, a call for re-collectivization has emerged in the guise of enlarging operational size to exploit returns to scale. In some localities, this call has resulted in contracts being disrupted before expiration without the consent of farmers (Jiang 1988). There is a concern that farmers may once again be deprived of the economic independence and increased freedom they have enjoyed over the past ten years (Johnson 1989). Nevertheless, the institutional reform of farming may have become irreversible. Any attempt to change the institution back to a collective system is doomed to fail.

Market and planning reform.   The third most important element of the reforms is the greater role given to markets, in place of planning, for guiding production in the rural sector. The prevalence of planning in agriculture before the reforms was a result of the emphasis placed on self-sufficiency in grain, which was a component of the Stalinist-type heavy-industry-oriented development strategy that the Chinese government pursued after 1953. Because state grain procurement prices were

---

20. Wen (1989) provides a theoretical investigation of the possible effects of tenure insecurity on long-term farm investments.
21. For an insightful critique of this doctrine, see Schultz (1964: Ch. 8).

kept at an artificially low level, the more grain an area exported, the more tax it effectively paid. Areas with a comparative advantage in grain production were thus reluctant to raise their levels of grain output. Consequently, grain-deficient areas had to increase grain production if grain demand increased with growth in population or income. National self-sufficiency thus degenerated into local self-sufficiency. To guarantee that each region would produce enough grain for its needs, the government embarked on extensive planning of agricultural production. Mandatory targets often specified not only the sown acreage of each crop, but also yields and levels of inputs. Because planners focused on grain, they gave insufficient attention to economic considerations. To increase grain output to meet state procurement quotas and local demands, local governments were often forced to expand grain-cultivation area at the expense of cash crops and to increase cropping intensity, even though these practices often resulted in net losses to farmers. Such measures undoubtedly caused land allocation increasingly to depart from the principle of comparative advantage. The loss of regional comparative advantage was especially serious in areas that traditionally depended on interregional grain trade to facilitate specialization in cash crops.[22]

The loss of allocation efficiency caused by the self-sufficiency policy was conceded at the beginning of the reforms. Although planning was still deemed essential, more weight was given to market considerations. The decision to increase grain imports, cut down grain procurement quotas, and reduce the number of products covered by planning reflected this intention.[23] Moreover, restrictions on private interregional trade in agricultural products were gradually loosened (Sicular 1988b). Special measures were also taken to encourage areas that traditionally had a comparative advantage in cotton production to expand cotton acreage.[24]

---

22. Cotton acreage dropped 16 percent nationally between 1957 and 1977/78 and fell even more in the northern provinces that initially had substantial comparative advantages in cotton production. For example, cotton acreage in Hebei, the province with the strongest initial comparative advantage, fell 58 percent between 1957 and 1977. Consequently, north China ceased to export cotton in the late 1970s (Lardy 1983: 62–63)

23. Net grain imports increased from 6.9 million tons in 1978 to 14.9 million tons in 1982 (Ministry of Agriculture, Planning Bureau, 1989: 522, 535). The grain purchase quota was reduced 2.5 million tons in 1979 (Ash 1988). For example, the number of planned product categories and obligatory targets was reduced from twenty-one and thirty-one, respectively, in 1978 to sixteen and twenty in 1981, and further to only thirteen categories in 1982 (Kueh 1984).

24. In 1979 a policy was instituted that rewarded above-quota delivery of

All of these policy changes reduced the role of direct state planning and increased the function of markets in guiding agricultural production. As a result, cropping patterns and cropping intensity changed substantially between 1978 and 1984. The area devoted to cash crops increased from 9.6 percent of total sown acreage in 1978 to 13.4 percent in 1984, a 41.6 percent increase. Meanwhile, the multiple cropping index declined from 151 to 146.9 (see Table 2.11).[25] Much of the change in crop patterns conformed with regional comparative advantages. For example, between 1978 and 1984, the seven provinces traditionally specializing in cotton production increased their cotton acreage by 2.33 million hectares, while the rest of the provinces reduced their cotton acreage by 1.19 million hectares.[26] Although cotton acreage increased only 25 percent nationally between 1978 and 1984, total output increased 189 percent. A substantial portion of this dramatic output surge was attributable to gains in comparative advantage.[27]

The climax of the market reforms was the declaration at the beginning of 1985 that the state would no longer set any mandatory production plans in agriculture and that obligatory procurement quotas were to be replaced by purchasing contracts between the state and farmers.[28] The restoration of household farming and the increase in market freedom prompted farmers to adjust their production activities in accordance with profit margins. The acreage devoted to cash crops further expanded from 13.4 percent of total acreage in 1984 to 15.6 percent in 1985, while grain acreage declined from 78.3 percent to 75.8 percent (see Table 2.11). Expansion in animal husbandry, fishery, and subsidiary production was even faster. As a result of these adjustments, ag-

---

cotton with low-priced grain. This policy made a huge expansion of cotton area possible in the traditional cotton-producing region.

25. The multiple cropping index indicates how many times a piece of land is sown for crops in a year. An index score of 151 indicates the land is sown 1.51 times a year. Because the cropping intensity might have exceeded a reasonable level in certain areas, the reduction in multiple cropping may increase the net revenue to farmers in those areas, though the gross output may decline.

26. The seven provinces traditionally specializing in cotton production are Hebei, Shanxi, Jiangsu, Shandong, Henan, Hubei, and Xinjiang (Lardy 1983: 58). The cotton acreage data are taken from the State Statistical Bureau (1984: 78), and the Editorial Board of China Agriculture Yearbook (1985: 150).

27. Another reason for this rapid growth was the introduction and diffusion in the early 1980s of a new high-yield variety called *lumian yihao*.

28. "Zhonggong zhongyang guowuyuan guanyu jinyibu huoyue nongcun jingji de shixiang zhengce" (Ten policies of the CCP Central Committee and the State Council for the further invigoration of the rural economy) in Editorial Board of China Agriculture Yearbook (1985: 1–3).

riculture output still grew at a respectable rate of 3.4 percent in 1985. Nevertheless, the aggregate output of the cropping sector declined 1.9 percent. In 1985, of the three most important agricultural products, grain output declined 6.9 percent and cotton 33.7 percent; only oil crops registered a 33.3 percent increase.[29] This stagnation of the cropping sector has lingered since 1985 (see Table 2.10).

The market-oriented reforms aroused anxiety in some sectors of the government from the very beginning. Concern over loss of control was widely reported in the early 1980s (Sicular 1988b). In the wake of the unprecedented successes between 1978 and 1984, the pro-market group was able to push the reforms further toward the market. When growth rates slowed down and grain output declined in 1985 and thereafter, however, the government retreated from its position and once again made the voluntary procurement contracts mandatory. The policy announced in 1985 has not formally been reversed, and the government still hopes to rely on market measures to stimulate grain production.[30] Nevertheless, administrative intervention in markets and production has been increasing. For example, to facilitate the fulfillment of procurement quotas, local governments often blockaded markets in grain, cotton, silk cocoons, tobacco, and other products. Intervention in production is revealed by the fact that the acreage devoted to cash crops declined after 1985 and the multiple cropping index increased to 151.3 in 1987, a level even higher than that reached in 1978 (see Table 2.11). The attempts to increase grain output were not successful until 1990. Faced with the stagnation in grain production, the state monopolies in regional grain trade and markets in chemical inputs were instituted again in 1989.

Summary of reforms.   The three types of reforms—price, institutional, and market reforms—all contributed to the remarkable output growth between 1978 and 1984. A careful econometric analysis, using province-level input-output data covering the period 1970 to 1987 and employing the production function approach, found that of the 42.2 percent output growth in the cropping sector in 1978–1984, about 48.6

---

29. However, the output of oil crops also declined sharply after 1985.

30. The government further reduced the quantity of grain procurement contracts by 22 percent in 1986 and again by 10 percent in 1987. This measure increased the quantity of grain sold to government at "negotiated prices," which are higher than contract prices and closer to market prices. The government also instituted a policy called "three-linkups," awarding subsidized credit, chemical fertilizer, and diesel for grain, cotton, and other selected crops (Sicular 1988a).

percent can be attributed to productivity growth due to reforms. Of the productivity growth, 96 percent is attributable to the institutional changes from the production team system to the household responsibility system, and the remaining 4 percent is attributable to changes in cropping patterns and cropping intensity. These last two factors are related to reforms in the role of markets and planning. The rise in state procurement prices also had a significant effect on output growth, but its effect was derived indirectly from the effect on input uses (Lin 1992).[31]

AGRICULTURAL PERFORMANCE SINCE 1952

Before the socialist takeover in 1949, China's agriculture had been ravaged by war for several decades. The success of the socialist revolution brought peace to rural areas. A consensus among students of the Chinese economy is that the economy had recovered from the war by 1952. In the following discussion, I will use 1952 as a base year.

Sources of Agricultural Output Growth

To evaluate agricultural performance in China, I will divide the period after 1952 into four subperiods: 1952–1965, 1966–1978, 1979–1984, and 1985–1988. The institutional structure of farming was changed from the household system to the collective system in the first subperiod. The collectivization movement resulted in an agricultural crisis in 1959–1961, and agricultural production did not recover its precrisis level until 1965. While the focus was on traditional technology in the first subperiod, more emphasis was given to modern technologies in the second subperiod. In the third subperiod, the institutional structure of farming was shifted from the production team to the household responsibility system. The last subperiod is the postreform period.

The performance of agriculture differs from one subperiod to another. Table 2.12 shows that in terms of output all crops—except soybeans, oil crops, and jute in the first subperiod and potatoes in the third subperiod—had positive average annual growth rates in the first to

---

31. Estimates using Solow-Denison-type growth accounting by McMillan, Whalley, and Zhu (1989) and Wen (1989) also find the household responsibility system reform to have been the main source of productivity growth in 1978–1984.

TABLE 2.12 AVERAGE ANNUAL GROWTH RATES OF CROPS IN CHINA 1952–1988 (PERCENTAGE)

Crop	1952–1965			1965–1978			1978–1984			1984–1988		
	Production	Area	Yield	Production	Area	Yield	Production	Area	Yield	Production	Area	Yield
Grain	1.33	-0.27	1.60	3.51	0.06	3.45	4.95	-1.09	6.04	-0.82	-0.62	-0.20
Rice	1.88	0.38	1.50	3.53	1.11	2.42	4.49	-0.61	5.10	-1.31	-0.91	-0.40
Wheat	2.57	-0.02	2.59	6.01	1.29	4.72	8.50	0.22	8.28	-0.69	-0.68	-0.01
Maize	2.65	1.71	0.94	6.84	1.88	4.96	4.63	1.23	3.40	1.32	1.52	-0.20
Soybeans	-3.32	-2.33	-0.99	1.62	-1.41	3.03	4.22	0.33	3.89	4.69	2.75	1.94
Potatoes	1.52	1.96	-0.44	3.67	0.42	3.25	-1.79	-4.43	2.64	-1.35	0.18	-1.53
Cotton	3.73	-0.83	4.56	0.25	-0.21	0.46	19.33	6.05	13.28	-9.76	-5.44	-4.32
Oil crops	-1.11	-0.77	-0.34	2.84	1.44	1.40	14.75	5.70	9.05	2.61	5.18	-2.57
Jute	-0.71	-2.83	2.12	11.04	10.44	0.60	5.40	-4.12	9.52	-7.80	-3.51	-4.29
Sugar crops	5.58	6.95	-1.37	3.42	4.10	-0.68	12.31	5.75	6.56	6.66	7.92	-1.26
Sugarcane	4.98	5.14	-0.16	3.56	3.50	0.06	11.01	4.83	6.18	5.56	6.14	-0.58
Beets	11.24	12.88	-1.64	2.40	5.22	-2.82	20.53	7.21	13.32	11.51	10.36	1.15
Tobacco	4.05	4.39	-0.34	8.32	4.99	3.33	6.59	2.62	3.97	10.94	16.20	-5.26
Fruit	2.19	n.a.	n.a.	5.59	n.a.	n.a.	6.97	n.a.	n.a.	14.06	n.a.	n.a.
Meat	3.82	n.a.	n.a.	3.45	n.a.	n.a.	10.28	n.a.	n.a.	9.24	n.a.	n.a.
Aquatic crops	4.56	n.a.	n.a.	3.50	n.a.	n.a.	4.85	n.a.	n.a.	14.42	n.a.	n.a.
Freshwater crops	5.05	n.a.	n.a.	4.59	n.a.	n.a.	1.52	n.a.	n.a.	11.36	n.a.	n.a.
Seawater crops	3.63	n.a.	n.a.	0.68	n.a.	n.a.	13.37	n.a.	n.a.	19.25	n.a.	n.a.

n.a. = not available.

Source: State Statistical Bureau, *Zhongguo tongji nianjian, 1989* (China statistical yearbook, 1989) (Beijing-China Statistics Press, 1989), pp. 192, 198–201, 213, 219.

third subperiods. The predominant source of output growth for foodgrains in these three subperiods was increased yield. This is a dramatic departure from the historical pattern found by Perkins (1969: 33), in which over 50 percent of grain output growth in the several centuries before the socialist revolution was attributable to the expansion of cultivated acreage. As with foodgrains, the main source of output growth for cotton in the first to the third subperiods was increased yield. For other cash crops, however—such as oil crops, jute, sugar crops, and tobacco—acreage expansions were the major source of output growth in the first and second subperiods, while yield increases played a more important role than acreage expansions in the third subperiod.

The average annual growth rates of yield for foodgrains in the second subperiod are about twice as high as those in the first subperiod. This reflects changes in the government's agricultural technology policy. In the first subperiod, the focus of the policy was the selection and promotion of best local varieties, while after the second subperiod the focus shifted to the green revolution—that is, the introduction of modern high-yield varieties and increases in the use of chemical fertilizer and other modern inputs. From the comparison of the growth rates of yields in the second subperiod, it is clear that the green revolution was confined largely to foodgrains.

In the third subperiod, the growth rates of output as well as yields of most crops outperformed the previous two subperiods. The average annual growth rate of yields for grain as a whole increased from 3.45 percent in the second subperiod to 6.04 percent in the third subperiod, mainly because of improvements in the yields of rice and wheat. Even more impressive were the improvements in cash crops. The average annual growth rates of yields for cotton, oil crops, jute, and sugar crops all outperformed those of grain. Part of the reason may be the diffusion of the green revolution from grain crops to cash crops.[32] Since the annual population growth rate in this period was only 1.3 percent, the per capita availability of grain, edible oil, fibers, and other agricultural products increased substantially.

The pattern of output growth in the last subperiod—the postreform period—was dramatically different from that of the first three subperiods. First of all, the yields of all crops except soybeans and sugar beets had a negative growth rate. The growth rates of sown acreage for rice,

---

32. For example, a new cotton variety, *lumian yihao,* was released in 1980 and widely adopted in northern China. This variety is reported to outperform the old varieties by a substantial margin.

TABLE 2.13 PRODUCTION OF MAJOR COMMODITIES IN CHINA, 1952–1988 (IN THOUSANDS OF TONS)

	1952	1965	1978	1984	1988
Grain	163,920	194,530	304,770	407,310	394,080
Rice	68,430	87,220	136,930	178,260	169,110
Wheat	18,130	25,220	53,840	87,820	85,430
Maize	16,850	23,660	55,950	73,410	77,350
Soybeans	9,520	6,140	7,570	9,700	11,650
Potatoes	16,330	19,860	31,740	28,480	26,970
Cotton	1,304	2,098	2,167	6,258	4,149
Oil crops	4,193	3,625	5,218	11,910	13,203
Jute	306	279	1,088	1,492	1,078
Sugar crops	7,594	15,376	23,819	47,804	61,875
Sugarcane	7,117	13,392	21,116	39,519	49,064
Beets	497	1,984	2,703	8,285	12,811
Tobacco	222	372	1,052	1,543	2,337
Fruit	2,443	3,239	6,570	9,845	16,661
Meat	3,385	5,510	8,563	15,406	21,936
Aquatic crops	1,670	2,980	4,660	6,190	10,610
Freshwater crops	1,060	2,010	3,600	3,940	6,060
Seawater crops	610	970	1,060	2,250	4,550

Source: State Statistical Bureau, *Zhongguo tongji nianjian, 1989* (China statistical yearbook, 1989) (Beijing: China Statistics Press, 1989), pp. 198–201, 213, 219.

wheat, cotton, and jute were also negative. As a result, the output growth rates for rice, wheat, cotton, and jute were negative. For the crops with a positive output growth rate, most rates were substantially lower than those in the previous subperiod. Nevertheless, for fruit, meat, and aquatic products, the average annual growth rates for output were several times the rates in the previous subperiods (see Table 2.12). As a result, the growth rate of the agricultural sector as a whole, measured at constant prices, stayed at an average rate of 4.1 percent per year in 1984–1988, which is remarkable compared with the growth rates in other countries in the same period.[33]

Table 2.13 documents output growth in absolute terms from 1952 to 1988. There was a net quadrupling of wheat and maize output, a

33. The coexistence of stagnation in the cropping sector and dynamism in the noncropping agricultural sector is a result of farming institutional reform and price reform. After the household responsibility system reform, a household's autonomy in making production decisions increased. Except for grains, oil crops, cotton, and a few other crops, most prices for agricultural products were decontrolled after 1984. The profit margin for those decontrolled products in general is higher. Therefore, it is natural that farmers allocated their resources away from crops to the more profitable noncrop agricultural products.

TABLE 2.14 DAILY PER CAPITA INTAKE OF CALORIES, PROTEIN, AND FAT IN VARIOUS COUNTRIES (ANNUAL AVERAGE FOR 1984–1986)

	Calories (kilocalories)	Protein (grams)	Fat (grams)
World	2,694	70.3	65.3
China[a]	2,565	68.8	41.3
India	2,204	53.9	35.7
Indonesia	2,513	53.4	42.9
Pakistan	2,244	59.1	53.1
Egypt	3,313	81.1	80.6
Brazil	2,643	61.1	57.5
Japan	2,858	88.0	84.5
United States	3,642	106.5	164.4

[a]1985 figures.
Source: Editorial Board of China Agriculture Yearbook, *Zhongguo nongye nianjian, 1989* (China agriculture yearbook, 1989) (Beijing: Agriculture Press, 1990), p. 631.

doubling of rice and foodgrains as a whole, a tripling of cotton and oil crops, and a more than sixfold increase in sugar crops, tobacco, fruit, meat, and aquatic crops. In the 1980s, thanks to this output growth, the daily nutritional intake of the Chinese population moved close to the world average, surpassing those of India and many other developing countries (see Table 2.14).

Farming Institutions and Agricultural Performance

The discussion of average annual growth rates of output and yield suggests that agriculture performed differently as a result of different institutional arrangements. Many factors, however, may affect the performance of agriculture. The rates of increase and the reliability of supplies of modern seed varieties, chemical fertilizers, pesticides, irrigation, tractors, and other inputs would also affect the rates of yield increase and output growth in each period. The best way to measure the effect of farming institutions on agricultural performance is to compare total factor productivity in each period. This approach first uses factor shares as weights to compile individual input series into a total input series, and then divides the aggregate output series by the total input series to obtain the total factor productivity index. Figure 2.1 depicts Wen's (1989) estimates of changes in total factor productivity in the 1952–1988 period. In Wen's estimates, the gross value of agricultural output is calculated from grains, cash crops, and livestock. Inputs include labor, land, capital, and current inputs. The weights used are 0.50 for labor, 0.25 for land, 0.10 for capital, and 0.15 for current inputs.

FIGURE 2.1   TOTAL FACTOR PRODUCTIVITY INDEX FOR CHINA, 1952–1988

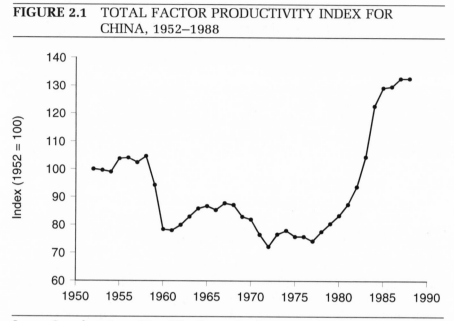

Source: Guanzhong James Wen, "The Current Land Tenure and Its Impact on Long-Term Performance of the Farming Sector: The Case of Modern China" (Ph.D. dissertation, University of Chicago, 1989).

Figure 2.1 shows that the total factor productivity indexes in 1952–1988 can be divided into four periods: 1952–1958, 1959–1978, 1979–1983, and 1984–1988. In 1952–1958, that is, during the period of voluntary collectivization, total factor productivity shows a rising trend, although the increments are small. Total factor productivity declined dramatically in 1959/60, when compulsory collectivization was first imposed, and throughout 1961–1978 stayed at a level about 20 percent below the level reached in 1952. The record improved dramatically after 1978, the period of decollectivization. By 1983 total factor productivity had regained its 1952 level. In 1985–1988, the post-reform period, total factor productivity remained about 30 percent higher than the 1952 level, though the rate of increase slowed.

Two puzzling questions must be addressed before we can draw conclusions about the different effects of farming institutions on agricultural performance: First, why did total factor productivity collapse in 1959–1961 and stay at a low level throughout the period 1961–1978? Second, why did increasing trends in total factor productivity take place during the transition periods both from the household farming system to the collective system in 1952 to 1958 and from the collective farming system to the household responsibility system in 1978 to 1984?

The commonly accepted explanations for the agricultural crisis of 1959–1961 are bad government policies, poor management in the communes, three successive years of bad weather, and poor incentives owing to the unwieldy size of communes (Perkins and Yusuf 1984: 79; Eckstein 1966: 379; Chinn 1980; Aston et al. 1984). As discussed in the previous section, all of these conditions had been eliminated by the time the commune system was replaced by the production team system in 1962. If these explanations were sufficient, then agricultural productivity should soon have recovered its pre-1958 level. The empirical evidence, however, indicates that total factor productivity did not return to its precrisis level until the production team system was abandoned.

In a recent paper, I argue that because of the difficulty of supervising agricultural work, the success of an agricultural collective depends on a self-enforcing contract, in which each member promises to discipline himself (Lin 1990). A self-enforcing contract, however, can be sustained only in a repeated game. In the fall of 1958, the right to withdraw from a collective was eliminated, thus changing the collective from a repeated to a one-time game. This change had a significant effect on the incentive structure of collectives. In the case of a repeated game, collective members can decide at the end of each production round whether they want to participate in the collective in the next round. If it is perceived as advantageous to be a member of the collective, members will retain their membership; otherwise, members will withdraw from the collective. Since in China a household's landholding is often highly fragmented and too small to allow a single household to raise a draft animal, farmers can achieve certain gains by pooling the land and farm tools of several households (Chinn 1980). Gains from economies of scale, however, are ultimately overshadowed by the incentive issue arising from the difficulties of supervision in agricultural production. To make a collective an efficient institution, some effective substitute for supervision is required. A self-enforcing agreement among collective members in which each one promises to provide as much effort as on his own household farm is an effective alternative when supervision is too costly.[34] Certainly, because of the heterogeneity of personal preferences, abilities, and endowments, a member may determine that he will be better off by reneging on the agreement. That is, the member may break the promise and not contribute as much to production as promised initially. When this is the

---

34. For further discussion of self-enforcing agreements, see Telser (1980).

case, the other collective members have to decide whether to stay in the collective and allow this member to continue to be derelict toward the agreement or to withdraw from the collective and resume household farming. If they find that the losses due to this member's default are larger than the gains from economies of scale, the collective will disintegrate. The possibility of the collective's collapse, however, obliges the would-be shirker to rethink his position: should he break his promise and let the collective collapse, or should he honor his commitment and prevent the disintegration of the collective? If he shirks in the current round, the member is definitely better off at the end of this round. If the collective collapses, however, the member will lose the gains from economies of scale from the second round on. If the discounted present value of future losses is larger than the one-time gains in this round, the member will honor the agreement. Therefore, it is the threat of a collective's collapse that greatly reduces the incidence of shirking. This implicit threat also guarantees that the production in a voluntarily formed collective will be at least as good as the sum of production of a group of households working separately.[35] Even in the worst case, if the collective collapses agricultural production will remain at the precollective level.

When a collective is imposed and withdrawal is prohibited, however, it becomes impossible to use withdrawal as a way of either protecting oneself or checking the possibility of shirking by other members. Consequently, the self-enforcing agreement cannot be sustained in the "one-time-game" collective (Telser 1980). Supervision becomes crucial in establishing work incentives and productivity levels in the collective. If the supervision of each member's work is perfect, the incentives to work will be excessive rather than insufficient (Lin 1988). This is due to the fact that the return on a member's additional effort has two components. First, the member will get a share of the increase in the collective output. Second, the member will get a larger share of the total net collective income, as now the member contributes a larger share of total effort and thus has a larger share of work points. The former itself provides insufficient incentives, but is overcompensated by the latter. On the other hand, if there is no monitoring of effort, a

---

35. This statement assumes that one's income is the only objective for joining a collective and that reorganization is cost-free. If a collective also provides services like risk sharing and if reorganization is costly, the productivity of a collective is allowed to be somewhat lower than the sum of the household farms. Moreover, if moral suasion is used in forming a collective, a member will also accept a somewhat lower income in the collective for fear of social opprobrium.

member will not get more work points for the additional contribution of effort. In this case, the return on a member's increase in effort has only one component, namely, a share of the increase in team output, which is in itself an insufficient incentive. The degree of increase in work point share for an additional unit of effort depends on the extent of supervision. Therefore, incentives to work in an imposed collective are positively correlated with the degree of supervision. The higher the degree of monitoring, the higher the incentive to work, and thus the more effort contributed.

Supervision, however, is very costly. The management of a collective thus needs to balance the gain in productivity from increased incentive and the rise in the cost of supervision. Other factors being equal, the optimum degree of supervision is higher if the work is easier to supervise in the production process and lower if the work is more difficult to supervise. Therefore, the degree of incentive to work depends on how difficult it is to monitor effort in the production process. Difficulty of supervision is affected by many factors. For example, all things being equal, the larger the size of a collective, the harder it is to monitor each peasant's effort. The nature of the production process, including spatial and temporal factors, also influences the ease of supervising effort.

The supervision of agricultural operations is particularly difficult because the processes involved typically span several months and many acres of land. Farming also requires peasants to shift from one kind of job to another throughout the production season. In general, the quality of work provided by a peasant does not become apparent until harvest time. Furthermore, it is impossible to determine each individual's contribution by simply observing outputs, owing to the random effects of nature on production. It is thus very costly to provide close monitoring of each member's contribution of effort in agricultural production. Consequently, the optimum degree of monitoring in a collective mainly engaging in agricultural production is necessarily low, and the incremental income for an additional unit of effort is only a small fraction of the marginal product of effort. Therefore, work incentives for peasants in an imposed collective must also be low, and agriculture in the collective system performs dismally.

In short, the collapse of agriculture in 1959–1961 and the dismal agricultural performance until 1978 was brought about by the abolishment of the right to withdraw in 1958 and the continued imposition of collectivization until 1978. Total factor productivity improved in the period 1952–1958 because collectivization was voluntary and in the period 1978–1984 because incentives to work were improved with the elimination of imposed collectivization.

Farming Institutions and Income Distribution

Although collectivization was ineffective in terms of the performance of agriculture, one often-mentioned favorable effect was its impact on income distribution (Riskin 1987: 225–32; Lippit 1987: 159–60; Lardy 1978). As Table 2.6 shows, the land reform program in the early 1950s confiscated and redistributed the landlords' property to poor peasants, significantly improving the distribution of income in rural areas. The formation of collectives further eliminated differences in income resulting from variations in the amounts of land owned by individual households. In a country as large as China, however, there are substantial cross-regional variations in agroclimatic and natural resource endowments. Moreover, for historical reasons, the development of urban centers, markets, and transportation varies significantly from region to region. Therefore, the major source of income differences in China is regional disparity, which cannot be eliminated by means of collectivization. A study based on simulation found that the Gini coefficients before and after collectivization were, respectively, .227 and .211 (Roll 1974: 72, quoted in Perkins and Yusuf 1984: 110). This estimate is supported by a recent study based on nationwide household survey data. It found that the Gini coefficient in 1978 was .2124 (see Table 2.15). The estimated Gini coefficients show that collectivization left nationwide income inequality basically unchanged.

The first row of Table 2.15 shows that inequalities in income distribution worsened after the rural reforms in 1978. The Gini coefficient increased from .2124 in 1978 to .3014 in 1988.[36] Since land owned by production teams was more or less equally distributed among team members in the household responsibility reform, the increasing disparity of household income after the reform may arise from other sources than the distribution of operational land. Table 2.15 shows that accompanying the reform were substantial changes in the composition of household income. In 1978, 85 percent of income derived from agricultural production. This share dropped to 63.4 percent in 1988. Meanwhile, the share from nonfarm sources, including rural industry, transportation, construction, and commerce, increased from 7 percent in 1978 to 27.3 percent in 1988. Since the opportunity to engage in nonfarm activities exhibits large regional variation, and the ability to capture such opportunity differs from household to household owing to differences in human capital and other endowments, the worsening of

---

36. Two studies using recently released provincial-level data also confirm that the regional disparities were not reduced in the collective period and that inequality increased after the reform (see Lyons 1991; Tsui 1991).

TABLE 2.15 GINI COEFFICIENT AND AVERAGE PER CAPITA
NET INCOME OF AGRICULTURAL HOUSEHOLDS
IN CHINA, 1978–1988

	1978	1980	1984	1985	1986	1987	1988
Gini coefficient	.2124	.2366	.2577	.2635	.2848	.2916	.3014
Average per capita net income (yuan)	133	191	355	398	424	463	545
Composition of income (%)							
Agricultural income	85.0	78.2	70.5	66.3	65.8	65.0	63.4
Nonagricultural income	7.0	8.8	18.2	21.7	22.6	25.4	27.3
Nonproductive income	8.0	13.0	11.3	12.0	11.6	9.6	9.3

Note: Agricultural income refers to income from crops, animal husbandry, forestry, fishery, and household handicraft production. Nonagricultural income refers to the income from township and village industries, construction, transportation, commerce, and the catering trade. Nonproductive income refers to remittances and transfers from the collectives and government.
Source: Gini coefficient is from State Statistical Bureau, Agricultural Household Survey Team, "Nonghu shouru chayi yanjiu" (A Study of Agriculture Household Income Difference) (Beijing: China Statistics Press, 1989, mimeo). The rest of the data are from State Statistical Bureau, *Zhongguo tongji nianjian, 1989* (China statistical yearbook, 1989) (Beijing: China Statistics Press, 1989), p. 743.

income inequality may arise from policies that encouraged the nonfarm activities rather than from the household responsibility reform itself. Without more detailed and careful studies, however, it is impossible to ascertain the main sources of the increase in income disparities.

The most important disparity in China is the gap in living standards between the urban and rural population, which existed at the beginning of the First Five-Year Plan. A natural way to reduce this disparity would be to allow the poor rural population to migrate into cities. The employment opportunities created by the heavy-industry-oriented development strategy, however, were not sufficient to absorb the increasing urban labor force. Thus, in the 1960s and 1970s, the government even had a program to send urban youth to rural areas and effectively blocked the rural-to-urban migration. It relaxed the restrictions on this migration only slightly during the 1980s.[37] As a result, the

---

37. Peasants are now allowed to find temporary jobs in the cities. However, they are not entitled to any of the subsidies given to the regular urban residents. Moreover, they are often forcibly sent back to rural areas when the urban economy suffers.

FIGURE 2.2   RELATIVE CONSUMPTION LEVELS OF PEASANTS
AND NONPEASANTS IN CHINA, 1952–1990

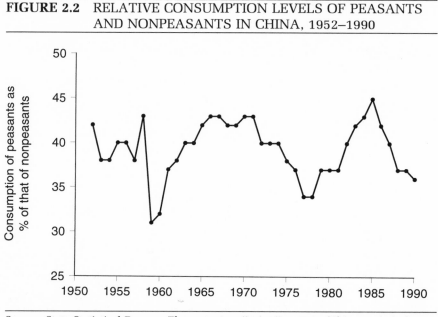

Source: State Statistical Bureau, *Zhongguo tongji nianjian, 1991* (China statistical yearbook, 1991) (Beijing: China Statistics Press, 1991), p. 270.

gap between urban and rural areas has persisted throughout the past
four decades. Figure 2.2 depicts the relative annual per capita consumption levels of peasants and nonpeasants. The consumption level
of peasants was only about 40 percent that of nonpeasants throughout
the period from 1952 to 1990. The situation reached its worst during
the 1959–1961 agricultural crisis and in 1978, the year before the
household responsibility system reform began. Although the gap was
narrowed substantially in the reforms up to 1984, it started to worsen
again in 1985. By 1990 the disparity in the relative consumption of
peasants and nonpeasants returned to its prereform level.

Although rural reforms did not reduce the consumption gap between peasants and nonpeasants, it did significantly improve peasants'
absolute level of consumption. Figure 2.3 shows that between 1952 and
1978 peasants' per capita consumption, measured at comparable prices,
increased only 57.6 percent, with an annual growth rate of only 1.8
percent. In contrast, the consumption level more than doubled between
1978 and 1988, increasing 8.1 percent per year, although it declined
slightly in 1989 and 1990. Similar improvement is also found in a comparison of peasants' per capita net income before and after the reforms.

FIGURE 2.3	CONSUMPTION LEVEL OF PEASANTS IN CHINA 1952–1990

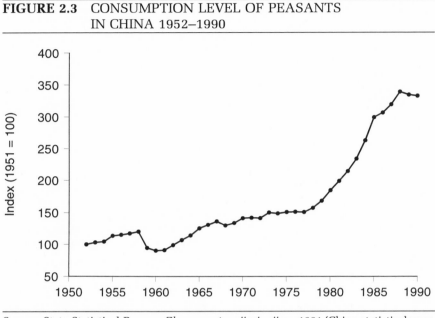

Source: State Statistical Bureau, *Zhongguo tongji nianjian, 1991* (China statistical year-book, 1991) (Beijing: China Statistics Press, 1991), p. 271.

As shown in Table 2.16, 65 percent of households in 1978 had per capita net incomes of less than 150 yuan, and only 2.4 percent had per capita incomes of more than 300 yuan. In 1988 only 2 percent of households had per capita incomes of less than 200 yuan, while more than 80 percent of households had per capita incomes of higher than 300 yuan. Even though the price index for consumption goods in rural periodic markets increased 112 percent between 1978 and 1988, the increase in per capita income still represents a substantial improvement. It is thus safe to conclude that, in terms of absolute level and rate of growth of consumption and income, peasants are much better off under the house-hold-based farming system than they were under the collective system.

ISSUES TO BE SOLVED FOR SUSTAINED AGRICULTURAL GROWTH

So far, China's agricultural reforms have been successful. Even the average growth rate of 4.1 percent per year after 1984 is remarkable. Two important, related issues, however, need to be addressed: (1) What is the future of the market-oriented reforms in rural areas? and (2) what is the

TABLE 2.16 PEASANTS' PER CAPITA NET INCOME IN CHINA, 1978–1988 (PERCENTAGE OF HOUSEHOLDS)

	1978	1980	1983	1984	1985	1987	1988
Above 500 yuan	0.0	1.6	11.9	18.2	22.3	35.7	47.0
400–500 yuan	0.0	2.9	11.6	14.1	15.8	17.2	16.7
300–400 yuan	2.4	8.6	22.1	24.5	24.0	21.3	17.5
200–300 yuan	15.0	25.3	32.9	29.2	25.6	17.5	13.5
150–200 yuan	17.6	27.1	13.1	9.4	7.9	5.0	3.3
100–150 yuan	31.7	24.7	6.2	3.8	3.4	2.4	1.5
Below 100 yuan	33.3	9.8	1.4	0.8	1.0	0.9	0.5

Source: State Statistical Bureau, *Zhongguo tongji nianjian, 1989* (China statistical yearbook, 1989) (Beijing: China Statistics Press, 1989), p. 742.

prospect for sustained growth in agriculture? A positive response to both of them cannot be assured until further reforms take place in the whole economy.

The stagnation of the cropping sector, especially grain production, during the 1984–1989 period hurt the momentum of market-oriented reforms. It is a deep-seated view among Chinese leaders and scholars that abundant grain production is a key to political and social stability. Therefore, the poor performance of grain production since 1984 has aroused some alarm and has even led to calls for collectivization in some circles.[38] The main reason for the cropping sector's poor performance, however, lies in its unfavorable price relative to other products after 1984. Improving the output of the cropping sector, including grain, does not involve recollectivization, but reform of current agricultural price policies.

The success of the reform toward household-based farming also brings with it issues that are potentially detrimental to sustained growth in the future. The beneficial effects of farming institutional reform on agricultural productivity is essentially a one-shot effect. Future agricultural growth will depend on conventional channels, namely, increases in inputs and improvements in technology. The speed with which the agricultural sector will be able to grow through conventional channels will be determined by public as well as private investment in agriculture. The household responsibility system reform, however, has negative effects on both types of investment. To improve incentives for public and private investment in agriculture will require some fundamental reforms in the overall economic development strategy.

---

38. In China the general public and most economists often regard agriculture as consisting only of grain production. Despite a respectable growth rate for agriculture as a whole in the past seven years, they often perceive agriculture as stagnating and in decline because of the grain situation.

Agricultural Price Policy Reform

The poor performance of the cropping sector—including grain, cotton, oilseeds, and sugar—in the postreform period is mainly due to the government's failure to change the pricing system for these products. Since 1984 the government has liberalized the control of most agricultural products. Grain, oilseeds, and sugar, however, are basic necessities for the rural population, and cotton is a major input for industry. The obligatory procurement quotas for these products remain, and their prices are regulated by the government. After the price liberalization, the production of vegetables, fruits, animal husbandry, and other non-crop products in most cases has higher profit margins than the production of the regulated products. Since the household responsibility reform offers farmers greater autonomy in production, the difference in profitability induces farmers to shift away from the cropping sector and to reallocate their time, effort, and other resources under their control to more profitable activities.[39] Therefore, a market-oriented price reform for grain, oilseeds, sugar, cotton, and other regulated agricultural products is the most fundamental way to break the production stagnation of these products.

The government's low prices for these regulated products are related to the early heavy-industry-oriented development strategy. The basic framework of the existing grain price policy, for example, was established in 1953 to secure the government's control of the grain supply on the one hand and to meet the demand of urban residents for low-priced grain on the other hand. Grain in China, as in many other countries, is more than just a commodity. Once the government becomes involved in grain distribution, any shift in the sale price of grain becomes a political event. Thus, to avoid possible political unrest, ration prices have changed little since the ration system was first instituted in 1953.[40]

When the quota system was introduced in 1953, procurement prices were set at a level under which the state grain procurement and marketing agency could make a small profit. After the great agricultural crisis of 1959–1961, however, grain procurement prices were raised an average of 25.3 percent to improve incentives for grain production.

---

39. In addition to the one-shot incentive effect of the institutional shift to household-based farming, in 1984, it is estimated that the outmigration of the labor force and the decline in the growth rate of chemical fertilizer use contributed to the stagnation of the cropping sector after 1984 (Lin 1992).
40. For example, between 1953 and 1986 the procurement price of rice increased 128.7 percent. The ration price of grain, however, increased only 9.4 percent in the same period.

After that, four more major price adjustments were made, in 1966, 1979, 1985, and 1988. Because ration prices were kept nearly constant, each raise in the procurement price resulted in an increase in the amount of the government subsidy.[41]

The existence of a gap between the government-set procurement price and the market price confronts the government with a dilemma. If the government tries to make the procurement price as competitive as the market price, its financial burden becomes unbearable. If, on the other hand, it attempts to limit the procurement price so that the amount of food subsidies can be controlled, the peasants' incentive to produce grain and to fulfill quota obligations is impaired. Since the household responsibility reform has given individual households more autonomy in production decisions and has weakened the government's enforcement measures, the issue of incentives has become particularly important.

Procurement prices have to be low because the sale price of rationed grain is low. Unless the urban food-rationing policy is eliminated and the sale price of grain is liberated, the dilemma cannot be solved. The attempt to keep the ration price at a low level was justifiable in the 1950s; in 1957 expenditures on grain alone represented 22.8 percent of total household expenditures for an average urban household. This share, however, had declined to 7.6 percent by 1987 (State Statistical Bureau, *China Statistical Yearbook,* 1986: 668, 1988: 807). Even if the sale price of grain doubled, expenditures on grain in an urban household's budget would not exceed 15 percent.

The obstacle to reforming the food-rationing policy, then, does not arise from urban residents' inability to pay the market price of grain. The low-priced food ration is, in effect, a vested interest of urban residents. As a rule, a reform will not be supported by a group of people whose vested interests are weakened by that reform, even though it may be beneficial to the economy as a whole and, indirectly, to this particular group of people. All workers in state enterprises and the majority of workers in the collective enterprises are entitled to food rations, and since over 90 percent of government income is obtained from state and collective enterprises, the government is particularly conscious of the support of workers and protective of their interests. Furthermore, all cadres in the government system itself enjoy the same

---

41. The subsidy per fifty kilos of grain sold at the government-set ration price was 2.65 yuan in 1965, 3.22 yuan in 1970, 3.56 yuan in 1978, 7.83 yuan in 1979, 15.11 yuan in 1984, and 18.67 yuan in 1987.

privilege. The government's reluctance to change the food-rationing policy in the past is thus understandable.

In 1991 the government for the first time substantially increased the retail price of grain in the urban areas by 40 percent. Although workers are compensated for the price increase and the retail prices are still not high enough to cover the procurement prices and transportation, storage, and other transaction costs, this is a big step toward the eventual liberalization of the retail price. It is reported that the retail prices of grain were further raised in 1992 to a level that can break even. So far, the dominant motives for the government are to reduce the burden of subsidies and to maintain a fixed retail price. As long as retail prices are fixed, however, the range for adjustment in the procurement prices is limited. Therefore, unless the government is willing to increase subsidies to farmers when the prices of other regulated agricultural products increase, it is unlikely that the production of grain can maintain a competitive profit margin. The production of grain may still stagnate. Therefore, the solution is to liberalize procurement and retail prices.[42] The government is finally moving toward this direction in 1993.

Public Investment

Improvements in technology, irrigation, and other infrastructure are crucial to modern agricultural development. Since investments in these activities have large externalities, governments need to play an important role in financing these activities. This is particularly true for China. Areas to which irrigation can easily be extended have been irrigated for decades, or even centuries. Yields for many crops, especially grains, are at or close to the highest levels in the world. Further increases in irrigation and improvements in seed varieties will require the government's active involvement.

Table 2.17 reports the shares of agriculture and water control in the Chinese government's annual investment in capital construction. The share of water control in total capital construction fell from about 7 percent before 1978 down to about 3 percent in the early 1980s, and further to about 1.5 percent in the late 1980s, while the share of agriculture dropped from about 10 percent to 6 and then 3 percent over the same period.

---

42. The government maintains low prices for oilseeds, sugar, and cotton for the same reason that it maintains low grain prices. Overcoming the stagnation in the production of these crops will require a solution similar to that for grain production.

TABLE 2.17   NATURAL CALAMITIES AND IRRIGATION IN
CHINA, 1953–1988

Year	Cultivated area hit by natural calamity[a] (%)	Share of government investment budget	
		Water control (%)	Agriculture (%)
1953	4.9	5.4	8.6
1954	8.5	2.3	4.2
1955	5.2	4.1	6.2
1956	8.2	4.5	7.7
1957	9.5	5.1	8.3
1958	5.2	7.3	9.8
1959	9.7	7.0	9.4
1960	15.3	8.2	11.6
1961	18.6	8.0	13.3
1962	11.9	11.6	20.2
1963	14.3	12.4	23.0
1964	8.8	10.4	18.6
1965	7.8	8.4	13.9
1966	6.7	n.a.	n.a.
1967	n.a.	n.a.	n.a.
1968	n.a.	n.a.	n.a.
1969	n.a.	n.a.	n.a.
1970	2.3	n.a.	n.a.
1971	5.1	n.a.	n.a.
1972	11.6	n.a.	n.a.
1973	5.1	n.a.	n.a.
1974	4.4	n.a.	n.a.
1975	6.7	6.3	9.3
1976	7.6	7.5	10.8
1977	10.2	7.4	10.8
1978	16.8	6.9	10.5
1979	10.2	6.7	11.0
1980	15.4	4.7	9.2
1981	12.9	3.0	6.5
1982	11.2	3.2	6.0
1983	11.3	3.5	5.9
1984	10.6	2.7	4.9
1985	15.8	1.7	3.3
1986	16.4	1.5	3.0
1987	14.1	1.6	3.1
1988	16.5	1.5	3.0

n.a. = not available.

[a]Sown acreage reported to have been hit by flood, drought, frost, or hail and to have had a yield 30 percent or more below normal.

Source: Ministry of Agriculture, Planning Bureau, *Zhongguo nongcun jingji tongji ziliao daquan, 1949–1986* (A comprehensive book of China rural economic statistics, 1949–1986) (Beijing: Agriculture Press, 1989), pp. 354–57; State Statistical Bureau, *Zhongguo guding zichan tongji ziliao, 1950–1985* (China fixed capital investment statistics, 1950–1985) (Beijing: China Statistics Press, 1987); State Statistical Bureau, *Zhongguo tongji nianjian, 1987, 1988,* and *1989* (China statistical yearbooks, 1987, 1988, and 1989) (Beijing: China Statistics Press, 1987, 1988, and 1989), p. 479 (1987), p. 572 (1988), and pp. 192, 229, 490 (1989).

The table also reports the percentage of total cultivated acreage reported to have been hit by natural disasters resulting in a 30 percent or more yield reduction compared with normal years. The percentages of disaster-hit area are significantly higher in the post-1978 reform period than in the pre-1978 reform period. The dramatic reductions in investments in water control are probably one of the main reasons for the weakening of agriculture's resistance to natural disasters.[43]

Along with the reductions in government agricultural investment have come reductions in government expenditures on agricultural research and extension services. Many extension workers find that the current government budget covers only their basic salaries, leaving no funds for trips to visit farmers. Since technological innovation and diffusion are fundamental to modern agricultural growth, a reduction in public expenditures on research and extension will undermine the long-term sustainability of agricultural growth.

When rural reforms were first conceived in 1978, the need for substantial increases in government funding for agriculture was a consensus among policy makers. The low allocation of state funds to agriculture and the high indirect taxes levied on agriculture through unfavorable state-manipulated terms of trade were believed to be primary causes of the low rate of agricultural growth. It was proposed that the share of agriculture in the government's investment in capital construction be increased from its then current rate of 11 percent to 18 percent. The government also endorsed an increase in the share of state budgetary expenditures allocated for noninvestment expenditures on agriculture. None of the planned increases in state budgetary support materialized, however, and the current levels of state support for agriculture are the lowest in history (Lardy 1986).

The dramatic reduction in government support for agriculture after 1978 has its roots in the policy environment created by the heavy-industry-oriented development strategy in the 1950s. Earlier in this paper I argued that the current policy environment—including low interest rates, overvalued exchange rates, low wage rates, and low agricultural prices—was designed to facilitate the rapid development of heavy industry. In such a policy environment, investment in industry

---

43. Another probable cause is that the prevention of floods, droughts, pests, and other natural disasters has strong externalities and requires the concerted efforts of farmers in a region. The household responsibility system has weakened local authorities' ability to mobilize farmers for disaster control. The individual household farms after the reform are thus more susceptible to natural disasters than collective farms.

is much more profitable than investment in agriculture.[44] Thus, the temptation to allocate more funds to industry always exists. Before the reform, however, the government needed to maintain investment in agriculture at a certain level because of dismal agricultural performance.[45] The output growth brought on by the household responsibility system reform reduced the pressure on the government to maintain its level of investment in agriculture. As a result, the government is once again diverting funds to the more profitable industrial sectors. The stagnation of grain production since 1984 has led again to a call to increase government investment in water control, agricultural research, and other support for agriculture. Once the output growth of agriculture as a whole, and grain production specifically, achieve satisfactory levels, however, this pressure will disappear. Therefore, if the basic policy environment favoring industrial expansion is not changed, a cyclic pattern in public agricultural investment and agricultural growth is inevitable.

Private Investment

The transition to the household responsibility system of farming has implications for private investment in human as well as physical capital. In the household responsibility system, farmers are residual claimants, giving them higher incentives to put effort into current production, which has resulted in a one-time jump in productivity. Furthermore, empirical evidence shows that, for the same reason, farmers in the household system also have higher incentives to obtain new information and learn new technology (Lin 1991). The increase in knowledge will contribute to agriculture's dynamic growth.

While the effect of the household responsibility system reform on human capital investment is positive, its effect on physical capital investment will probably be negative. In the household responsibility system the collectively owned land is leased to individual households for periods up to fifteen years. The average size of a household farm is only about 0.5 hectare. In addition, landholdings were fragmented into an average of nine tracts each to compensate for differences in land

---

44. The Chinese government's main source of budgetary revenue is the income of state enterprises. Therefore, the government has higher incentives to invest its limited resources in more profitable sectors.
45. The agricultural disaster in 1959–1961 caused government investment in agriculture to reach a historical peak in 1960–1965 (see Table 2.1). The heavy-industry-oriented strategy was also temporarily replaced by an "agriculture-first" strategy. As agriculture recovered from the crisis, state investment in agriculture gradually dropped to precrisis levels.

quality when the household-based farming system was first adopted. Such fragmentation and small farm size make investment in certain forms of machinery, equipment, tools, and draft animals unprofitable. Since land is still collectively owned and the ideological heritage of collectivism is strong, there is a risk that farmers will revert to certain forms of collective farming. Moreover, since a given tract of land may not be reassigned to the same household in the next contract, tenure is insecure. This may reduce incentives for investments in land improvement such as maintenance of land fertility. To provide better incentives for physical investment, the policy of improving tenure security and facilitating the consolidation of landholding through market exchanges, which was introduced in 1985, should be strengthened.[46]

CONCLUSION

China's experience in agricultural development, both its successes and its failures, provides many valuable lessons for other developing countries. China has been able to feed over one-fifth of the world's population with only one-fifteenth of the world's arable land and to transform a predominantly agrarian economy into an industrial power. Before the 1979 reform, however, China paid a high price for these achievements. The collective farming system was so detrimental to work incentives that, despite sharp improvements in technology and increases in modern inputs in the 1960s and 1970s, grain production in China barely kept up with population growth. The performance of agriculture just matched its performance in the six centuries before the socialist revolution.

The shift toward the household responsibility system of farming in 1979 greatly improved peasants' work incentives. Grain production and the agricultural sector as a whole registered unprecedented growth between 1979 and 1984. The increase in work incentives resulting from the institutional reform of farming, however, had mainly a one-time discrete impact on agricultural productivity. While the average annual growth rate of 4.1 percent for Chinese agriculture from 1984 to 1988 was remarkable compared with the agricultural growth rates of other developed and developing countries, grain production in China stagnated after reaching its peak in 1984. This stagnation is mainly due to

---

46. Collectivization should be ruled out as an alternative for solving the problems of fragmentation, small size, and tenure insecurity, although it is appealing to some decision makers in China. The collapse and stagnation of agriculture after collectivization in 1959 provide a lesson that should not be forgotten.

the fact that food policy reform has lagged behind institutional reform. Individual households now have more autonomy in production decisions, so farmers in the household responsibility system will allocate more resources to crops that command higher profits. Reforms have freed the marketing of most cash crops and other products of animal husbandry and fishery. Grain, however, is among the exceptions. In many counties, farmers are still required to meet grain quota obligations at government-set prices. In addition, local governments often impose blockades on grain markets, thus reducing grain prices in areas with comparative advantages in grain production. The stagnation of grain production in the postreform period, contrasted with the sizable growth of agriculture as a whole, can be attributed mainly to the decline in profitability of grain compared with other crops.

Most people in China, including political leaders and economists, believe that China should be self-sufficient in grain. Because of the stagnation of grain production, the optimism about Chinese agriculture that developed in the first six years of reform has been quickly replaced by pessimism. The small farm size and the fragmentation of cultivated land in the household-based farming system are often wrongly blamed for the poor performance of grain production after 1984. Some areas have begun to recollectivize the household responsibility system, under the guise of pursuing economies of scale in agricultural production.[47] This practice is especially appealing to local officials, because it simplifies the task of procuring grain under state quotas.

The lessons of the period before the 1979 reform demonstrate that collectivization is not a solution to the increasing demand for grain arising from population growth and industrial expansion. The final way to break the current stagnation of grain production is to let prices carry the right signal to farmers. As long as the grain price brings farmers profits as attractive as those from other crops, the individual household-based farmers in China will be able to produce enough grain to feed the Chinese population. Grain, however, is a land-intensive product, and China's land endowment is extremely scarce. This makes grain self-sufficiency a costly policy. A better policy for China would be to rely on comparative advantages and allow the nation to produce other labor-intensive crops in exchange for part of the grain requirement through international trades. Crop patterns and resource allocation in

---

47. See the report by Jiang Yaping, "Wo men bu guo yao zhong di: beijing shungyixian yiqi chengbao tudi hetong jiufen jishi" (All we want is to cultivate land: an on-the-spot report of a dispute of land contract in Shungyi County, Beijing), Renmin ribao (People's daily), October 26, 1988.

each region and in the nation as a whole would be greatly improved if 5 percent of the grain requirement (about 20 million tons) were imported. This policy is inconceivable, however, until the government gives up the ideology of grain self-sufficiency and allows urban residents to face, at least partially, world price fluctuation.

Agriculture is a supporting sector in the existing development strategy, receiving public attention only when a poor harvest constrains industrial development. Under such a strategy, the contribution that agriculture makes to modern economic growth is systematically undervalued, and a cyclic pattern in agricultural production is inevitable. Sustained agricultural growth will be possible only when China replaces its current policy environment, which was shaped by its heavy-industry-oriented development strategy, with a policy environment that allows the economy to exploit its regional as well as international comparative advantages. In the latter policy environment, both the prices of commodities and factors of production will reflect their relative scarcities in the economy. Such prices can only be obtained through demand and supply in undistorted markets.

REFERENCES

Agricultural Cooperativization in China Editorial Office. 1987. "Chronicle of Events in Agricultural Cooperativization in Modern China II." *Zhongguo nongye hezuoshi zillao* (Historical material of agricultural cooperativization in China), no. 3 (June): 4–12.

Ash, Robert F. 1988. "The Evolution of Agricultural Policy." *China Quarterly,* no. 116 (December): 529–55.

Aston, Basil, Kenneth Hill, Allan Piazza, and Robin Zeitz. 1984. "Famine in China, 1958–61." *Population and Development Review* 10 (December): 613–45.

Barker, Randolph, and Robert W. Herdt. 1985. *The Rice Economy of Asia.* Washington, D.C.: Resources for the Future.

Barnett, A. Doak. 1981. *China's Economy in Global Perspective.* Washington, D.C.: Brookings Institution.

Chinn, Dennis L. 1980. "Cooperative Farming in North China." *Quarterly Journal of Economics* 95 (March): 279–97.

Crook, Frederick W. 1985. "The *Baogan Daohu* Incentive System: Translation and Analysis of Model Contract." *China Quarterly* 102 (June): 291–305.

Du Runsheng. 1985. *China's Rural Economic Reform.* Beijing: Social Science Press.

Eckstein, Alexander. 1966. *Communist China's Economic Growth and Foreign Trade: Implication for U.S. Policy.* New York: McGraw-Hill.

Editorial Board of the Almanac of China's Foreign Economic Relations and Trade. 1986. *Almanac of China's Foreign Economic Relations and Trade, 1986.* Beijing: Zhongguo Zhanwang Press.

Editorial Board of China Agriculture Yearbook. 1981–1990. *Zhongguo nongye nianjian, 1980* to *1989* (China Agriculture Yearbook, 1980 to 1989). Beijing: Agriculture Press.

Field, Robert Michael. 1988. "Trends in the Value of Agricultural Output, 1976–86." *China Quarterly,* no. 116 (December): 556–91.

Hartford, Kathleen. 1985. "Socialist Agriculture Is Dead; Long Live Socialist Agriculture! Organizational Transformations in Rural China." In E. J. Perry and C. Wong, eds., *The Political Economy of Reform in Post-Mao China.* Cambridge, Mass.: Harvard University Press.

Jiang, Yaping. 1988. "Wo men bu guo yao zhong di: beijing shungyixian yiqi chengbao tudi hetong jiufen jishi" (All we want is to cultivate land: an on-the-spot report of a dispute of land contract in Shunyi County, Beijing). *Renmin ribao* (People's daily), October 26.

Jingjixue zhoubao (Economic Weekly). 1982. January 11.

Johnson, D. Gale. 1989. "Economic vs. Noneconomic Factors in Chinese Rural Development." Paper No. 89:13. Chicago: Office of Agricultural Economics Research, University of Chicago.

Kojima, Reeitsu. 1988. "Agricultural Organization: New Forms, New Contradictions." *China Quarterly,* no. 116 (December): 706–35.

Kueh, Yak-Yeow. 1984. "China's New Agricultural-Policy Program: Major Economic Consequences, 1979–1983." *Journal of Comparative Economics* 8, no. 4 (December): 353–75.

_____. 1985. "The Economics of the 'Second Land Reform' in China." *China Quarterly,* no. 101 (March): 122–31.

Lardy, Nicholas R. 1978. *Economic Growth and Income Distribution in the People's Republic of China.* New York: Cambridge University Press.

_____. 1983. *Agriculture in China's Modern Economic Development.* Cambridge: Cambridge University Press.

_____. 1986. "Prospects and Some Policy Problems of Agricultural Development in China." *American Journal of Agricultural Economics* 68, no. 2 (May): 451–57.

Latham, Richard J. 1985. "The Implications of Rural Reforms for Grass-Roots Cadres." In Elizabeth J. Perry, ed., *The Political Economy of Reform in Post-Mao China.* Cambridge, Mass.: Harvard University Press.

Lin, Justin Yifu. 1987. "The Household Responsibility System Reform in China: A Peasant's Institutional Choice." *American Journal of Agricultural Economics* 69, no. 2 (May): 410–15.

_____. 1988. "The Household Responsibility System in China's Agricultural Reform: A Theoretical and Empirical Study." *Economic Development and Cultural Change* 36 (April): S199–S224.

_____. 1989. "Rural Factor Markets in China after the Household Responsibility Reform." In Bruce Reynolds, ed., *Chinese Economic Policy.* New York: Paragon.

_____. 1990. "Collectivization and China's Agricultural Crisis in 1959–1961." *Journal of Political Economy* 98 (December): 1228–52.

_____. 1991. "The Household Responsibility System Reform and the Adoption of Hybrid Rice in China." *Journal of Development Economics* 36, no. 2 (July): 353–72.

_____. 1992. "Rural Reforms and Agricultural Growth in China." *American Economic Reform* 82, no. 1 (March): 34–51.

Lin, Justin Yifu, Cai Fang, and Shen Minggao. 1989. "On Economic Reform and the Choice of Development Strategy." *Jingji Yanjiu* (Economic Research Monthly), no. 3 (March): 28–35.

Lippit, Victor D. 1974. *Land Reform and Economic Development in China: A Study of Institutional Change and Development Finance.* White Plains, N.Y.: International Arts and Sciences Press.

_____. 1987. *The Economic Development of China.* Armonk, N.Y.: Sharpe.

Luo Hanxian. 1985. *Economic Changes in Rural China.* Beijing: New World Press.

Lyons, Thomas P. 1991. "Interprovincial Disparities in China: Output and Consumption, 1952–1987." *Economic Development and Cultural Change* 39, no. 3 (April): 471–506.

McMillan, John, John Whalley, and Li Jing Zhu. 1989. "The Impact of China's Economic Reforms on Agricultural Productivity Growth." *Journal of Political Economy* 97, no. 4:781–807.

Ministry of Agriculture. 1989a. *Zhongguo nongye tongji ziliao, 1987* (China agriculture statistical material, 1987) Beijing: Agriculture Press.

Ministry of Agriculture, Planning Bureau. 1984. *Nongye jingji ziliao, 1949–1983* (Material of agricultural economy, 1949–1983). Beijing: Ministry of Agriculture.

_____. 1989b. *Zhongguo nongcun jingji tongji ziliao daquan, 1949–1986* (A comprehensive book of China rural economic statistics, 1949–1986). Beijing: Agriculture Press.

Perkins, Dwight H. 1969. *Agricultural Development in China 1368–1968.* Chicago: Aldine.

_____. 1988. "Reforming China's Economic System." *Journal of Economic Literature* 26, no. 2 (June): 601–45.

Perkins, Dwight, and Shahid Yusuf. 1984. *Rural Development in China.* Baltimore: Johns Hopkins University Press.

Perry, Elizabeth J. 1985. "Rural Collective Violence: The Fruits of Recent Reforms." In Elizabeth J. Perry and Christine Wong, eds., *The Political Economy of Reform in Post-Mao China.* Cambridge, Mass.: Harvard University Press.

Perry Elizabeth J., and Christine Wong, eds. 1985. *The Political Economy of Reform in Post-Mao China.* Cambridge, Mass.: Harvard University Press.

Riskin, Carl. 1987. *China's Political Economy.* New York: Oxford University Press.

Robinson, Joan. 1964. "Chinese Agricultural Communes." *Co-Existence* (May): 1–7. Reprinted in Charles K. Wilber, ed., *The Political Economy of Development and Underdevelopment.* New York: Random House, 1973.

Roll, C. Robert. 1974. "The Distribution of Rural Income in China: A Comparison of the 1930s and the 1950s." Ph.D. dissertation, Harvard University.

Schultz, Theodore W. 1964. *Transforming Traditional Agriculture*. New Haven: Yale University Press.

Sicular, Terry. 1988a. "Agricultural Planning and Pricing in the Post-Mao Period." *China Quarterly*, no. 116 (December): 671–705.

_____. 1988b. "Plan and Market in China's Agricultural Commerce." *Journal of Political Economy* 96, no. 2: 283–307.

State Statistical Bureau. 1980. *Jianguo 30 nian chuanguo nongye tongji ziliao 1949–1979* (National agricultural statistics for the 30 years since the founding of the People's Republic of China 1949–1979). Beijing: State Statistical Bureau.

_____. 1981–1991. *Zhongguo tongji nianjian, 1981* to *1991* (China Statistical yearbook, 1981 to 1991). Beijing: China Statistics Press.

_____. 1984. *Zhongguo maoyi wujia tongji ziliao, 1952–1983* (China trade and price statistics, 1952–1983). Beijing: China Statistics Press.

_____. 1987a. *Guominshouru tongji ziliao huibian* (A compilation of national income statistical data). Beijing: China Statistics Press.

_____. 1987b. *Zhongguo guding zichan tongji ziliao, 1950–1985* (China fixed capital investment statistics, 1950–1985). Beijing: China Statistics Press.

_____. 1987c. *Zhongguo laodong gongzi tongji ziliao, 1949–1985* (China labor and wage statistics, 1949–1985). Beijing: China Statistics Press.

Telser, L. G. 1980. "A Theory of Self-Enforcing Agreements." *Journal of Business* 53, no. 1 (January): 27–44.

Tsao, James T. H. 1987. *China's Development Strategies and Foreign Trade*. Lexington, Mass.: Lexington Books.

Tsui, Kai Yuen. 1991. "China's Regional Inequality, 1952–1985." *Journal of Comparative Economics* 15, no. 1 (March): 1–21.

Wen, Guanzhong James. 1989. "The Current Land Tenure and Its Impact on Long-Term Performance of the Farming Sector: The Case of Modern China." Ph.D. dissertation, University of Chicago.

Wiens, Thomas B. 1983. "Price Adjustment, the Responsibility System and the Agricultural Productivity." *American Economic Review: Papers and Proceedings* 73, no. 2 (May): 319–24.

3

Indian Agriculture: Policies and Performance

T. N. Srinivasan

India is a largely rural nation of agriculturalists consisting of owner-cultivators, tenants, and landless agricultural workers. Agriculture is still the occupation of a little less than two-thirds of the population of working age, a proportion that has declined slowly over the century since the first population census of 1881. The share of agriculture in gross domestic product, however, has declined much more rapidly, particularly since independence in 1947, from over three-fifths to less than one-third in 1990/91, thus considerably widening the disparity in the average product of labor in agriculture and that in the rest of the economy. Primary exports including agriculture constituted 20 percent of the total value of exports in 1990/91. Food and fiber products from agriculture are the basic raw materials for food processing, jute, and cotton textiles industries, which have a weight of about 22 percent in the index of industrial production with the base year of 1980/81.

Arable land per capita is extremely modest, at 0.25 hectares in the mid-1980s, although it is higher than that of China. As would be expected of a country that has been under settled agriculture for millennia, the scope for expanding cultivated area by bringing new land under the plow is limited. Of course the same land could be cropped more

I thank Robert Evenson and Sudhin Mukhopadhyay for their comments on an earlier draft, without implicating them in any errors that remain.

than once a year if moisture was available. Although the rulers of India have invested in irrigation since ancient times and such investment has accelerated since independence, cultivators in many parts of India are still subject to the vagaries of the monsoon. Thus, expanding cropped area through multiple cropping is constrained by the extent of irrigation and moisture availability. Nonetheless in the first two decades after independence, cropped area grew at about 1.6 percent per year on the average. In the subsequent two decades this growth slowed to 0.8 percent per year.

With slow and decelerating growth in cultivated area, growth in output depends on the use of land-augmenting inputs such as fertilizers and technical change in the form of the introduction of better crop varieties. Indeed, the use of chemical fertilizers per unit of cropped area has increased substantially from virtually nothing before 1950 to about 62 kilos per hectare in the late 1980s (and pesticide use increased as well). Still, this is not a very high dosage, and Indian crop yields are low in comparison with other land-scarce countries such as China.

An overwhelming majority of landholdings are small, less than 2.5 hectares in size (see Tables 3.1 and 3.2). Farms, even small ones, are fragmented into many smaller parcels located at some distance from each other. A significant proportion of the rural households consist of landless laborers. With small and fragmented landholdings and modest crop yields per unit of area, a significant portion of the cultivators are poor. The landless are even poorer. Until recently, the proportion of poor among rural households did not diminish over time but fluctuated from year to year depending on agricultural output. The fall in this proportion in the late 1980s to less than 30 percent compared with over 50 percent in earlier years, if sustained, would constitute a welcome break from the past. In any case, the importance of rapid agricultural growth for alleviating poverty cannot be exaggerated.

India is a mixed economy in which agriculture is in private hands. The decisions of millions of individual farmers regarding cropping patterns, input use, and investment determine agricultural performance. Even though subsistence agriculture characterized by production largely for the cultivator's own use is still of some significance, it is fair to say that the prices farmers receive for the output they sell in the market and the prices they pay for purchased inputs greatly influence these decisions. Thus government intervention in the markets for inputs and outputs, public investments in irrigation and infrastructure (particularly in transport and communication), and public expenditures on agricultural research and extension are extremely important in determining the pace and character of agricultural development. The institutional structure, particularly credit arrangements, property

TABLE 3.1   SIZE OF HOUSEHOLD OWNERSHIP HOLDINGS IN
RURAL INDIA, 1953/54–1982

Size of household ownership holdings (hectares)	1953/54		1961/62		1971/72		1982	
	Cumu-lative % of house-holds	Cumu-lative % of land owned	Cumu-lative % of house-holds	Cumu-lative % of land owned	Cumu-lative % of house-holds	Cumu-lative % of land owned	Cumu-lative % of house-holds	Cumu-lative % of land owned
0.00	23.09	0.00	11.68	0.00	9.64	0.00	11.33	0.00
Below 0.21	41.10	0.45	37.90	0.54	37.42	0.69	39.93	0.90
Below 0.41	47.26	1.37	44.21	1.59	44.87	2.07	48.21	2.75
Below 1.01	61.24	6.23	66.06	7.59	62.62	9.76	66.64	12.22
Below 2.03	74.73	16.32	75.22	19.98	18.11	24.44	81.34	28.71
Below 3.04	82.55	26.28	83.51	31.55	86.00	37.14	88.61	42.55
Below 4.05	87.23	34.72	88.08	40.52	90.05	46.36	92.12	52.09
Below 6.08	92.28	47.50	93.17	54.49	94.67	60.93	96.02	66.73
Below 8.10	94.94	57.07	95.64	64.15	96.71	70.19	97.66	75.55
Below 10.13	96.40	63.83	97.15	71.75	97.88	77.09	98.57	81.92
Below 12.15	97.40	69.55	98.01	77.08	98.55	81.89	99.01	85.73
Below 20.25	99.06	82.46	99.40	88.87	99.59	92.14	99.76	94.57
All sizes	100.00	100.00	100.00	100.00	100.00	100.00	100.00	100.00
Concentration ratio		0.75		0.73		0.71		0.71

Source: National Sample Survey, "A Note on Some Aspects of Household Ownership Holding: NSS 37th Round (January–December 1982)," *Sarvekshana* 11, no. 2:1–18.

rights in land, and the existence and functioning of markets for tenancies, can also affect agricultural performance negatively or positively.

In this chapter, I provide an analytical description of India's agricultural policies and performance, taking into account the institutional setting, the major policies and programs relating to agricultural production, and crop output and input use since 1950. I will assess the impact of the public distribution system and poverty alleviation policies in rural areas and will conclude the chapter with a brief look at future prospects.

INSTITUTIONAL DEVELOPMENTS
IN INDIAN AGRICULTURE

The leaders of the struggle for political independence from British rule viewed ameliorating the poverty and misery of the bulk of the rural population as one of the major objectives of the postindependence state. This poverty was ascribed to the extreme inequality in the own-

TABLE 3.2   SIZE OF HOUSEHOLD OPERATIONAL HOLDINGS
IN INDIA, 1953/54 AND 1961/62

Size of household operational holdings (hectares)	1953/54		1961/62	
	Cumulative % of households	Cumulative % of area operated	Cumulative % of households	Cumulative % of area operated
Below 0.20	34.24[a]	0.44	8.55	0.32
Below 0.40	40.23	1.25	17.13	1.27
Below 1.01	54.80	5.93	39.07	6.86
Below 2.02	70.71	16.79	61.69	19.18
Below 3.04	79.95	27.31	74.53	30.91
Below 4.05	85.58	36.42	81.49	39.88
Below 6.07	91.11	49.00	89.44	54.08
Below 8.09	94.42	59.71	93.19	63.66
Below 10.12	96.09	66.72	95.48	71.05
Below 12.14	97.28	72.81	96.79	76.35
Below 20.23	99.09	85.57	98.97	88.40
All sizes	100.00	100.00	100.00	100.00
Estimated number of holdings (thousands)	66,659[a]		50,765	

[a]Including households possessing less than 0.02 hectare (numbering 4.162 million) and possessing below 0.04 hectare (numbering 6.995 million).
Source: National Commission on Agriculture, *Agrarian Reforms*, Part XV of the Report of the National Commission on Agriculture (New Delhi: Ministry of Agriculture, 1976), Appendix 67.6.

ership of land and the existence of a layer of intermediaries between the tiller and the state who claimed rights to the produce from land. After independence, the Indian National Congress, the dominant political party of the freedom struggle, formed the government. It soon constituted a committee to make recommendations on agrarian reforms as well as on cooperative farming, methods of improving agricultural production, and the condition of various rural classes such as tenants, subtenants, and landless laborers. This committee strongly held the view that land must belong to the tiller and that all intermediary rights between the tiller and the state ought to be abolished. It recommended that, barring certain relatively minor exceptions, the subletting of land be prohibited, tenants be given the right to purchase the holdings they were leasing at a reasonable price, occupancy rights be conferred on those who had been cultivating a piece of land continuously for a period of six years or more, and owners be allowed to resume personal cultivation of tenanted land only under certain well-defined conditions, including that they put in a minimum amount of physical labor and participate in actual agricultural operations (Dantwala 1987).

After considering the committee's report, the central and state governments (the latter have primary responsibility for matters relating to agriculture under the Indian Constitution) enacted a number of laws regulating agriculture. In some ways these laws had their precedents in the laws enacted during the brief period in the late 1930s when popular ministries ruled the provinces under the Government of India Act of 1935 enacted by the British Parliament. In the new laws tax farming rights that had been conferred in perpetuity to the so-called zamindars by the British were abolished after paying compensation. Other laws provided security of tenure, regulated the rents payable by tenants, and consolidated fragmented holdings. Laws establishing a ceiling on the size of land ownership were also enacted. Many of these laws were successfully challenged in the courts and were named unconstitutional deprivations of private property rights, leading the government to amend the Constitution within a year of its adoption to exclude land reform legislation from the purview of the judiciary. Yet, other than zamindari abolition and legislation on tenancy in some of the states, the remaining laws, particularly the ceiling laws, were not effective. Ceiling laws were largely evaded through subdivision of large holdings among members of an extended family and others. One study concluded that "the impact of ceiling laws in terms of surplus land released was virtually negligible . . . at 25 acres (10 hectares) ceiling about 11 million hectares of surplus land should have become available for distribution. But even under the scaled-down ceiling limits, only 0.35 million hectares were declared surplus by 1971/72 of which only 0.16 million hectares had been acquired for distribution. . . . The position had not improved up to 1977" (ICSSR 1980: 38).

The same study noted that in spite of the failure of ceiling laws, a relative shift occurred in favor of small and medium owners. This shift is confirmed by the available data on the size distribution of ownership and operational holdings (land owned plus land leased in minus land leased out) given in Tables 3.1 and 3.2. The concentration ratio of the distribution of ownership holdings has declined a bit and the share of land in ownership holdings exceeding 10.13 hectares (25 acres) fell from about 36 percent in 1953/54 to 18 percent in 1982. At the same time, the share of holdings below 2.02 hectares (5 acres) increased from about 16 percent in 1953/54 to 29 percent in 1982. Whether there has been a significant increase in the proportion of rural households that have no access to land (either through ownership or through various tenancy arrangements) and depend on wage income from manual labor for more than half their income has not been conclusively established, though some have asserted that it is the case and see an unmistakable trend toward proletarianization of the agricultural economy. Table 3.1

shows that the proportion of households that did not own any land has decreased from 23 percent in 1953/54 to 11 percent in 1982. The data in Tables 3.1 and 3.2 taken together indicate that the distribution of operational holdings is less concentrated than that of ownership holdings, suggesting that the land lease market has had a favorable redistribution effect. Of course, these data are based on responses to questions in schedules of inquiry canvassed in sample surveys. To the extent the respondents deliberately falsify the information they provide in order to conceal fraudulent transfers and partitions of the large holdings, the data will be biased. Unless both transferors and transferees have to falsify in a consistent way, however, this bias may not be quantitatively significant.

Apart from reform of the rights of land ownership that the laws discussed above addressed, the issue of the organization of production also confronted the policy makers. When the First Five-Year Plan for national development was formulated in 1951, it was thought that each village community would manage the entire area of the village, both cultivated and uncultivated, as if it were a single farm. Although actual cultivation would be arranged in family holdings, planners also envisaged a form of cooperative farming by households. It turned out that the idea of cooperative farming did not find political acceptance. A 1976 report of the National Commission on Agriculture compared three alternative organizations, with privately owned, large, capitalist, mechanized farms run with family and hired labor at one end and perhaps equally mechanized, collectively owned farms run with communal labor at the other. The report named small peasant farms run with family labor supplemented with labor exchange with other families and occasional hired labor as most appropriate under Indian conditions (National Commission on Agriculture 1976b: 154). In many ways this conclusion is essentially a reiteration of the view expressed by the Royal Commission on Agriculture in its report in 1928: "India is still preeminently the land of small holders and the typical agriculturist is still the man who possesses a pair of bullocks and who cultivates a few acres with the assistance of his family and occasional hired labour. He requires all the help that science can afford, and which organisation, education and training can bring within his reach" (National Commission on Agriculture 1976a: 126–27). The actual trends in the size distribution of farms have not quite conformed to this preferred pattern, however, mainly because of the nature of the technical change in agriculture.

The introduction of the high-yielding dwarf varieties of rice and wheat (and hybrids for other cereal crops) in the mid-1960s placed middle-sized farms in an advantageous position relative to both very small and very large farms. Although this technology was by and large scale neutral, access to a controlled source of water, to credit for the purchase of fertilizer, and to electricity or diesel for running irrigation pumps was decidedly not. Middle peasants had considerably better access to subsidized formal credit and informal credit than did very small farmers, while government policy precluded the provision of subsidized credit to very large farmers. The fragmentation of holdings and lumpiness of investment in a deep tubewell or in energizing a shallow well made such investment infeasible for small farmers. On the other hand, very large farms, except those located in the command areas of major irrigation reservoirs, did not have adequate irrigation potential. Thus, the middle peasants, aptly named bullock capitalists by the political scientists Rudolph and Rudolph (1987), have prospered economically with the advent of the new technology. Unsurprisingly, they have also organized themselves politically to safeguard their prosperity by ensuring that various public subsidies, investments, and expenditures benefiting them are maintained and expanded.

The available data on the extent of tenancy suggest that it has been declining. ICSSR (1980: 37) reports that the area under tenancy declined from nearly a fifth of the total operated area in 1953/54 to about a tenth in 1971/72, most of the decline having occurred by 1961/62. In 1982, according to the National Sample Survey (1987), the proportion of area leased out to total area owned by those owning some land was 4.30, and the proportion of area leased into total area owned was 7.47. These figures imply that tenanted area was roughly 7 percent of operated area. The ICSSR (1980) report recognizes that the data may overstate the extent of the decline, since in those states where tenancy had been legally abolished it was known to exist under informal arrangements. There may even have been an increase in tenancy since the early 1980s. The comparative advantage of middle-sized farms with respect to the green revolution technology may have induced the middle farmers to lease in land from both large and small owners. Unlike tenants in earlier years, however, who had little land of their own and were at the mercy of the landlords, the middle-farmer-cum-tenant has more bargaining power with the owners of tenanted land.

Another major institutional feature of the rural scene in the immediate postindependence years was that the commercial banks and other institutions providing formal credit were virtually absent from rural areas except possibly the land mortgage banks in some states. This meant that the rural population, including farmers, tenants, and laborers, depended on the informal markets for their credit needs. Traditionally the informal lenders included the proverbial moneylenders and the richer members of the community, particularly the landlords.

**TABLE 3.3   SHARE OF INSTITUTIONAL CREDIT IN
OUTSTANDING DEBT IN INDIA,
1951/52–1981 (PERCENTAGE)**

Year	Institutional credit	Noninstitutional credit
1951/52	12.3	87.7
1961	18.4	81.6
1971	31.7	68.3
1981	63.3	36.7

Source: D. K. Desai, "Institutional Credit Requirements for Agricultural Production—2000 A.D.,"
Indian Journal of Agricultural Economics 43, no. 3 (1988): Table I.

The bulk of the borrowing was for consumption purposes. The conventional wisdom about such borrowings was that lenders charged usurious interest rates and caused poor, illiterate, and uninformed borrowers to become so heavily indebted that they would never be able to repay as a way of alienating land and other assets that borrowers may have pledged as collateral. Also, when landlords and traders were lenders, they tended to link their credit transactions with tenancy, labor, and output marketing transactions so that the terms of lending, crop share, wage rates, and price of output became interrelated. There is a considerable literature that views such interlinking as exploitation by the economically powerful of the economically weak. A more modern view is that interlinking need not necessarily be exploitative but may simply represent the response to moral hazards and default risks in a world of asymmetric information and incomplete markets (Stiglitz 1988). Be that as it may, the decennial surveys of rural indebtedness conducted by the Reserve Bank of India show that since 1969, when all major commercial banks were nationalized and initiated a policy of expanding banking into hitherto unserviced rural areas, the dependence of the rural population on noninstitutional informal credit appears to have been weakened considerably. Table 3.3 provides the relevant data. Bell (1990), however, has questioned the reliability of these data. It should also be recalled that the adoption of the green revolution technology introduced in the mid-1960s requires substantial credit, both for long-term investment in irrigation and draft power and for working capital for the purchase of chemical fertilizers, pesticides, fuel and power, and even for wage payments for hired labor. Thus, besides an apparent shift away from informal sources, there was also a shift after the early 1970s toward borrowing for production purposes rather than for consumption.

It was mentioned earlier that the National Commission for Agricul-

TABLE 3.4   DISTRIBUTION OF PERSONS AGE FIVE AND ABOVE
BY CURRENT WEEKLY ACTIVITY STATUS IN INDIA,
1977/78 AND 1983 (PERCENTAGE)

	Rural		Urban		All India	
	1977/78	1983	1977/78	1983	1977/78	1983
Working	44	40	36	34	42	38
Self-employed	29	25	15	14	25	23
Regular employee	4	4	16	15	6	6
Casual labor	11	11	5	5	10	9
Unemployed	2	3	3	4	2	3
Not in labor force	54	57	61	62	56	58
Total population	100	100	100	100	100	100
Share of wage labor in working population	34	38	59	59	38	39

Source: National Sample Survey, "Results of the Second Quinquennial Survey on Employment and Unemployment," *Sarvekshana* 5, nos. 1 and 2 (1981); "Preliminary Results of the Third Quinquennial Survey on Employment and Unemployment, Based on First Two Subrounds Data," *Sarvekshana* 9, no. 4 (1986).

ture opted for peasant farming as a production organization and expected that by and large the labor requirements for cultivation would be met by household labor. The occupational pattern of the population of working age in rural areas is consistent with this view of the labor market. Most of the participants in the labor force are self-employed (Table 3.4). Wage employment is the occupation of about a third of those working, although, as briefly mentioned earlier, some see an increasing trend in this proportion. It is clear that the labor market as an institution has functioned efficiently in the sense of generating a diverse set of arrangements to suit the risks associated with the diverse agroclimatic conditions of Indian agriculture and the differential factor endowments (land labor and draft power) of rural households. These include employment and self-employment as cultivators, as casual agricultural laborers on a daily basis, as attached farm servants for a whole crop season or crop year, as semiattached laborers with an obligation to serve the employer when called but otherwise free to engage in any other activity, and as part of a team of contract laborers. In addition to migrating to nearby towns and distant cities within a state, rural workers from one state migrated to other states in search of employment in agriculture. The most cited example of such migration is that of migrant agricultural workers from the slower-growing and poorer eastern state of Bihar to the faster-growing and richer northwestern states of Haryana and Punjab since the advent of the green revolution.

AGRICULTURAL DEVELOPMENT POLICIES
SINCE INDEPENDENCE

Policies that affected or were expected to affect the pace and character of agricultural growth can be broadly divided into six categories ranging from broad-based to specific and from direct to indirect:

1. official campaigns to augment agricultural output, selective area-based programs, and package programs around nontraditional technologies

2. public investment and public sector outlays, including current expenditures devoted to agriculture in the five-year plans

3. direct and indirect taxes affecting agriculture, including various taxes, subsidies, and quantitative restrictions affecting production, consumption, and foreign trade; and the public distribution system (PDS) of subsidized rations of foodgrains, sugar, and edible oils provided to urban residents, the supplies for which are obtained in part from purchases at below open market prices from producers

4. other price and inventory policies, including price support policies, crop insurance schemes for encouraging adoption of risky technologies that raise average output, and a buffer stock policy that is meant to stabilize prices

5. credit policies

6. poverty alleviation policies that work primarily through the income generation process in agriculture

General and Selective Production-Oriented Policies

During World War II, with the Japanese occupation of Burma and the disruption of shipping lanes, imports of essential food articles including foodgrains became risky and uncertain. The colonial government responded to this in two ways. It controlled demand by instituting statutory rationing of scarce agricultural commodities in urban areas, cordoning off rural areas with agricultural surplus, and regulating the exports of the surplus to other areas. It encouraged production under a Grow-More-Food Campaign initiated during the second half of the war. This campaign was later modified, extended to include cotton and jute, and renamed the Integrated Production Programme. In 1946, a year before independence, the colonial government issued a statement on agriculture and food policy in India, whose overriding objective was "to lead the country away from the menace of famine to a new vigour and prosperity." The statement included ten cardinal objectives running the gamut from production, equity and efficiency, and consumption to prices and research. It also identified ten priority measures and twenty-six other measures in a program of action and assigned specific roles to the central and provincial governments (Sarma 1974). The partition of the country at independence in 1947 and the related dislocations made this statement largely nonoperational.

The First Five-Year Plan (1951–1956), into which the Integrated Production Programme had been essentially merged, accorded the highest priority to agriculture, including irrigation. Policy measures relating to land reform and tenancy reform were included in the plan, as discussed in the previous section. Largely because of favorable weather conditions, the production targets of the plan were more than achieved. This perhaps led to some complacency on the part of the planners when they put together the considerably more ambitious Second Five-Year Plan (1956–1961). As the weather turned less favorable, the production of foodgrains fell from its peak value in 1953/54 and stagnated for the next few years. With the growth in demand arising from growth in per capita income and population, a situation of excess demand and consequent upward pressure on food prices developed, coinciding with the foreign exchange shortage arising from massive imports that the ambitious second plan generated. With little foreign exchange available to pay for food imports at world market prices, concessional imports under U.S. Public Law 480 had to be sought. The emerging food crisis led the Ford Foundation to assemble a team of experts to inquire into India's food problem.

The team gave its report in 1959 (Ministry of Community Development and Cooperation 1959). Based on this report, the government initiated a program known as the Intensive Agricultural District Programme (IADP) in 1960 in seven districts and later extended it to sixteen districts. This program was aimed at increasing food output in a relatively short time and hence focused on those districts that had the highest potential for rapid growth. The policy innovation consisted of providing a package of inputs that would raise the profitability of cultivation. Indeed the program was popularly called the Package Programme. The idea of the application of a package of practices was then extended to larger areas with either irrigation or assured rainfall. It came to be called the Intensive Agricultural Area Programme (IAAP) and covered about 1,200 community development blocks in addition to the 300 blocks already covered under IADP. A number of studies evaluating the IADP and IAAP are available. The quantitative effects of the two programs on aggregate output were not large, for without technical change, the potential for increasing yields through intensive cultivation of traditional varieties using heavy doses of fertilizers and other inputs was limited.

The technological breakthrough came with the importation of seeds of dwarf varieties of wheat and rice in the mid-1960s. Because of their short stature, these varieties did not lodge when heavy with grain, and hence could withstand heavy doses of fertilizers and provide high yields. Indian agricultural scientists and plant breeders then devised other varieties, based on these seeds, that suited Indian agroclimatic conditions and the tastes of the Indian population. These rice and wheat varieties and improved varieties of corn and sorghum formed the foundation of the New Agricultural Strategy launched in 1965.

Although the new varieties gave somewhat higher yields than traditional varieties even on unirrigated land with little or no use of chemical fertilizer, their potential was greatest with controlled irrigation and adequate use of fertilizers. It was natural that the new strategy focused on those areas with controlled irrigation. Whether the use of available fertilizers should be concentrated on these varieties or should be spread thin over all varieties was debated. Given diminishing marginal returns to fertilizer use, spreading would have been more appropriate. The strategy, however, called for concentration. Since farmers using these varieties had a greater requirement for purchased inputs and hence for credit, access to credit became an important issue. Although early on there was some apprehension that the new strategy would accentuate income inequalities within the agricultural community and regional disparities arising from differences in irrigation and other endowments, the evidence accumulated over the two and a half decades since the introduction of the strategy has shown that these apprehensions were exaggerated.

It should be mentioned that even before the Ford Foundation team's report, the government had decided to establish agricultural universities based on the model of land-grant colleges in the United States. The first of these universities was established in Pant Nagar in the state of Uttar Pradesh. Since then each of the major states has established its own agricultural university. Although not all are equally effective, the contributions of the Punjab Agricultural University at Ludhiana and the Pant Nagar University to the success of the green revolution have been significant.

Agriculture in the Five-Year Plans

Western economists and others have persistently criticized the planners of Indian five-year plans for neglecting agriculture until the steep fall in food output in the two disastrous drought years of 1965/66 and 1966/67. The consequent need to import food at a high political cost, say the critics, forced Indian planners to change. This view is at best an exaggeration and at worst a distortion of history. This neglect is often inferred from the decline in the share of agriculture in the plan outlays since the first plan. It is not obvious that the only measure of emphasis or neglect of a sector is the proportion of total investment allocated to that sector. Nor is it demonstrable (at any rate it has not been demonstrated by the critics) that additional investment in agriculture would have yielded substantial returns before the availability of the new technology in the mid-1960s. Even based on this admittedly crude and arguably inappropriate comparison, however, the planners could not be accused of neglect of agriculture. On the basis of data provided by the Planning Commission, the World Bank put together the sectoral composition of real outlays and actual output levels in comparison with targets in all the plans. These data are presented in Tables 3.5 and 3.6. Remarkably, except for the First Five-Year Plan, which in many well-known ways is an exception, the share of agriculture together with irrigation and flood control has remained virtually constant, within the range of 21–24 percent. Even the share of agriculture alone does not vary much. Further, agriculture does not do worse than other sectors in the ratio of achievements to targeted output levels in successive plans. Thus, the alleged "neglect" of agriculture cannot be traced to a declining share of plan outlays or to its failure to achieve targets to a greater extent than other sectors.

A major part of public investment in agriculture went for the construction of irrigation reservoirs and distribution systems. Irrigated areas increased from about 22 million hectares in 1950/51 to about 74 million hectares in 1990/91. In the official statistics any plot of land that is irrigated at least once in a crop season is counted as an irrigated plot. Since no information about the adequacy and intensity of irrigation from the perspective of the crop yields is available, the official statistics of irrigated area might overstate the contribution of irrigation to output growth. For a number of reasons, there has also been an increasing gap between the irrigation "potential" created by investment and its actual use. For example, as of the end of the sixth plan in 1984/85 the potential created was 68 million hectares, while the use was 60 million hectares. To some extent this difference may be more apparent than real, because of the overestimation of the potential under the mistaken assumption that farmers will spread irrigation water over a large area to protect crops against stress when deprived of moisture owing to a lack of rainfall. Instead, farmers, in their choice of risk-return combinations, often opted for using water more intensively to

TABLE 3.5 ACTUAL PLAN OUTLAYS FOR AGRICULTURE AND IRRIGATION IN INDIA, 1951/52–1990 (ANNUAL AVERAGES AT CONSTANT 1970/71 PRICES)

	First Plan (1951/52–1955/56)	Second Plan (1956/57–1960/61)	Third Plan (1961/62–1965/66)	Annual plans (1966/67–1968/69)	Fourth Plan (1969/70–1973/74)	Fifth Plan (1974/75–1978/79)	Sixth Plan (1980/81–1984/85)	Seventh[a] Plan (1985–1990)
1. Agriculture and allied programs								
Billions of rupees	1.09	1.79	2.66	2.64	3.02	5.33	9.46	33.38
% of total outlays	12.04	9.71	9.98	10.24	10.68	12.33	13.85	14.17
2. Irrigation and flood control								
Billions of rupees	1.75	2.07	2.90	3.05	3.35	4.25	6.88	17.64
% of total outlays	19.34	11.23	10.89	11.84	11.85	9.83	10.07	7.49
3. 1 + 2								
Billions of rupees	2.84	3.86	5.56	5.69	6.37	9.58	16.34	51.02
% of total outlays	31.38	20.94	20.87	22.08	22.52	22.16	23.92	21.66
4. All sectors								
Billions of rupees	9.05	18.43	26.64	25.77	28.28	43.23	68.30	235.6

[a]Provisional.
Source: World Bank, private communication.

TABLE 3.6 ACHIEVEMENT OF PLAN TARGETS IN INDIA, 1951/52–1990 (PERCENTAGE OF PLAN TARGET)

	First Plan (1951/52–1955/56)	Second Plan (1956/57–1960/61)	Third Plan (1961/62–1965/66)	Fourth Plan (1969/70–1973/74)	Fifth Plan (1974/75–1978/79)	Sixth Plan (1980/81–1984/85)	Seventh Plan (1985–1990)
Plan outlays (in constant 1970/71 prices)							
Agriculture and allied programs	77	78	78	69	123	91	110
Irrigation and flood control	93	84	92	93	83	65	76
Industry and minerals	54	110	80	68	124	80	105
Power	92	91	107	95	71	82	89
Transport and communications	96	79	111	76	118	81	120
Social services	90	69	87	78	98	70	8
Total	88	85	92	79	95	80	90
Infrastructure (increase over plan period)							
Fertilizer consumption (per year)	n.a.	n.a.	39	28			
Gross irrigation area	30	34	48	89			
Electricity							
Installed capacity	51	64	65	47			
Generation (per year)	n.a.	75	66	n.a.			
Railway freight (per year)	n.a.	66	52	−31			
Annual production (increase over plan period)							
Foodgrains	187[b]	136[b]	−14[b]	19[b]			
Coal and lignite	119	76	31	27			
Finished steel	75	37	46	6			
Fertilizers	71	18	19	24			
Petroleum products	n.a.	400	92	41			
Cement	95	38	62	43			
Cotton cloth	120	32	42	3			
Gross domestic product (annual growth rate over plan period)[c]							
Agriculture	n.a.	82	2	34			
Mining and manufacturing	n.a.	68	55	56			
Other sectors	n.a.	119	108	67			
Total	178	87	56	52			

n.a. = not available.
NOTE: Targets and achievements have been compared on an annual average basis. Source does not give data for Fifth through Seventh plans.
[b] Actual increase in foodgrain production has been calculated as difference between average production in three years centered on last year, and production in base year of each plan.
[c] For actual domestic product, trend growth rates have been calculated by least squares estimation.
Source: World Bank, private communication.

raise the yields of high-value crops in a smaller area. Another reason is the lack of coordination between public investment in reservoirs and main channels and private investment in field channels. To the extent there is a time lag between the creation of potential and its use, to that extent the return from irrigation investment is lower than it could have been.

Investment in railways, roads, electricity generation, and communications, while providing the infrastructure for the whole economy, also furthered agricultural growth. Given the priority accorded to food production in the various plans, whenever there was a power shortage, nonagricultural users were made to absorb most of it. Radio programs for farmers that disseminate knowledge about better agricultural practices and newer technologies have been broadcast for several decades. Since the introduction of television, community television sets have been provided in many villages and once again special programs for farmers are telecast. Given the high adult illiteracy among the rural population, the radio and television broadcasts are important means of communicating new knowledge.

Current public expenditures on agriculture include those on crop production, irrigation, livestock and dairy development, area development, and soil conservation as well as on community development and cooperatives. These expenditures have grown substantially faster than real income and are estimated to account for about 3 percent of gross domestic product in 1990/91. Only a part of the expenditure is recovered from farmers (see the following section for estimates of subsidies). The current expenditures include expenditures on agricultural research, training, and extension. The establishment of agricultural universities has already been mentioned. Even before independence, higher education in agriculture was organized in Coimbatore in south India in 1878 and Pune in west India in 1890. An agricultural research institute was established in Pusa in the eastern state of Bihar in 1905. This institute was later shifted to Delhi and became the major research organization devoted to agriculture. Under its auspices several experimental stations were established in different parts of the country. In the postindependence era the institute carried out several experiments on different crops and varieties to determine their response to various doses of fertilizers (nitrogenous, phosphoric, and potassic), both under the strictly controlled environment of experiment stations and on farmers' fields. As mentioned earlier, the plant scientists at this institute contributed significantly to the development of a number of high-yielding dwarf varieties of rice and wheat that were resistant to droughts and pests and yielded grain that met the requirement of Indian tastes. An extension network was also created to provide knowledge and advice about the new varieties and better methods of cultivation. It used the services of a trained worker, called the village level worker (VLW) in each village, though extension was only one of the many responsibilities of the VLW.

Taxes, Subsidies, and Quantitative Restrictions in Agriculture

Agricultural income at the personal level has been largely exempt from central income taxes, and state agricultural income taxes are minor. Taxes on landholdings, which used to be important sources of revenue, have been vastly reduced. In 1950/51 land taxes accounted for nearly 8 percent of the tax revenue of the central and state governments. By 1990/91, this percentage had fallen to less than 1 percent. Estate duties and wealth taxes have raised only limited revenue from farmers. Thus the direct tax burden on agriculture is relatively light and getting lighter.

Among the indirect taxes, taxes on exports of jute, raw cotton, tea, and a few other minor agricultural commodities were significant in the 1950s and 1960s. But export duties have been negligible at least since the early 1970s. Although some of the excise and sales taxes at the state level may involve agricultural commodities, they are unlikely to be of major significance. Thus agricultural output is largely free of explicit indirect taxes as well. Of course, the rural population and agriculturalists among them bear their share of indirect taxes on manufactured consumer and intermediate goods. And, above all, the indirect effects of industrial protection and overvalued exchange rates on agriculture have been considerable.

Before turning to explicit and implicit taxes and subsidies on output and consumption of agricultural commodities, I will turn to taxes and subsidies on agricultural inputs. First of all, irrigation water from public reservoirs is heavily subsidized. Irrigation charges levied on farmers do not even cover the cost of maintaining irrigation reservoirs and canals, let alone contribute to an adequate return on capital invested. The estimated losses on irrigation projects, defined as the difference between current expenditure on the operation of the projects and irrigation charges, amounted to about 0.5 percent of GDP in 1989/90. Obviously, this is an underestimate since it did not allow for an adequate rate of return on capital invested in computing operational expenses. Second, concessions granted on electricity sold by the state electricity boards accounted for a large part of their losses amounting to over 1 percent of GDP in 1989/90. Once again these are underestimates, for the same reason as mentioned in the case of irrigation losses. Third, subsidies on fertilizers amounted to nearly 1 percent of GDP in 1989/90. Fourth, subsidies on livestock development and assorted poverty alleviation programs that are agriculture based are estimated at about 1.5 percent of GDP again in 1989/90. At a minimum, therefore, agriculture-related subsidies accounted for 4.0 percent of GDP in 1989/90.

The only implicit tax on agricultural output is that associated with procurement at below-market prices of foodgrains and a few processed agricultural commodities including sugar for the public distribution system. It has been suggested, most notably by Dantwala (1967), that the overall effect on producers of the procurement and public distribution system is a price subsidy to producers of grain. He argued that the subsidized distribution of a limited quantity of foodgrains removes poor consumers with price-elastic demand from the market, so that the price received by the producers on their open market sales to price-inelastic consumers can raise their total revenue from procurement and open market sales above what they would have been in the absence of the system. One need not take a stand on this empirical issue, since in recent years procurement prices have not been significantly below market prices and as such the implicit tax, if any, has been negligible. The difference between the price of a so-called levy sugar that manufacturers are required to deliver to the public distribution system and the open market price is significant, but this is at the first instance a tax on sugar manufacturers rather than on sugarcane cultivators. The subsidy on the public distribution of foodgrains, however, has been substantial. In 1989/90 these amounted to about 0.7 percent of GDP.

The more important quantitative restrictions affecting agriculture presently are those relating to foreign trade. In the immediate postindependence period, however, interstate (and even interdistrict) movements of foodgrains by private traders from surplus areas were prohibited. This prohibition was meant to make it easier for the public authorities to procure grains for the public distribution system from surplus districts since the ruling market prices would be lower than what they would have been with no such prohibition assuming that the amounts procured fall short of what would have been exported from these areas. Of course this blunted incentives for production in surplus areas and encouraged production in deficit areas by raising market prices above what they would have been under free movements. The market segmentation and violation of regional comparative advantage arising from such a prohibition imposed a deadweight loss, and many economists argued the case for and succeeded in achieving its abolition.

Foreign trade in several agricultural commodities (raw and processed) is canalized through state trading agencies. Canalization meant that world market prices and prospects did not necessarily determine the trading decisions—indeed the domestic market was to a considerable extent insulated from movements in world prices. For

FIGURE 3.1   INDEX OF RICE PRICES IN INDIA, 1971/72–1987/88

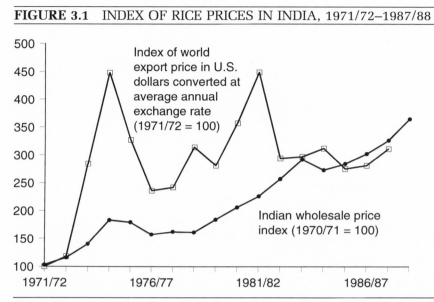

Source: International Rice Research Institute (IRRI). *World Rice Statistics, 1987.* (Los Banos, The Philippines: IRRI, 1988), Table 93; Ministry of Finance. *Economic Survey 1991–92.* (New Delhi: Controller of Publications, 1992), Table 5.2.

example, in Figures 3.1 and 3.2 the trends in world export and Indian wholesale prices of rice and wheat are shown. The movements in the two prices do not match for either crop, although the two seem to be converging for rice. It is clear that domestic prices fluctuated much less around an increasing trend compared with world prices. Even those commodities that were not so canalized were subject to arbitrary restrictions at times; a notorious example is the ban on onion exports at the time of the general elections in 1980. Onions are an essential ingredient in Indian cuisine, and a spurt in domestic prices on the eve of the elections due to strong export demand from West Asia was viewed with alarm by the party in power!

Price and Buffer Stock Policies

Apart from setting procurement prices for purchases for the public distribution system from producers and issue prices at which rations are sold to urban consumers, the government also sets minimum support prices for a number of grain and fiber crops and statutory minimum prices that processors are required to pay growers for sugarcane, jute, and tobacco. The support prices were prices at which the government stood ready to buy whatever quantities were offered. The ratio-

FIGURE 3.2 INDEX OF WHEAT PRICES IN INDIA, 1971/72–1987/88

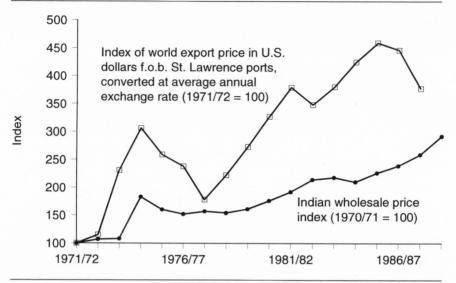

Source: International Rice Research Institute (IRRI). *World Rice Statistics, 1987.* (Los Banos, The Philippines: IRRI, 1988), Table 93; Ministry of Finance. *Economic Survey 1991–92.* (New Delhi: Controller of Publications, 1992), Table 5.2.

nale for the policy of price supports is to reduce the risk from a collapse of market prices in a bumper harvest in part because of the belief that anticipation of such a collapse would keep producers from adopting yield-raising innovations. The statutory minimum prices are meant to ensure that relatively few and powerful processors do not exploit millions of relatively weak producers.

The procurement prices for wheat and paddy were set at a level higher than support prices because they applied to limited purchases for the public distribution system in all years, good and bad, while support prices were meant to be effective for unlimited purchases in those good years of very large harvests. Indeed, until the onset of the green revolution the support prices were never invoked and the open market prices were sufficiently above procurement prices that purchases for the public distribution system involved taxation of producers. With the rapid rise in the output of wheat (and later rice) that accompanied the onset of the green revolution, however, market prices began to drift toward procurement prices. At the same time a newly organized farm lobby campaigned successfully for raising procurement prices so that the government in fact bought whatever was offered at those prices and not just the amount needed for public distribution.

With purchases exceeding the needs of the public distribution system, the government was forced to accumulate increasing foodgrains stocks, particularly after the mid-1970s. Stocks reached a peak of 25 million tons at the end of 1984/85. With the shortfall in purchases and an increase in the off-take from the public distribution system during the severe drought years of 1987 and 1988, the stocks were depleted to less than 10 million tons. As of the end of 1991 the stocks were only 14.7 million tons. Given the high cost of storage and the losses due to spoilage, however, not to mention the consumption by rodents because the grain was often stored in open areas, it is debatable whether the social benefit of such a stock policy exceeded that of other alternative policies including the use of foreign trade and exchange reserves as a means of smoothing domestic consumption of grain in the face of fluctuating output.

Before closing this section, I should make a brief reference to the continuing debate about the feasibility and efficacy of influencing the terms of trade between agriculture and industry (or alternatively between rural and urban areas) to extract the food and other surpluses needed to support rapid industrialization. An early contribution to this debate was Evgenii Alexeyevich Preobrazhensky's entrance into the Soviet policy discussion in the 1920s. It was resumed in the development economics literature in the 1950s (see Sah and Stiglitz 1984 for a recent discussion). In the Indian context, a distinguished political economist on the left of the political spectrum, Ashok Mitra, argued that "in recent years the domestic terms of trade in the country have moved continuously in favour of farm products in general, and within the agricultural sector in favour of those specific crops that are marketed by . . . the richer sections of the peasantry." This shift in terms of trade can be viewed as "mirroring a political arrangement entered into by the urban bourgeoisie with the rural oligarchy" (Mitra 1977: 141). I have shown elsewhere that this view had little empirical support and the terms of trade shifted against agriculture soon after Mitra's book was published (Srinivasan 1986)!

Credit Policies

The National Commission on Agriculture (1976a) traced the evolution of the institutional financing system for agriculture to the adoption of the Cooperative Credit Societies Act of 1904 by the colonial government. The various enquiries and studies during the preindependence era pointed out that almost all farm credit was supplied by moneylenders at high interest rates. The government periodically passed measures for debt relief and attempted to control moneylending through ceilings on chargeable rates of interest and prohibition of the seizure of land and other specific property items of agriculturists in default to moneylenders.

In the postindependence period until the nationalization of commercial banks, the cooperative system was viewed as the most suitable for administering farm credit. By the time the first All India Rural Credit Survey was undertaken in the early 1950s, however, the cooperative system accounted for only 3.1 percent of the total borrowings of cultivators. The National Development Council, which included the prime minister and the chief ministers of the states, recommended in 1958 that conditions should be created so that every rural peasant and worker would be attracted to join the village cooperative. After a committee appointed in 1961 devised policies in this regard, the government declared that cooperatives were to be the sole institution to provide agricultural credit. Five years later another committee (appointed in July 1966), called the All India Rural Credit Review Committee, came to the conclusion that noninstitutional sources still accounted for over 80 percent of total agricultural credit in 1961/62. Based on the recommendation of this committee, the government took several steps to provide administrative, technical, and supervisory support to the cooperative system. An Agricultural Refinance Corporation (ARC) was set up in 1963 to help cooperatives and commercial banks expand their term lending and to assist them in project formulation, appraisal, and refinance. In spite of supervision by the Reserve Bank of India and support from other government agencies, the cooperative system has succeeded only in some parts of the country. In others, cooperative credit societies are in a moribund state burdened by overdues, most often of members who wield political and economic power.

The commercial banks were nationalized in 1969 and were directed to open new rural and semiurban branches. Each district was associated with one of the nationalized commercial banks and had a lead bank for the district that would plan for and provide agricultural credit. In 1975 the ARC was reorganized into the Agricultural Refinance and Development Corporation and was given special responsibility for meeting the credit requirements of less-developed regions and weaker sections of the rural society. At the same time Regional Rural Banks were established to focus exclusively on the weaker sections. Finally, with the establishment of the National Bank for Agriculture and Rural Development in 1982, an institution at the apex of the network of rural credit agencies was created (Gadgil 1986).

According to Desai (1988), total institutional credit grew at a compound rate of over 16 percent a year in the decade after 1974/75, with credit from commercial banks growing at a faster rate of 22 percent a year. Further, the share of cooperatives declined from 84 percent of short-term credit in 1974/75 to 64 percent in 1984/85, while the share of commercial banks increased from 16 percent to 36 percent. The

TABLE 3.7 INSTITUTIONAL CREDIT IN INDIA, 1980/81
AND 1981/82

Size of farm	Credit per hectare, 1980/81 (rupees)	Percentage of area operated, 1981/82	Percentage of total credit, 1981/82
Marginal (up to 1 hectare)	311	26[a]	43[a]
Small (1–2 hectares)	261		
Medium (2–4 hectares)	196	51	24
Large (above 4 hectares)	120	23	33
Total	179	100	100

[a]Includes both small and marginal farms.
Source: D. K. Desai, "Institutional Credit Requirements for Agricultural Production—2000 A.D.;" *Indian Journal of Agricultural Economics* 43, no. 3 (1988): Tables V and VI.

change with respect to longer-term credit was even more dramatic. The share of cooperatives declined from 69 percent to 30 percent during the same decade. The distribution of credit per hectare of land owned (though not total amount) was heavily in favor of small farms (see Table 3.7). Desai also found significant correlation coefficients of 0.6 and 0.8 across states between his index of agricultural development based on twenty-nine indicators and short- and long-term credit supply respectively.

Poverty Alleviation Policies and Agriculture

In an economy in which nearly 75 percent of the people live in rural areas and two-thirds of the labor force depends on agriculture for employment, it is hardly surprising that an overwhelming majority of the poor live in rural areas and that their futures are significantly affected by agricultural development. Indeed, as mentioned earlier, the proportion of the rural population deemed poor (having a monthly per capita household consumption expenditure of Rs. 15, or US$3, at 1960/61 prices) fluctuated between a low of 39 percent in 1960/61 and a high of 56.5 percent during the second successive drought year of 1967/68 with no significant time trend over the years 1956/57 to 1973/74. The fluctuations were closely correlated with fluctuations in real agricultural output per capita. The proportions of rural poor in 1977/78 and 1983 were 40 percent and 33 percent respectively (Tendulkar 1987). The official figures for the proportion of rural poor for 1977/78, 1983/84, and 1987/88 are respectively 48.3 percent, 37.4 percent, and 29.9 percent (Ministry of Finance 1992: 126). It has been suggested that these three figures in fact represent a downward trend attributable to the impact of an increasing amount of resources spent on policies to alleviate rural poverty. Since the poor among the rural population are mostly agricultural laborers and cultivators of small holdings, it is natural that the specific programs were designed to provide additional employment opportunities to workers and to increase net income from cultivation.

A number of such rural development programs were executed through a plethora of agencies. The Small Farmers Development Agency (SFDA) was initiated in 1969/70 to meet the credit needs of small farmers. The Agency for Development of Marginal Farmers and Agricultural Laborers (MFAL) was initiated in 1969/70 but later merged with SFDA; it was devoted to raising land productivity and creating income-earning opportunities in activities allied to agriculture, such as animal husbandry. The Drought Prone Areas Programme (DPAP) began in 1969/70 aimed at "optimum utilization of land, water and livestock resources, restoration of ecological balance and stabilization of the incomes of people" in areas prone to frequent drought. The Crash Scheme for Rural Employment was launched in the early 1970s with a view to generating employment and creating durable assets. The Employment Guarantee Scheme was initiated by the Maharashtra State Government in 1972/73 and ensured employment for a specified period and wage to anyone who wished. And the Food for Work Programme started in 1977 to provide employment and create durable assets; part of the wages were to be paid in kind in terms of foodgrains.

Many of these programs were later reorganized and combined. At the time of the formulation of the Seventh Five-Year Plan (1985–1990) the major rural development programs were (1) the Integrated Rural Development Programme (IRDP), designed to develop self-employment opportunities in a variety of activities, such as sericulture, animal husbandry, land improvement, handicrafts, and small business enterprises; (2) the Training of Rural Youth and Self Employment (TRYSEM), with the objective of providing technical skills to rural youth; (3) the National Rural Employment Programme (NREP), which is essentially the same as the earlier Food for Work Programme; (4) the Rural Landless Employment Guarantee Programme (RLEGP), which is a nationwide extension of the Maharashtra State Programme mentioned above; and (5) the DPAP.

Since 1989/90 all these schemes have become part of a new employment program called the Jawahar Rozgar Yojana. It covers the whole country, with more intensive coverage for poorer districts. The employment projects are identified and managed by local bodies with the help of a number of junior engineers to ensure high-quality execution. Local bodies also select the beneficiaries, with preference given to socially disadvantaged groups, namely the so-called scheduled castes and tribes as well as women.[1] Workers are paid the statutory minimum wage.

The achievements of many of the programs have been modest. According to the Planning Commission (1985), the IRDP benefited 1.65 million persons during 1980–1985, of which 40 percent belonged to the economically and socially weak scheduled castes and tribes. Nearly a million rural youth were trained under TRYSEM during the same period. Around 350 million man-days of employment were generated under NREP in 1984/85 in creating assets such as roads, irrigation works, and schools. RLEGP created another 260 million man-days of employment in 1983/84 and 1984/85. The DPAP generated 177 million man-days of employment in 1985. To put these figures in perspective, total employment in the country was estimated at 186 million standard person-years. More recent estimates suggest that these schemes backed by the central government have generated an average of 1.76 million jobs a day.

Authorities have encountered a number of problems in the implementation of these programs. For example, according to the Planning Commission (1985), problems with the NREP stemmed from (1) poor supply and distribution of foodgrains, (2) excessive time taken in the preparation of a shelf of projects for implementation, (3) nonavailability of technical manuals and guidebooks in local languages, (4) difficulties in mobilizing local resources, and (5) inadequate maintenance of assets created and their low durability. Corruption and leakages of benefits to nontarget groups were also prevalent. These problems have led some observers, such as Guhan (1980), to question the likely quantitative impact of the program on rural unemployment and others, such as Dantwala (1978), to view these only as transitional in the development process. Not all assessments, however, have been negative; MHJ (1980), Reynolds and Sundar (1977), Bagchee (1984), and Dandekar and Sathe (1980) all suggest that the objectives of some of the programs have been achieved in a significant measure.

Subsequent evaluation reports suggest that the above-mentioned problems persist. The coverage of the projects has been uneven across states with just over half of the villages per block benefiting from NREP projects since 1980. Projects have not been successful in getting poor

---

1. Scheduled castes and tribes are those castes and tribes that are entitled by the Constitution to a certain number of places in legislatures and educational institutions and to a certain proportion of government jobs.

TABLE 3.8   AVERAGE ANNUAL GROWTH OF CROPS IN INDIA, 1891–1989/90 (PERCENTAGE)

Crop	1891–1947 (preindependence)		
	Area	Production	Yield
Foodgrains	0.3	0.2	0.1
Non-foodgrains	0.4	1.3	0.9
All crops	0.4	0.4	—[a]

	1949–1986 (postindependence)								
	1949/50 to 1964/65			1967/68 to 1989/90			1949/50 to 1989/90		
	Area	Produc-tion	Yield	Area	Produc-tion	Yield	Area	Produc-tion	Yield
Rice	1.33	3.49	2.16	0.57	2.74	2.19	0.83	2.58	1.73
Wheat	2.68	3.99	1.27	1.91	5.12	3.14	2.53	5.82	3.21
Coarse cereals	0.90	2.23	1.29	−0.98	0.57	1.57	−0.19	1.23	1.42
Pulses	1.90	1.39	−0.22	0.28	0.78	0.50	0.26	0.40	0.14
Foodgrains	1.41	2.93	1.43	0.20	2.74	2.53	0.59	2.67	2.07
Oilseeds	2.69	3.11	0.20	0.16	2.15	1.99	0.82	2.11	1.28
Fibers	2.57	4.45	1.68	−0.31	2.07	2.39	0.22	2.08	1.86
Sugarcane	3.27	4.26	1.12	1.34	2.78	1.43	1.76	2.97	1.19
All crops	1.61	3.13	1.30	0.26	2.74	2.47	0.67	2.66	1.98

[a]Increases in yield were negligible.
Source: For preindependence period, George Blyn, *Agricultural Trends in India 1891–1947: Output, Availability and Productivity* (Philadelphia, University of Pennsylvania Press, 1966); for postindependence period, Directorate of Economics and Statistics (1992), Appendix B, Table (iv).

women to participate. Of the rural works constructed under the program, only 75 percent have been inspected by state and district officials. Many works remained incomplete or in poor shape because of lack of maintenance. The RLEGP has done no better and has failed to achieve its announced objective of providing up to 100 days of work a year to at least one member of each rural landless household. In sum, there are a number of problems, some financial and others organizational and institutional, that have yet to be satisfactorily resolved.

AGRICULTURAL PERFORMANCE SINCE INDEPENDENCE

Indian agricultural performance in the four decades since independence has been spectacular relative to the stagnation in the five decades before independence. As can be seen from Table 3.8, the trend rate of growth of production of all crops in the period from 1949/50 to 1985/86 was 2.64 percent per year contrasted with 0.4 percent per year during 1891–1947. The average rate of growth of production of foodgrains in the same two periods was 2.64 percent and 0.2 percent per year respectively. The source of growth in the preindependence period was mostly expansion of cultivated area, with virtually no growth in yield per unit area except in nonfood commercial crops. By contrast, yield per unit area of all crops grew at an average rate of 1.54 percent per year and that of foodgrains grew by 1.73 percent per year. Indian performance, however, is unspectacular both in comparison with other developing countries and in per capita terms. With the rate of population growth exceeding 2 percent per year since 1951, output per capita of all crops and foodgrains has grown only at about 0.64 percent per year. According to the World Bank (1989), the rate of growth of real gross value added by agriculture in India was 2.8 percent per year during 1965–1980 and 0.8 percent per year during 1980–1987. The corresponding figures for China were 3 percent and 7.4 percent, for Pakistan 3.3 percent and 3.4 percent, and for Sri Lanka 2.7 percent and 3.1 percent.

Table 3.8 also depicts the markedly different growth performance between the pre– and post–green revolution periods. Thus, during the period 1949/50 to 1964/65, nearly half the growth in the production of foodgrains as well as of all crops put together was accounted for by growth in cultivated area. In the post–green revolution period of 1967/68 to 1985/86, the contribution of area growth to output growth fell sharply to less than one-eighth in the case of foodgrains and a little over one-seventh in the case of all crops. The green revolution did not significantly change the trend in the growth of output (if anything, there was a slowdown in aggregate output in the period after the green revolution). It did, however, enable India to maintain the growth of foodgrain output in spite of considerably slower growth in cultivated area by sharply increasing the rate of growth of yield per unit of area.

It is also clear from Table 3.8 that at least in India, the green revolution was largely confined to increases in cereal yields, mostly wheat and rice. These two crops (particularly wheat) and sugarcane attracted more land area at the expense of coarse cereals in absolute terms and all other crops in relative terms in the context of slow growth in aggregate crop area.

Table 3.9 documents output growth in absolute terms during roughly four decades beginning in 1950/51. Wheat output showed a ninefold increase; rice, oilseed, and overall foodgrain output tripled; and sugarcane output quadrupled. The table also shows the growth of inputs. Between 1950/51 and 1990/91, while cultivated area increased by only 39 percent, irrigated area more than tripled. With the advent of the green revolution, the proportion of the area under cereal crops that

TABLE 3.9   PRODUCTION OF MAJOR CROPS AND GROWTH OF
INPUTS IN INDIA, 1950/51–1990/91

Crop	Volume of output			
	1950/51	1964/65	1987/88	1990/91[a]
Rice (10⁶ metric tons)	20.6	39.3	56.9	74.6
Wheat (10⁶ metric tons)	6.5	12.3	46.2	54.5
Coarse cereals (10⁶ metric tons)	15.4	25.4	26.4	33.1
Pulses (10⁶ metric tons)	8.4	12.4	11.0	14.0
Foodgrains (10⁶ metric tons)	50.8	89.4	140.4	176.2
Sugarcane (10⁶ metric tons)	57.1	121.9	196.7	240.3
Oilseeds (10⁶ metric tons)	5.2	8.6	12.7	18.4
Cotton (10⁶ bales of 170 kilos)	3.0	6.0	6.4	9.8
Jute and mesta (10⁶ bales of 180 kilos)	3.3	7.7	6.8	9.1
Tea (10³ metric tons)	275	372	665	700[b]
Coffee (10³ metric tons)	25	47	123	100[b]

Input	Amount of inputs			
	1950/51	1964/65	1987/88	1990/91
Gross cropped area (10⁶ hectares)	132	159	173	188
Gross irrigated area (10⁶ hectares)	23	31	56.2	74[c]
Consumption of fertilizers (10⁶ tons)	0.07	0.77	8.78	12.57
Consumption of fertilizers per hectare of cropped area (kgs/ha)	0.5	5	51	67
Share of high-yielding varieties in cereal cropped area (%)	0.0	0.0	55	62

[a]Provisional.
[b]1989–90.
[c]Forecast.
Source: Directorate of Economics and Statistics (1992), Table 1.3, Appendix E, Table (i); Ministry of Finance, *Economic Survey 1991–92* (New Delhi: Controller of Publications, 1992), Appendix Tables 1.10, 1.12, and 1.16.

were devoted to the cultivation of high-yielding varieties rose from nil in 1964/65 to 62 percent in 1990/91. Associated with this is the thirteenfold increase in the use of chemical fertilizers, from five kilos per hectare in terms of nutrients in 1964/65 to sixty-eight kilos per hectare in 1990/91. It is also the case that other current and capital inputs such as pesticides, pumpsets, tractors, threshers, and combines also grew significantly during the period. An indication of the growing importance of modern inputs, including fertilizers, is the fact that while in 1970/71 the share of value added in gross value of output of agriculture was 89 percent, it fell to 72 percent in 1987/88 according to national

TABLE 3.10 AGRICULTURAL OUTPUT IN INDIA AND THE
WORLD, 1987–1989

	India's share of world output, 1987–1989 (percentage)	Yield, 1989 (kilos/hectare)			
		India	China	Brazil	United States
Rice (paddy)	20.6	2,617	5,537	2,106	6,444
Wheat	9.3	2,244	3,054	n.a.	2,203
Cereals	n.a.	1,916	4,014	1,995	2,138
Pulses	n.a.	582	1,203	472	1,666
Sugarcane	21.0	65,375	52,909	64,832	78,914
Groundnuts	33.9	933	1,737	1,753	2,757
Cotton	8.5	265	731	350	694
Jute and substitutes	42.3	1,656	2,093	1,155	0
Tobacco	6.5	1,307	1,641	1,599	2,376

n.a. = not available.
Source: Directorate of Economics and Statistics (1992), Appendix J, Tables (i) and (ii).

accounts statistics. Table 3.10 compares the yield per hectare of important crops in India with that in other countries. It also gives India's share in world output. It is evident from this table that India is one of the major world producers of rice, wheat, groundnuts, sugarcane, cotton, jute, and tobacco. To the extent that Brazil and the United States can be viewed as land-rich countries, it is not surprising that they have yields per unit of land comparable to the levels obtaining in India, a relatively land-poor country whose agriculture sector is not yet fully modernized. Indian yields are low, however, relative to those in China, which is also land-poor, a difference that is unlikely to be fully accounted for by the difference in the agroclimatic conditions and the availability of irrigation.

It was pointed out earlier that the output of foodgrains on a per capita basis grew at a snail's pace of about 0.64 percent per year. Even this meager growth, however, was not allowed to augment per capita availability. As shown in Table 3.11, there was no trend, but only fluctuations in the per capita availability of foodgrains, because the growth in output was used to substitute for imports. Although this apparent self-sufficiency in food is viewed by many, certainly in India but also outside, as an important achievement, the fact that average consumption of grains has remained at a low level has to be set against this so-called success.

The picture with respect to the availability of other agricultural commodities is much brighter. As can be seen from Table 3.11, per capita availability of sugar, edible oils, and tea has increased substan-

TABLE 3.11   PER CAPITA NET AVAILABILITY OF
AGRICULTURAL COMMODITIES IN INDIA,
1951–1990/91

	Foodgrain (grams/day)	Sugar (kilos/year)	Edible oils (including vasiaspati) (kilos/year)	Tea (grams/ year)	Coffee (grams/ year)
1951–1956	426	4.38	n.a.	n.a.	n.a.
1956–1961	479	4.89	3.60[a]	272[a]	73.5[a]
1961–1966	448	5.38	3.64	309	70.6
1966–1971	446	5.56	3.98	367	77.0
1971–1976	434	6.20	3.98	425	61.0
1976–1981	448	7.68	4.66	490	73.8
1981–1986	460	9.80	5.18	534	74.2
1986–1989	457	11.60	5.33	583	75.7
1989/90	474	12.40	5.30	571	68.0
1990/91	510	12.50	5.40	606	n.a.

n.a. = not available.
[a]Average of 1955–1966 and 1960/61.
Source: Ministry of Finance, *Economic Survey 1991–92* (New Delhi: Controller of Publications, 1992), Appendix Tables 1.18 and 1.20.

tially. In evaluating the increase in per capita availability, however, one has to keep in mind that it is an average. There is no necessary presumption that the poor have shared in the increase. Of course the fact that the public distribution system provided a certain minimum amount of foodgrains, sugar, and edible oils at subsidized prices to all urban residents meant that at least the urban poor were better off relative to the rural poor.

In a country of subcontinental size such as India, it is not surprising that agroclimatic and natural resource endowments vary substantially among states. Besides variation in resource endowments, for historical reasons the size distribution of land, land tenure, and labor market arrangements varied significantly among states at the time of independence. For example, some of the states into which a number of former princely states had been merged inherited almost feudal agrarian structures. The extent of area under the permanent revenue settlement (the zamindari system) also varied among states. In the early 1960s the value of crop production (in nineteen major crops) per head of rural population ranged from a third of the national average in Kerala to more than 2.3 times in southern Punjab (Vaidyanathan 1986). According to Mahendra Dev (1985), at one end of the spectrum, in 39 out of the 289 districts he considered, the rate of growth of crop output exceeded 4.5 percent per year between 1962–1965 and 1975–1978 and these

TABLE 3.12   GROWTH IN PRODUCTION OF SELECTED CROPS
IN INDIAN STATES, 1967/68–1984/85 (ANNUAL
COMPOUND GROWTH RATE, PERCENTAGE
PER YEAR)

	Cereals	Pulses	5 major oilseeds[a]	Sugarcane	Cotton
Andhra Pradesh	1.63	3.59	1.23	−0.18	11.32
Assam	1.46	2.41	4.16	3.67	0.00
Bihar	1.52	−2.45	0.99	−0.38	0.00
Gujarat	2.34	8.06	2.19	9.91	1.49
Harvana	5.33	−7.32	5.74	0.57	2.51
Himachal Pradesh	0.51	−4.00	0.00	1.71	0.00
Jammu & Kashmir	3.77	−1.68	4.16	4.16	0.00
Karnataka	1.98	1.45	3.18	4.03	5.03
Kerala	0.55	0.00	−6.26	3.24	0.00
Madhya Pradesh	1.34	1.99	−0.32	3.62	−1.35
Maharashtra	2.15	1.80	0.99	5.57	0.16
Orissa	1.73	6.86	8.50	4.30	0.00
Punjab	7.20	−6.95	−2.84	0.53	2.46
Rajasthan	1.45	−0.61	7.51	9.13	3.63
Tamil Nadu	1.12	7.65	2.05	4.90	2.36
Uttar Pradesh	4.28	−1.03	−2.81	3.73	−2.36
West Bengal	3.11	−3.01	9.67	−2.48	0.00
All India	2.86	0.05	1.76	3.58	2.28

[a] Groundnut, rapeseed, mustard seed.
Source: World Bank, private communication.

districts accounted for 15 percent of total crop area of all the 289 districts. At the other end, in eighty-eight districts accounting for 31 percent of total crop area the growth rate was less than 1.5 percent per year. In the latter set of districts with population growing at about 2 percent per year, per capita crop output of cereals and pulses are shown in Table 3.12. It is clear from this table that the northwestern states of Haryana and Punjab and the northern state of Uttar Pradesh, in which the green revolution technology of wheat cultivation was rapidly adopted, experienced rapid growth in the output of cereals.

In his wide-ranging analysis of regional disparities in agricultural development in India, Vaidyanathan (1986) concludes that interstate disparities are not only large but are also increasing over time, although the evidence on the latter is not very robust. His analysis suggests that these disparities are largely accountable in terms of differences in demographic pressure, agroclimatic environment, and the extent of irrigation development. He is careful not to infer a causal link from the observed association among land productivity, population growth, and some aspects of agrarian structure. From a sociopolitical perspective, interstate disparities in agricultural development are of serious concern since the bulk of the rural population will be dependent on agriculture in the foreseeable future. To a significant extent, public investment in irrigation and other production-oriented public expenditure can be allocated in a way that offsets initial interstate differences in irrigation development. However, a strategy of reducing interstate disparities in incomes originating in agriculture to address disparities in income *accruing* to residents of different states can be costly if it seriously undermines regional specialization in crop production based on comparative advantage. Clearly, an allocation of investment among states, whether it is in irrigation or other capital, which is based on meeting other objectives besides productivity, will not generate the maximum return possible. The issue is whether alternative policies, such as encouraging interstate migration, for example, are not only feasible but also more cost-effective in reducing income disparities than a nonoptimal (from the point of view of maximum returns) investment allocation.

The trends in rural poverty and the effects of poverty-oriented policies in the agricultural sector on employment were discussed in the previous section. In concluding this section, it is worth noting the trends in real wages. The data compiled by Lucas (1988) shown in Figure 3.3 suggest no upward or downward trend in real agricultural wages between 1960/61 and 1979/80. Using a longer time series, Lal (1989) concludes, after noting some of the limitations of the series, that there was no clear trend in real agricultural wages in the nineteenth century. He finds some evidence of a mild rise in the rural real wage from 1912 to 1933, a collapse during the period 1933–1942, and a rapid rise back to the level of the early 1930s at independence in 1947. For the period 1950–1978, Lal's analysis suggests a statistically significant trend rate of growth in real wages of 0.36 percent per year. Given the slow growth in per capita output and the fact that the import-substituting industrialization strategy did not generate rapid growth in nonagricultural employment, and with the rural labor force growing at more than 2 percent per year since 1950, it is not surprising that there was little to no growth in real agricultural wages.

CONCLUSION

It should be clear from the discussion in the previous sections that the Indian government intervened actively in agriculture ostensibly to achieve a rapid growth in output and the equitable sharing of the benefits of such growth. Public investment in irrigation and agriculture as

FIGURE 3.3 TRENDS IN REAL AGRICULTURAL WAGES IN
INDIA, 1960/61–1979/80

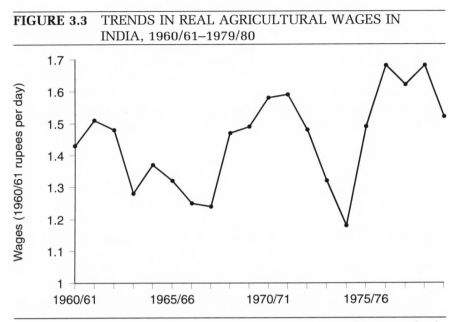

Source: R. E. B. Lucas. "India's Industrial Policy," In R. E. B. Lucas and G. Papaneck, eds.
The Indian Economy: Recent Development and Future Proposals. (Boulder, Colo.: Westview Press, 1988), Table 9.5.

well as public expenditures for operating the irrigation, research, and
extension systems have been substantial. Inputs of modern agriculture,
such as better seeds, fertilizers, pesticides, electricity and fuel, and
irrigation water, have increased and their cost has been subsidized
through the public budget. Besides, a number of rural poverty alleviation programs that worked through the employment and income generation processes in agriculture have been publicly funded. Supply of
institutional credit to agriculture has vastly expanded and has nearly
replaced informal credit.

The performance of the agricultural sector as a whole in the postindependence era has been significantly better than that in the colonial
era. Yet overall growth has barely kept ahead of the growth in population. This slow growth, together with the policy of import substitution
in foodgrains, has kept per capita availability of foodgrains at the low
levels that prevailed in the immediate postindependence years. The
per capita availability of other commodities, however, has increased
significantly. Although resources allocated to agriculture and agricultural output have clearly increased, it is an open question whether the
allocation of resources within the agricultural sector among crops, regions, and programs and *between* agriculture and other sectors has

been socially optimal. There has been no in-depth study of this issue, although some of the early linear programming models of Indian Planning in the 1960s (for example, Eckaus and Parikh 1968 and Chakravarty and Lefeber 1965) did address the issue of intersectoral allocation.

Maintaining the trend rate of growth of output of 1950–1988 in the future will likely require the allocation of a larger quantity of resources to agriculture, for several reasons: first, major irrigation, which has been the main source of growth in the past, is likely to be more costly in the future, partly because the relatively inexpensive potential sites have already been exploited and partly because there is increased awareness of the environmental costs of large reservoirs. As for minor irrigation, opportunities still exist in some areas for relatively inexpensive exploitation of groundwater resources. But in other areas, overexploitation has resulted in water mining and a consequent fall in the water table and a rise in the cost of pumping. And in many areas irrigated by canals and tubewells, lack of drainage and increased soil salinity are of serious concern. Second, no significant new developments in plant breeding have occurred since the introduction of dwarf varieties of cereals. Because cultivation of these varieties (particularly wheat and also rice to a lesser extent) has been extended to all areas where they can be profitably cultivated—that is, areas with irrigation or assured rainfall—no further growth in output can be expected from this source. Crops such as pulses and oilseeds did not figure in the green revolution of the late 1960s. Unless new high-yielding varieties of other major crops and of cereals that grow well in semi-arid areas with little or no irrigation are developed, future growth in agricultural output may be slower than in the past. Development of such varieties would also redress regional imbalances.

Indian agriculture has been largely insulated from the world market. It is time to modify, if not abandon, this policy. Now that India has become largely self-sufficient in food, and in view of the likely increase in the resource cost of future rises in total output, the country should examine whether greater specialization within agriculture in crops in which India is likely to have a dynamic comparative advantage would be better from the point of view of saving scarce resources. Of course, letting world market price trends pass through may mean greater instability in producer prices. But it is not necessarily the case that secure incomes for farmers are achieved at a lower cost by insulating domestic markets from world market trends.

One-third to one-half of the rural population still lives in abject poverty. It is true that more rapid agricultural growth that is widely shared among crops and regions will alleviate rural poverty. However, the important and unfortunate consequence of the inward-oriented, capital-intensive development strategy that India has pursued since the Second Five-Year Plan has been that the share of agriculture in GDP has fallen rapidly without an accompanying decline in the share of low-productivity agricultural employment in total employment. Unless and until the economic development strategy itself is changed radically toward outward orientation and internal liberalization, the prospects for a rapid reduction in rural poverty are slight.

REFERENCES

Bagchee, S. 1984. "Employment Guarantee Scheme in Maharashtra." *Economic and Political Weekly* (Bombay) (September 15).

Bell, Clive. 1990. "Interactions between Institutional and Informal Credit Agencies in Rural India." *The World Bank Economic Review* 4, no. 3.

Chakravarty, S., and L. Lefeber. 1965. "An Optimising Planning Model." *Economic and Political Weekly* (Bombay) Annual Number (February):237–52.

Dandekar, K., and M. Sathe. 1980. "Employment Guarantee Scheme and Food for Work Programme." *Economic and Political Weekly* (Bombay) (April 12).

Dantwala, M. L. 1967. "Incentives and Disincentives in Indian Agriculture." *Indian Journal of Agricultural Economics* 22, no. 2: 1–25.

_____. 1978. "Some Neglected Issues in Employment Planning." *Economic and Political Weekly* (Bombay) Annual Number (February).

_____. 1987. "Growth and Equity in Agriculture." *Indian Journal of Agricultural Economics* 42, no. 2: 149–59.

Desai, D. K. 1988. "Institutional Credit Requirements for Agricultural Production—2000 A.D." *Indian Journal of Agricultural Economics* 43, no. 3: 326–55.

Dev, Mahendra S. 1985. "Direction of Change in Performance of All Crops in Indian Agriculture in the Late 1970's." *Economic and Political Weekly* (Bombay) (December 21–28):A-130–36.

Directorate of Economics and Statistics. 1992. *Area and Production of Principal Crops in India: 1989–90.* New Delhi: Controller of Publications.

Eckaus, R. S., and K. S. Parikh. 1968. *Planning for Growth: Multi-Sectoral Intertemporal Models Applied to India.* Cambridge, Mass.: MIT Press.

Gadgil, M. V. 1986. "Agricultural Credit in India: A Review of Performance and Policies." *Indian Journal of Agricultural Economics* 41, no. 3: 282–309.

Guhan, S. 1980. "Rural Poverty: Policy and Play Acting." *Economic and Political Weekly* (Bombay) (November 22).

Indian Council for Social Science Research (ICSSR). 1980. *Alternatives in Agricultural Development.* New Delhi: Allied Publishers.

International Rice Research Institute (IRRI). 1988. *World Rice Statistics, 1987.* Los Banos, The Philippines: IRRI.

Lal, D. 1989. *The Hindu Equilibrium.* Vol. 2. Oxford: Clarendon Press.

Lucas, R. E. B. 1988. "India's Industrial Policy." In R. E. B. Lucas and G. Papaneck, eds., *The Indian Economy: Recent Development and Future Proposals.* Boulder, Colo.: Westview Press.

MHJ. 1980. "Maharashtra-II: Employment Guarantee Scheme—An Evaluation." *Economic and Political Weekly* (Bombay) (December 6).

Mitra, A. 1977. *Terms of Trade and Class Relations.* London: Frank Cass and Company.

Ministry of Community Development and Cooperation. 1959. *India's Food Crisis and Steps to Meet It.* New Delhi: Government of India.

Ministry of Finance. 1992. *Economic Survey 1991–92.* New Delhi: Controller of Publications.

National Commission on Agriculture. 1976a. *Review and Progress.* Part I of the Report of the National Commission on Agriculture. New Delhi: Ministry of Agriculture.

_____. 1976b. *Agrarian Reforms.* Part XV of the Report of the National Commission on Agriculture. New Delhi: Ministry of Agriculture.

National Sample Survey. 1981. "Results of the Second Quinquennial Survey on Employment and Unemployment." *Sarvekshana* 5, nos. 1 and 2: 1–49.

_____. 1986. "Preliminary Results of the Third Quinquennial Survey on Employment and Unemployment, Based on First Two Subrounds Data." *Sarvekshana* 9, no. 4: S-103–24.

_____. (1987). "A Note on Some Aspects of Household Ownership Holding: NSS 37th Round (January–December 1982)." *Sarvekshana* 11, no. 2: 1–18.

Planning Commission. 1985. "Seventh Five Year Plan 1980–85." New Delhi: Government of India.

Reynolds, N., and P. Sundar. 1977. "Maharashtra's Employment Guarantee Scheme: A Programme to Emulate?" *Economic and Political Weekly* (Bombay) (July 16).

Rudolph, L. I., and S. H. Rudolph. 1987. *In Pursuit of Lakshmi.* Chicago: University of Chicago Press.

Sah, R., and J. E. Stiglitz. 1984. "The Economics of Price Scissors." *American Economic Review* 74, no. 1: 125–38.

Sarma, J. S. 1974. "Agricultural Policy in India." *Indian Journal of Agricultural Economics* 29, no. 1: 1–15.

Srinivasan, T. N. 1986. "Was Agriculture Neglected in Planning?" In D. K. Bose, ed., *Review of the Indian Planning Process.* Calcutta: Indian Statistical Institute.

Stiglitz, J. E. 1988. "Economic Organisation, Information and Development." In H. B. Chenery and T. N. Srinivasan, eds., *Handbook of Development Economics.* Vol. 1. Amsterdam: North-Holland.

Tendulkar, S. D. 1987. "Economic Inequalities and Poverty in India: An Interpretive Overview." In P. R. Brahmananda and V. R. Panchamukhi, eds., *The Development Process of the Indian Economy.* New Delhi: Himalaya Publishing House.

Vaidyanathan, A. 1986. *India's Agricultural Development in a Regional Perspective.* Calcutta: Centre for Studies in Social Sciences.

World Bank. 1989. *World Development Report 1989.* New York: Oxford University Press.

4

An Appraisal of China's Foreign Trade Policy, 1950–1992

Yun-Wing Sung

Since the Communists took power in China in 1949, the development strategy and trade policy of China have been heavily influenced by ideology. The state monopolized foreign trade beginning in 1950, well before the collectivization of agriculture and nationalization of industry, and pursued a largely Stalinist development strategy characterized by the unbalanced growth of industry, especially heavy industry. Resource allocation was centralized through quantitative controls. The rates of investment and labor participation were raised through the strategy of extensive growth, that is, growth coming largely from increases in inputs (labor and capital) rather than from increases in productivity.

China centralized its foreign trade to serve its economic strategy. All international trade was conducted by nine national foreign trade corporations (NFTCs) under the control of the Ministry of Foreign Trade. The foreign trade corporations operated according to mandatory plans, purchasing fixed quantities of domestic goods at fixed prices for export and importing fixed quantities of foreign goods for domestic distribution at fixed prices. All foreign exchange earnings were remitted to Beijing. Because the *renminbi* was overvalued, corporations usually incurred losses on exports and earned profits on imports. This situation has not been a matter of concern, for the Ministry of Foreign Trade has borne the losses and siphoned off the profits. Centralized financial responsibility implies, however, that producers and trading enterprises have little incentive to be cost-conscious and efficient.

The system enabled planners to enforce their priorities at the cost of inhibiting international trade. Buyers and sellers could conduct business only through an intermediary. The lack of direct contact between producers and end-users obstructed the transfer of technology that usually occurs through such contacts. Moreover, the rigid system could not respond to rapid changes in the international market.

The open door policy that has evolved in China since 1979 involves not only a rapid expansion of foreign trade, foreign loans, and foreign investment. It also involves a significant decentralization and marketization of China's external sector, facilitating direct contacts between producers and end-users. In fact, the open door policy was carried out simultaneously with the reforms of the entire economy.

This chapter will discuss China's trade policy both before and after its adoption of the open door policy in 1979. It will analyze the reforms of the external sector and evaluate the achievements and deficiencies of the open door policy. Finally, it will gauge the impact of China's accession to the General Agreement on Tariff and Trade (GATT) and the prospects of the open door policy.

TRADE POLICY BEFORE 1979

Although the organization of the foreign trade system was quite stable until 1979, foreign trade policy has alternated between self-reliance and a reliance on trade for industrial plant imports. The fluctuations in the volume of trade were closely connected with ideological or political campaigns. Table 4.1 shows the value of China's exports and imports from 1950 to 1992, and Tables 4.2 and 4.3 show the composition of China's exports and imports.

The period 1949–1952 was devoted to economic recovery and land reform. By 1952 agricultural and industrial output had recovered to the prewar level. Trade also recovered. From 1952 until the break with the Soviet Union in 1960, China depended heavily on the Soviet bloc for trade and economic assistance, and trade expanded rapidly. During this period, agricultural products (food and raw materials) constituted over 70 percent of China's exports (Table 4.2), and machinery constituted the chief item of imports. The years 1958–1960 saw the Great Leap Forward and the break with the Soviet Union. Rather than bringing a dramatic economic advance, the ultraleft Great Leap strategy led

TABLE 4.1   VALUE OF CHINA'S FOREIGN TRADE, 1950–1992

Year	Exports Millions of US$	Exports % of China's GDP	Exports % of world exports	Imports (millions of US$)	Trade balance (millions of US$)
1950	552	4.10	0.91	583	−31
1951	757	4.21	0.92	1,198	−441
1952	823	3.98	1.02	1,118	−295
1953	1,022	4.24	1.23	1,346	−324
1954	1,146	4.62	1.33	1,287	−141
1955	1,412	5.34	1.50	1,733	−321
1956	1,645	5.46	1.58	1,563	82
1957	1,597	5.19	1.42	1,506	91
1958	1,981	5.18	1.82	1,890	91
1959	2,261	5.52	1.95	2,120	141
1960	1,856	4.48	1.44	1,953	−97
1961	1,491	4.15	1.11	1,445	46
1962	1,490	4.41	1.05	1,173	317
1963	1,649	4.32	1.07	1,266	383
1964	1,916	4.11	1.10	1,547	369
1965	2,228	3.93	1.19	2,017	211
1966	2,366	3.60	1.15	2,248	118
1967	2,135	3.42	0.99	2,020	115
1968	2,103	3.52	0.88	1,945	158
1969	2,204	3.20	0.80	1,825	379
1970	2,260	2.55	0.72	2,326	−66
1971	2,636	2.85	0.75	2,205	431
1972	3,443	3.35	0.83	2,858	585
1973	5,819	4.36	1.01	5,157	662
1974	6,949	5.13	0.83	7,619	−670
1975	7,264	4.94	0.83	7,487	−223
1976	6,855	4.80	0.69	6,578	277
1977	7,590	4.57	0.67	7,214	376
1978	9,745	4.67	0.75	10,893	−1,148
1979	13,658	5.30	0.83	15,675	−2,017
1980	18,272	6.12	0.92	19,550	−1,278
1980	18,120	6.07	0.91	20,020	−1,900
1981	22,007	7.70	1.11	22,015	−8
1982	22,321	7.97	1.20	19,285	3,036
1983	22,226	7.55	1.22	21,390	836
1984	26,139	8.34	1.34	27,410	1,271
1985	27,350	9.45	1.40	42,252	−14,902
1986	30,942	11.16	1.46	42,904	−11,962
1987	39,437	13.01	1.62	43,216	−3,779
1988	47,540	12.56	1.69	55,251	−7,711
1989	52,486	12.23	1.74	59,142	−6,656
1990	62,063	16.67	1.83	53,350	8,713
1991	71,910	19.39	2.06	63,791	8,119
1992	85,000	19.58	2.35	78,000	7,000

Source: Data for 1950–1980 are from the Ministry of Foreign Economic Relations and Trade. Data for 1980–1992 are from Economic Information Agency, *China Customs Statistics* (Hong Kong, various issues). World exports are from United Nations, *Monthly Bulletin of Statistics* (New York, various issues).

TABLE 4.2 COMMODITY COMPOSITION OF CHINA'S EXPORTS 1953–1991 (PERCENTAGE)

| Year | Raw materials | | | | Manufacturing | | | | | | Total |
	Food (0,1)	Textile Fibers (26)	Fuel (3)	All raw materials	Chemicals (5)	Textile fibers (65)	Machinery (72)	Clothing (84)	Other (9)	All manufacturing	
1953–1955	42.7	9.0	n.a.	39.2	2.8	6.6	n.a.	n.a.	6.3	18.1	100.0
1956–1958	29.3	6.5	n.a.	42.2	2.8	15.7	n.a.	n.a.	7.7	28.5	100.0
1959–1961	19.3	6.9	n.a.	31.7	1.7	33.1	n.a.	n.a.	4.2	49.0	100.0
1962–1964	22.2	4.1	n.a.	24.5	2.8	35.5	n.a.	n.a.	3.6	53.3	100.0
1965–1967	28.9	4.9	n.a.	24.2	3.9	16.1	n.a.	8.6	4.3	46.9	100.0
1968–1970	29.8	5.1	n.a.	21.5	4.6	15.3	n.a.	8.8	2.2	48.7	100.0
1970	31.6	4.9	2.7	21.3	5.4	18.2	0.9	4.7	0.1	47.0	100.0
1975	29.7	3.3	14.3	26.6	4.8	14.5	1.1	5.1	0.3	43.6	100.0
1977	24.9	3.9	14.2	27.4	4.9	15.2	1.4	7.2	0.3	47.8	100.0
1979	20.1	3.7	17.9	30.1	5.7	16.6	1.4	7.7	0.3	49.9	100.0
1981	13.6	2.1	23.8	33.0	6.1	12.2	1.3	8.5	4.1	53.4	100.0
1983	13.3	3.0	21.0	30.0	5.6	13.1	1.7	9.3	8.8	56.7	100.0
1985	14.5	4.3	25.9	36.3	5.0	12.3	1.5	11.9	6.8	49.3	100.0
1987	12.6	4.0	11.5	21.2	5.7	15.0	4.3	14.5	11.3	66.2	100.0
1989	12.5	2.9	8.0	16.4	6.1	13.7	9.5	15.4	5.2	71.1	100.0
1990	11.4	1.8	5.7	14.4	6.0	11.6	10.5	15.4	6.6	74.2	100.0
1991	9.9	1.6	4.8	12.4	5.3	11.1	11.7	16.9	6.2	77.7	100.0

NOTE: Numbers in parentheses are Standard International Trade Classification (SITC) numbers.
n.a. = not available.
Source: Data for 1953–1979 are from the Ministry of Foreign Economic Relations and Trade. Data for 1981–1991 are from Economic Information Agency, *China Customs Statistics* (Hong Kong, various issues).

TABLE 4.3 COMMODITY COMPOSITION OF CHINA'S IMPORTS, 1953–1991 (PERCENTAGE)

Year	Raw materials			Manufactures						Total
	Food (0,1)	Textile fibers (26)	All raw materials	Chemicals (5)	Textile fibers (65)	Iron and steel (67)	Machinery (7)	Other (9)	All manufacturing	
1953–1955	0.1	n.a.	15.8	8.0	1.1	n.a.	n.a.	0.7	84.1	100.0
1956–1958	0.9	5.4	22.1	8.6	1.6	n.a.	n.a.	2.7	77.0	100.0
1959–1961	5.7	5.5	23.7	6.3	1.6	n.a.	41[a]	1.3	70.6	100.0
1962–1964	25.8	8.0	25.0	12.5	2.8	n.a.	5[b]	1.2	60.0	100.0
1965–1967	19.7	8.6	17.0	14.1	2.4	14.0	21.5	1.0	63.3	100.0
1968–1970	18.9	5.1	16.7	16.2	2.0	16.0	15.4	0.7	64.4	100.0
1970	16.1	4.8	13.9	14.9	1.9	18.9	20.0	0.1	70.0	100.0
1975	11.8	5.9	13.5	11.9	1.3	21.6	29.2	0.3	74.7	100.0
1977	16.1	7.7	19.6	13.1	2.6	23.3	17.7	0.5	64.3	100.0
1979	12.8	0.8	15.5	10.1	2.1	23.9	26.7	0.7	71.8	100.0
1981	17.1	12.7	19.3	11.3	8.8	7.3	25.5	1.1	63.6	100.0
1983	12.9	6.4	14.5	12.2	5.5	18.0	23.4	1.1	72.6	100.0
1985	5.1	3.0	8.0	9.4	5.7	16.4	42.0	1.0	86.9	100.0
1987	6.8	3.5	10.2	12.2	8.2	10.9	36.5	1.0	83.0	100.0
1989	7.4	4.1	12.7	12.8	8.0	9.8	30.8	8.7	79.9	100.0
1990	6.5	3.7	14.1	12.5	9.9	5.3	31.6	11.8	79.4	100.0
1991	4.7	3.8	12.6	14.5	10.6	4.2	30.7	12.3	82.7	100.0

NOTE: Numbers in parentheses are Standard International Trade Classification (SITC) numbers.

[a] 1959 only.

[b] 1962 only.

Source: Data for 1953–1987 are from U.S. Central Intelligence Agency, National Foreign Assessment Center, *China: International Trade*, various issues. Data for 1989–1991 are from *China Customs Statistics*. Data for machinery exports in 1959 and 1962 are from Christopher Howe, *China's Economy*, (London: Paul Elek, 1978), p. 151.

to famines and economic depression. Trade fell sharply in 1961 and 1962, and China was forced to import large amounts of grain, as reflected in the dramatic rise in the share of food imports from 1959 onward. Imports of machinery had to be cut correspondingly (Table 4.3). China's exports stagnated in money terms and fell significantly as a percentage of its GDP and world exports until 1970. Isolated in a hostile world, China pursued a policy of self-reliance.

The years 1963–1965 were a period of economic readjustment and pragmatism. China recovered from the crisis of the Great Leap, and trade revived as well; in 1966 it approached its 1959 level in money terms.

In 1966–1969 China was engaged in the Cultural Revolution, and trade stagnated. By 1970 the tumult of the Cultural Revolution was over, and two years later China ended its isolation with the dramatic breakthrough in Sino-American relations. Trade expanded rapidly until 1974 and stagnated in 1975 and 1976 owing to the worldwide energy crisis and a domestic political struggle.

After Mao's death and the downfall of the Gang of Four in 1976, Hua Guofeng adopted his overambitious modernization plan, which involved an unbalanced growth strategy focused on industry, massive imports of industrial plants, and an explicit commitment to an open door policy. Hua's plan soon resulted in structural imbalances and hasty and inappropriate plant imports, and its failure led to a fundamental reorientation of China's development strategy. To improve economic efficiency, the government initiated economic reforms and a program of marketization. Let us look at the various phases of trade policy before 1979 in more detail.

"Leaning to One Side" (1952–1959)

The period 1952–1959, which covers both the First Five-Year Plan and the Great Leap Forward, was one of the fastest-growing periods in the history of the Chinese economy. From 1952 until the break with the Soviet Union in 1960, China relied heavily on Soviet loans (valued at US$1.4 billion), technicians, turnkey projects, and blueprints, in a strategy Mao Zedong described as "leaning to one side." At least 150,000 Chinese technicians and workers were trained in the Soviet Union. Joint stock companies with the Soviet Union also existed. It has been estimated that Soviet plant exports and technical assistance were responsible for half of the growth of China's national product during the First Five-Year Plan of 1952–1957 (Howe 1978: 134).

To manage this massive technology transfer from the Soviet Union, China had to commit itself to long-term foreign trade plans and to squeeze agriculture for exports to exchange for imports of industrial plants. China ran trade deficits from 1950 to 1955, reflecting the role of Soviet loans, and began loan repayment in 1956 (Table 4.1). The Stalinist emphasis on industrial investment, however, led to weak agricultural performance. By 1957 the weak performance was undermining China's trade strategy of exchanging agricultural exports for imports of industrial equipment. Table 4.1 shows that China's exports in 1957 were below that of 1956.

To bypass the agricultural bottleneck, Mao initiated the Great Leap Forward in 1958. The Leap relied on mass mobilization of peasant labor for rural irrigation projects, rural infrastructural construction, and increased steel production through the backyard furnaces. The state continued to reserve its investment for industry, and the agricultural sector was expected to perform miracles through mass mobilization, psychological appeals, and indoctrination. During the Great Leap, Mao's strategy of mass mobilization, developed through years of guerilla warfare, was grafted onto the Stalinist development model.

The techniques of warfare mobilization were ill suited to the delicate and complicated tasks of economic management and coordination, however, and the Great Leap brought catastrophe to the Chinese economy. Natural disasters, the Sino-Soviet rift, and the withdrawal of Soviet assistance in 1960 compounded the crisis, and famine became widespread as grain production fell. Forced to abandon the trade strategy of exchanging agricultural exports for imports of industrial equipment, China started to import grains on a large scale.

Crisis, Recovery, and Cultural Revolution (1960–1969)

The 1960s were above all a period of self-reliance. Trade stagnated in money terms and shrank relative to China's gross domestic product (GDP) and world trade. As China became isolated, the much-publicized policy of self-reliance made virtue out of necessity and corresponded more closely with Mao's ideology. At a pragmatic level, China reoriented its trade from the Soviet bloc to capitalist countries, especially Japan. As the Chinese economy recovered from the crisis of the Great Leap under the pragmatic policies of Liu Shaochi and Deng Xiaoping, the sharp fall in trade reversed. China began to import complete industrial plants from Japan during 1962–1965, and trade approached the 1959 level again in 1966. In Zhou Enlai's address to the Third National People's Congress in 1964, he urged that China pursue the "Four Modernizations" (of industry, agriculture, defense, and science and technology).

Mao, however, believed that the pragmatist retreat from the Great Leap amounted to revisionism, and he unleashed the Cultural Revolution to purge the leaders of pragmatism, namely Liu Shaochi and Deng Xiaoping. The expansion in trade was halted in 1966 with the outbreak of the Cultural Revolution, and trade stagnated from 1966 to 1969. As the dust of the Cultural Revolution settled in 1970, China's volume of trade was equal only to that of 1959 in money terms. Though China had achieved ingenious technological breakthroughs in selected areas under the policy of self-reliance, many crucial industrial sectors, including fertilizers, transport, iron and steel, and coal were technologically backward and required modernization. The economic need coincided with the thaw in Sino-American relations in 1970 and the dramatic improvement in China diplomatic relations in other countries. These diplomatic openings set the stage for another round of trade expansion.

Revival of Growth With Trade (1970–1979)

After its rapprochement with the United States in the early 1970s, China resumed imports of industrial plants from capitalist countries on a large scale. In 1973 the State Council approved a plan to spend US$4.3 billion (the Four Three Program) on plant imports over a four-year period. At the Fourth National People's Congress in January 1975, Premier Zhou Enlai reiterated his proposal that China should pursue the Four Modernizations. The Gang of Four, however, resisted this policy of massive plant imports financed by oil exports and accused Zhou, Deng, and their supporters of selling out China's resources. Moreover, in the world recession following the energy crisis, demand for Chinese exports were weak and China suffered trade deficits in 1974 and 1975. During the political struggle between the Zhou-Deng group and the Gang of Four, trade stagnated from 1975 to 1976.

Deng was purged for a second time after Zhou Enlai's death in April 1976. But when Mao died in September 1976 and the Gang of Four was arrested, Deng was rehabilitated once again.

As already mentioned, Hua's grafting of massive plant imports onto the Stalinist model of unbalanced and extensive growth soon ran into trouble. Excessive attention to heavy industry led to structural imbalances, bottlenecks, and trade deficits from 1978 to 1980. The neglect of efficiency and the centralization of imports led to hasty and inappropriate plant imports. Often, contracts on plant imports were concluded without feasibility studies and without estimates of the demand for complementary domestic inputs, as in the case of the giant Baoshan General Iron and Steel Works near Shanghai.

Evaluation of the Centralized Trading System

Both the periods of "leaning to one side" (1952–1959) and Hua's open door policy (1977–1978) involved rapid export expansion and massive plant imports under centralized planning. China's trading system succeeded in the first case but failed in the second.

China's centralized system of foreign trade enabled planners to enforce their priorities at the cost of cutting the direct contacts between products and end-users. In the 1950s China traded mostly with Communist countries that also had a centralized trading system. Under such circumstances, the centralization of China's trading system was an advantage. Moreover, the program of economic and technical assistance from the Soviet Union required China to commit itself to long-term foreign trade plans to repay Soviet loans. Centralization was also an advantage here.

China managed to expand its exports rapidly in the 1950s. The majority of its exports were agricultural products sold to the Soviet bloc. In the export of agricultural products, quality is not as important as in the export of manufactures. In any case, competition was not keen in the state-controlled markets of the Soviet bloc. It is thus not surprising that China succeeded with its centralized trading system in the 1950s.

In the 1960s China reoriented its trade to the capitalist countries. The share of manufactures in China's exports rose from less than 30 percent in the late 1950s to close to 50 percent in the 1960s. In the export of manufactures to the competitive world market, efficiency, quality, and direct contacts between producers and end-users are crucial. The problems were manageable only because China's trade stagnated in money terms and declined in real terms in the 1960s.

With the rapid expansion of trade in the 1970s, China's centralized trading system became less and less satisfactory. The rapid expansion of oil exports and rising oil prices in the 1970s eased the problem temporarily by allowing China to increase its export earnings quickly. But the sudden rise in the share of oil in China's exports led to stagnation and decline in the share of manufactures (Table 4.3), and China experienced its version of the Dutch disease. China's oil production stagnated in the 1980s, and falling oil prices beginning in 1985 led to a drastic drop in the share of oil. The share of manufactures in exports rose to 70 percent in 1987. The falling oil prices increased pressure for the reform and decentralization of China's trading system.

EVOLUTION OF THE OPEN DOOR POLICY

The open door policy is a vital part of China's new development strategy of intensive growth through adaptation and diffusion of technology, especially foreign technology. Although China imported foreign technology, including capitalist technology, in Mao's era, the "open door" signals a new willingness to acquire technology through foreign investment. Moreover, foreign technology is broadly interpreted to include not only technology embodied in plant and equipment, but also knowledge, including management skills and even the practices and ideas of a modern society. The traditional mechanism of arm's-length trade does not suffice for the transfer of knowledge; rather, close interaction with foreigners through direct foreign investment is required. This accounted for the willingness of the Chinese to adopt special trade and industrial cooperation agreements.

Another vital aspect of China's modernization drive is the reform and partial marketization of the country's Stalinist economic system. The open door policy and the reform drive are mutually reinforcing, for the commitment to the open door policy forces China to modify its rigid economic system to facilitate economic interaction with world markets. Successful foreign enterprises in China and ideas and examples from the outside world have significant demonstrative effects; the external sector has been a leader in China's reform drive. As Eastern European experiences indicate, however, reforming a Stalinist economy is a long and tortuous process. China's door to the outside world will not be genuinely open until it has successfully reformed its economic system.

As mentioned, the failure of Hua's overambitious plan led to a fundamental reorientation of China's developmental strategy. At its historic Third Plenum in December 1978, the Party abandoned Hua's Stalinist strategy and introduced a program of readjustment and reform to achieve balanced and intensive growth. The government initiated economic reforms and marketization to improve economic efficiency. To rectify the imbalances engendered by the strategy of unbalanced growth, it introduced readjustment, involving a shift in emphasis from heavy industry to agriculture and light industry and a lowering of the savings rate. The willingness to accept foreign investment, the most often-noted feature of the open door policy, can be explained by the change in development strategy. The rise in consumption following readjustment reduces the resources available for investment and exports, and the Chinese thus accept foreign investment to relieve savings and balance of payments constraints. Because debt financing can lead to repayment problems in hard times, China also accepts equity financing.

Equity financing is also more effective in transferring technology. Under the new strategy of intensive growth, China's economic authorities are paying attention to the form and effectiveness of technology transfer. The importing of complete plants, as in Hua's era, has slowed, and priority is being given instead to technology imports aimed at modernizing China's existing plants. China's awareness of the importance of disembodied and undocumented technology explains its willingness to cope with the frictions and tensions typical of joint ventures.

The open door policy should not be confused with free trade. Strict foreign exchange controls exist, and China is still trying to avoid importing goods that can be produced domestically. The novel aspect of the open door is that China is trying to untap the positive effects of exports on efficiency to promote its strategy of intensive growth. As Zhao Ziyang emphasized: "Putting China's products to the test of competition in the world market will spur us to improve management, increase variety, raise quality, lower production costs and achieve better economic results" (Beijing Review, December 21, 1981: 24). Chinese exports as a proportion of national product rose to a record level of 19 percent in 1991, compared with 4.6 percent in 1977 and a low of 2.6 percent in 1970.

The open door policy has gone through several cycles of liberalization and retrenchment. Decentralization of the trading and investment systems were undertaken simultaneously with domestic economic reforms in 1979–1980, 1983–1984, and 1988. In each reform drive, selected regions of the country were opened up—that is, given substantial autonomy in international trade and investment. All three reform drives led to inflation and balance of payments difficulties, and a period of retrenchment followed each reform and liberalization drive. In early 1992 Deng Xiaoping launched a fourth reform drive with his tour of Southern China, and signs of inflation were emerging in late 1992.

The First Reform Drive (1979–1980)

When Hua Guofeng's modernization plan led to a trade deficit in 1978 (Table 4.1), it was replaced by a program of readjustment and reform at China's Third Plenum. In 1979 the reform drive gained momentum: the Ministry of Foreign Trade was reorganized and industrial ministries were given more power in foreign trade. Moreover, special autonomy in trade and investment was given to the provinces of Fujian and Guangdong and the three central municipalities, Beijing, Tianjin, and Shanghai. Guangdong and Fujian were given the authority to operate special economic zones (SEZs). SEZs are areas where planning controls are relaxed to promote foreign investment and the growth of market forces. Tax exemptions and other incentives are given to foreign investors operating in SEZs. Guangdong has three SEZs: the Shenzhen and Zhuhai SEZs, which are adjacent to Hong Kong and Macau respectively, and the Shantou SEZ, which has close links to overseas Chinese populations, including a community in Hong Kong that originated in Shantou. Fujian operates the Xiamen SEZ, which is opposite Taiwan and only a few miles from two coastal islands controlled by Taiwan. The reforms in the domestic and external sectors, however, led to a loss of central control, and internal and external balances continued to deteriorate during 1978–1980 (Table 4.1). China's leaders concluded that the 1979 policy of readjustment had failed and that severe retrenchment was needed (Sung and Chan 1987: 8). In December 1980 they announced a second readjustment, involving recentralization with an emphasis on slow and balanced growth. Foreign exchange controls were strengthened and the Ministry of Foreign Trade regained control over a few commodities, but export decentralization remained basically intact. (Kueh and Howe 1984: 832).

The Second Reform Drive (1983–1984)

The balance of trade was restored in 1981, and China accumulated a sizable surplus in 1982–1983. Fiscal balance was restored in 1982, and China embarked on another reform drive in 1983/84 (Sung and Chan 1987: 11). In 1983 Hainan Island, an island only slightly smaller than Taiwan, was granted a degree of autonomy exceeding that of the special economic zones. In April 1984 fourteen coastal cities along the entire Pacific coast were declared open.[1] These cities provide virtually all of the port facilities in China and accounted for 97 percent of turnover in Chinese ports in 1983. They are also relatively industrialized, accounting for nearly one quarter of China's gross value of industrial output, although their population share was only 8 percent (Kueh 1987: 454). In January 1985 China announced its intention to open the entire Chinese Pacific basin. The first step was the opening of the Changjiang delta, the Zhujiang delta, and the south Fujian triangle containing the historic ports of Xiamen, Zhangzhou, and Quanzhou in February 1985. The opening of the Liaoning and Shandong peninsulas was originally on the agenda for March 1985 (Kueh 1987: 450), but the speed of events

---

1. They are Dalian, Qinhuangdao, Tianjin, Yantai, Qingdao, Lianyungang, Nantong, Shanghai, Ningbo, Wenzhou, Fuzhou, Guangzhou, Zhanjiang, and Beihai.

led to confusion, and the opening of the two peninsulas was shelved. In September 1984 the State Council approved a radical proposal to reform the foreign trade system, giving autonomy to foreign trade corporations, which were to become responsible for their own profits and losses. In view of the sizable foreign exchange reserves built up since 1982, foreign exchange controls were relaxed in 1984 (Qi 1985: 47).

The radical reform proposals had barely been implemented when a massive trade deficit and runaway inflation forced planners to recentralize. Domestic reforms led to a loss of control over investment and monetary expansion. The trade deficit was caused primarily by the relaxation of foreign exchange and import controls, especially in the open areas, leading to a surge of imports (Qi 1985: 47). To rectify the imbalance, planners imposed severe administrative controls on bank loans, foreign exchange, and investment in early 1985. Although the foreign trade reforms proposed in 1984 remained largely unimplemented, there was active discussion on economic and political reforms in 1984–1985, and the reformers appeared to be preparing for another reform drive. The *renminbi* was devalued twice in 1985–1986, and another devaluation was reportedly scheduled for 1987. However, the radical proposals on economic and political reforms and student unrest in December 1986 provoked a strong conservative backlash, culminating in the forced resignation of the liberal leader Hu Yaobang and a campaign against "bourgeois liberalization." Following student demonstrations, price reforms and the planned devaluation of the *renminbi* were shelved in response to social discontent over inflation (Sung and Chan 1987: 19).

The Third Reform Drive (1988–1989)

The campaign against "bourgeois liberalization" held up reforms only temporarily, and reformers gained the upper hand in the Thirteenth Party Congress in November 1987. A third reform drive was launched in 1988. Hainan Island become a separate province in mid-1988, with a higher degree of autonomy than before. The opening of the entire Chinese Pacific basin continued with the opening of the Liaoning and Shandong peninsulas, the entire provinces of Guangdong (previously limited to the Zhujiang delta) and Fujian (previously limited to the south Fujian triangle), parts of Guangxi province and Hebei province, and eighteen additional coastal cities (*Hong Kong Economic Times,* June 14, 1988). The areas opened in 1988 were as large as all the areas opened in the nine years from 1979 to 1987. By 1988 the population in the open areas totaled 160 million. The open areas form a three-tier structure, with coastal open areas having the least autonomy, coastal open cities having an intermediate level of autonomy, and SEZs having the greatest autonomy. The huge trade deficit of 1984–1986 declined rapidly in 1987, and China's trade was close to balanced in the first half of 1988. The radical 1984 trade reforms that had stalled in 1985 were resumed in 1987–1988.

The most noticeable event of 1988 was price reform. Carried out in an overheated economy plagued by excessive investment and monetary growth, the price reforms precipitated panic buying and bank runs. In September the reforms were shelved, and the State Council imposed severe controls on investment and credit. A trade deficit again emerged in the second half of 1988, and trade controls were stiffened. The Tiananmen incident of June 1989 led to the downfall of the liberal party secretary, Zhao Ziyang, and a severe setback for economic reforms. In the second half of 1989 Beijing tried to recentralize and placed severe restrictions on private enterprises. It reversed such policies in early 1990, however, because of resistance on the part of provincial authorities as well as Beijing's fears of rising unemployment.

The Fourth Reform Drive (1991–1992)

Though economic reforms stalled on many fronts after the Tiananmen incident, economic reforms of the external sector have continued. Foreign loans and investment and tourism earnings dwindled after the Tiananmen incident, and China had to expand its commodity exports to meet its import needs and debt obligations. The *renminbi* was devalued by 21 percent against the U.S. dollar in December 1989 and by 9.6 percent in November 1990. Pudong was declared open in April 1990. Trade subsidies were abolished in early 1991, and foreign trade corporations became financially independent. China's exports grew by 18 percent and 16 percent in 1990 and 1991. The fourth reform drive gathered momentum in early 1992 when Deng Xiaoping dramatized his dissatisfaction with the pace of economic reforms in his tour of Guangdong and Shenzhen. After Deng's tour, new reforms were launched rapidly. Besides the myriad open areas along the coast, numerous areas were opened along the major waterways and along the borders with Russia and Vietnam. China's tertiary sector was opened to foreign investment. Foreign trade was further liberalized, and the *renminbi* was devalued by 9 percent against the U.S. dollar in 1992. Contracted foreign investment in 1992 was more than four and a half times that of 1991, setting a record of US$58 billion, and exports grew by 18 percent. In early 1993, double-digit inflation emerged owing to an investment boom, and Beijing tightened credit to fight inflation. China appeared to be heading toward retrenchment.

INSTITUTIONAL CHANGES
IN THE EXTERNAL SECTOR

The traditional Chinese system of foreign trade was inadequate for the demands of the increasing variety of economic interactions that arose under the open door policy. Organizational changes and new incentive structures were adopted beginning in 1979.

The First Reform Drive and Retrenchment (1979–1981)

In 1979 new central agencies for trade and investment were created by the State Council in response to the need for functional specialization in implementing the open door policy. These included the Foreign Investment Administrative Commission (FIAC), the Import-Export Administration Commission (IEAC), the State Administration of Foreign Exchange Control (SAFEC), and the China International Trust and Investment Corporation (CITIC). The functions of FIAC and SAFEC were self-evident. IEAC was responsible for special trade not involving direct foreign investment. CITIC was a ministerial-rank multinational company formed to court foreign investment and finance. It had unprecedented autonomy in the communist world and was led by an old-style millionaire, Rong Yiren, who had refused to leave China during the communist takeover in 1949. In March 1982 the FIAC and IEAC were merged with the Ministry of Trade and the Ministry of Foreign Economic Relations into an umbrella organization called the Ministry of Foreign Economic Relations and Trade (MOFERT).

In addition to the creation of new agencies at the central level, powers of trade and investment have been decentralized. Industrial ministries under the State Council are allowed to establish their own import-export corporations. Ministerial foreign trade corporations (MFTCs) usually export the ministry's own products and handle imports required by the ministry. The reforms facilitated direct technical contacts between Chinese and foreign enterprises.

Beginning with Guangdong, Fujian, and the three central municipalities, an increasing number of provinces have set up provincial import-export corporations since 1979. A handful of producer enterprises have also achieved autonomy in exports. The total number of corporations and enterprises with autonomy to export numbered several hundred in 1980.

Despite these reforms, the Chinese trading system was still highly centralized, with official approval required for all exports and imports, although applications could be processed more quickly as some of them were approved by ministerial or provincial authorities instead of the Ministry of Foreign Trade. Exports were classified into three categories. Category I commodities, under the control of the Ministry of Foreign Trade (such as grain, coal, crude oil, and finished steel), continued to be handled by the national foreign trade corporations and accounted for 80 percent of China's total exports in 1980/81 (at the height of the first decentralization drive) (Kueh and Howe 1984: 832). Less important Category II commodities were handled by local authorities under central guidance, and locally established export prices were within centrally stipulated ranges. Category III goods were usually outside the plan, allowing local authorities to issue export licenses, set the prices, and handle exports (Ho and Huenemann 1984: 41–44). Imports were even more centralized than exports because of strict foreign exchange controls.

The 1979/80 decentralization did, however, cause some confusion. Local authorities cut export prices to compete, especially in the Hong Kong market (Xue 1986: 4). The prices of native products in which China had a monopoly fell appreciably, and China reacted by instituting an export licensing system in 1981 (Sung 1991: 46). The recentralization measures were part of the retrenchment program of the second readjustment, though export decentralization remained basically intact.

The Second Reform Drive and Retrenchment (1983–1985)

The second reform drive of 1983/84 led to the opening of Hainan Island and fourteen coastal cities as well as the radical proposal to decentralize foreign trade to foreign trade corporations. The reform package, approved by the State Council in September 1984, called for the separation of the functions of government and enterprises. That is, the MOFERT and local trade authorities would concentrate on the overall management of foreign trade without interfering in the business of foreign trade corporations (NFTCs, MFTCs, and provincial foreign trade corporations), and the foreign trade corporations would gradually become independent of their administrative superiors, assuming responsibility for their own profits and losses. Furthermore, an agency system would be introduced, whereby foreign trade corporations would function as intermediaries in foreign trade for producers and users, collecting service charges in the process. The producers and users would be responsible for the profits and losses involved. Lastly, foreign trade plans would be simplified. Mandatory planning would be restricted to key commodities, and guidance planning would be used for secondary commodities (Zheng 1984: 27–33).

The 1984 reform, if fully implemented, would have revolutionized the Chinese foreign trade system. The 1979/80 reform had given trading authority to ministerial and provincial authorities, which could easily be controlled by administrative means, whereas the 1984 reform sought to make foreign trade corporations independent of administrative controls.

A prime objective of the 1984 reform proposal was to cut the huge subsidies to exports. Because the *renminbi* was overvalued, the state had to subsidize exports according to their costs. Though the *renminbi* had been devalued repeatedly against the U.S. dollar since 1979, the "cost of earning foreign exchange" (COEFE) or the *huanhui chengben* (the cost in *renminbi* of earning one unit of foreign exchange) often exceeded the official exchange rate. Table 4.4 shows the average COEFE of China's exports and the official exchange rate in recent years. Though the 1979/80 reforms partially decentralized the power to trade, the financial responsibility was still centralized; that is, exports were subsidized up to their costs. The system encourages foreign trade corporations to procure goods at high prices for export to meet mandatory export targets, leading to a rapid rise of the COEFE.

To lower costs, Chinese planners have been using the COEFE in well-run enterprises as an efficiency norm. In view of the rapid rise of the COEFE in 1983, the State Council established ceilings of COEFE for different goods and banned the export of goods that cost more than the stipulated ceilings in December 1983 (*Almanac of China's Foreign Economic Relations and Trade 1985:* 241) The COEFE declined temporarily in 1984 but shot up again in 1985. Given mandatory export targets and soft budget constraints, administrative controls on the COEFE failed to hold down the cost of exports.

The 1984 reform proposal attempted to shift the financial responsibility from the state Treasury to enterprises, as foreign trade corporations, producers of exports, and users of imports took responsibility for their own profits and losses. Producers and foreign trade corporations would thus be encouraged to be cost-conscious, and end-users would be forced to economize on the use of imports.

The 1984 reform proposal was stalled by the severe macroeconomic imbalance of 1984/85. The price of export procurement was lowered in 1984 following the ban on high-cost exports in December 1983, but domestic inflation was high because of the macroeconomic imbalance. Many export producers thus diverted their production capacity to the domestic market (Zhao and Liu 1986: 36). From March to July 1985, China's exports declined by 5 percent over the same period in 1984,

TABLE 4.4   CHINA'S AVERAGE COST OF EARNING FOREIGN
EXCHANGE (COEFE) IN EXPORTS, 1980–1991
(YUAN/US$)

Year	Cost of earning foreign exchange (COEFE)		Official exchange rate
	National	Guangdong	
1980	2.31	n.a.	1.50
1981	2.48	2.84	2.80
1982	2.67	3.18	2.80
1983	3.07	3.44	2.80
1984	2.80	3.15	2.80
1985	3.19	3.65	2.94
1986	4.18	4.78	3.50
1987	4.70	5.37	3.73
1988	4.52	5.17	3.72
1989	5.06	5.79	3.72
1990	n.a.	n.a.	4.81
1991	n.a.	n.a.	5.33

Note: The internal settlement rate is used for the official exchange rate in 1981–1984.
n.a. = not available.
Source: For Guangdong, the 1981–1986 and 1988–1989 data were obtained through interviews, and
the 1987 data came from E. F. Vogel, *One Step Ahead in China* (Cambridge: Harvard University Press,
1989), p. 378. For the nation, the 1980–1984 data came from Wang Shenzhong, "Changes in the
Exchange Rate and Economic Development in the External Sector (in Chinese)," *Jingji Yanjiu* (Economic Research) (April 1984), pp. 44–51; data since 1985 were estimated by regressing the national
COEFE on Guangdong's COEFE from 1981 to 1984:

$$Y(t) = 0.8743\ X(t),\ R^2 = 0.9994$$
$$(70.982)$$

where $Y(t)$ was the national COEFE and $X(t)$ was Guandong's COEFE. The regression was highly
significant. The national COEFE since 1985 was then predicted from Guandong's COEFE by using the
above equation. The standard errors of prediction were small:

Year	Predicted $Y(t)$	Standard error	
		$E(Y(t))$	$Y(t)$
1985	3.1912	0.0910	0.1198
1986	4.1792	0.2977	0.3077
1987	4.6950	0.4057	0.4131
1988	4.5202	0.3691	0.3772
1989	5.0622	0.2328	0.3691

though the decline was halted in August 1985 as a result of stabilization measures that had been taken in March. Imports rose by 54 percent
in 1985 and China ran a huge trade deficit. The *renminbi* was devalued
several times against the U.S. dollar in 1985 and 1986, but the devaluations were not big enough to keep pace with the rapid rise of the
COEFE. The state Treasury continues to assume most of the financial
responsibility in foreign trade (Tian, Li, He, and Zhang 1986: 37), and
the 1984 reform proposal remained largely unimplemented.

One aspect of the 1984 reform that has been widely adopted was the agency system, which permitted direct contact between producers and end-users. This is especially important for the import of appropriate technology. Though the agency system was widely implemented on the import side, it covered only 10 percent of exports as exports were still heavily subsidized. Moreover, the NFTCs play a larger role than do such intermediaries in other countries because the producers have little experience in exporting, and export prices are negotiated by the NFTC and the end-user (*Ta Kung Pao,* May 30, 1987). The total number of corporations and enterprises with autonomy to export continued to grow, reaching three thousand by 1986. In 1986, however, mandatory export targets still accounted for 70 percent of all exports (*Wen Hui Pao,* June 6, 1987). NFTCs, which were responsible for the key commodities controlled by the MOFERT, still handled 80 percent of all imports and 90 percent of all exports in 1986.[2] Decentralization of foreign trade has not made much headway since 1980/81, when NFTCs handled 80 percent of China's exports.

The Third Reform Drive and Retrenchment (1988–1990)

The third reform drive led to the opening of more coastal cities and coastal areas, including the establishment of Hainan as a province and an SEZ. In March 1988 MOFERT started to restructure the foreign trade system, and power was decentralized from the head offices of the NFTCs in Beijing to local foreign trade corporations (LFTCs), which were formerly local branches of the NFTCs. The LFTCs became financially independent companies. The reform represented an application of the contract responsibility system in foreign trade (*South China Morning Post,* October 10, 1988). Under the new system, each province or municipality must sign an annual contract with MOFERT specifying three targets: foreign exchange earnings, amount of foreign exchange earnings to be turned over to the state, and profits (or losses). To meet these obligations, the provincial or municipal governments will enter into contracts with the LFTCs, which act as import and export agents for the local enterprises. The role of NFTCs diminished greatly, and the number of commodities subject to exclusive trading by NFTCs was limited to a few items.

Along with the decentralization of power, financial responsibility was also decentralized from the state to provincial governments and

---

2. Information obtained in interviews with Chinese trade officials.

foreign trade corporations (NFTCs, MFTCs, and LFTCs), which were required to be financially independent. To enable provincial governments and foreign trade corporations to cover the losses from exports, they were allowed to retain 80 percent of their foreign exchange earnings that exceeded planned targets. This was in addition to the customary 25 percent retention of within-target foreign exchange earnings, which had been allowed since 1979. Since the *renminbi* was overvalued, the right to retain foreign exchange served as a powerful incentive. The restrictions on the sale of foreign exchange earnings at prices above the official rate were also relaxed in early 1988. The foreign exchange retention scheme and restrictions on the transfer of such foreign exchange are complicated subjects that will be discussed in greater detail below. The generous foreign exchange retentions together with other economic incentives such as the exemption of domestic taxes for exports, have enabled foreign trade corporations to come close to financial independence, which was the goal of the 1984 reform proposal. However, because the problem of a soft budget constraint is deeply rooted in socialist economies (including marketized socialist economies), the complete financial independence of state enterprises in China has to wait for the full implementation of the bankruptcy law passed in 1988.

The Fourth Reform Drive (1991–1992)

Though the Tiananmen incident led to temporary recentralization of many activities, the 1988 trade reforms remained basically intact. As mentioned earlier, reforms of the external sector continued because soft loans dried up after the Tiananmen incident and Beijing was under great pressure to expand its exports. The government abolished subsidies on exports in early 1991 and raised the rate of foreign exchange retention to 80 percent of export earnings.

Incentives to Promote Trade

Starting in 1979, China adopted incentives to promote trade, especially exports. Measures adopted included devaluation of the *renminbi;* permission for local governments, ministries, and export enterprises to retain a portion of the foreign exchange earned in exports; tariff exemption for imported inputs used in producing exports; and rebates of indirect taxes for exports. These new measures were introduced in addition to the established practice of priority allocation of scarce materials to export enterprises.

In 1979/80 the official exchange rate of roughly 1.5 yuan per dollar could not cover the exporters' costs, since the average COEFE was around 2.5 yuan per dollar (Table 4.4). The variations in the COEFE among localities and goods were large. In 1979 77.2 percent of Guangdong exports incurred losses, and the COEFE of some goods was ten times the official rate (Kueh and Howe 1984: 845). A dual rate system was adopted at the beginning of 1981. Commodity trade was settled at the internal rate of 2.80 yuan per dollar, and the official rate of 1.53 yuan per dollar continued to apply to noncommodity transactions. Table 4.4 shows the COEFE and exchange rate of China in recent years. From 1980 to 1981, the internal settlement rate exceeded the COEFE.

The dual rate system was strongly criticized by the United States as an export subsidy. As the U.S. dollar appreciated against other currencies in 1981–1984, the *renminbi* was gradually devalued against the dollar, and the official exchange rate approached the internal rate. The dual rate system was abolished on January 1, 1985, when the official exchange rate was 2.84 yuan per dollar. By then the COEFE of Chinese exports was 4.00 yuan per dollar, and huge subsidies were still required for exports.

From January 1 to September 30, 1985, the *renminbi* was gradually devalued by a total of 12.5 percent to 3.2 yuan per dollar and remained steady at this level for ten months until July 4, 1986, when it was further devalued by 14 percent to 3.70 yuan per dollar. The yuan was still overvalued, but the continued weakness of the U.S. dollar in 1986–1987 helped to ease the extent of overvaluation.

The foreign exchange retention scheme was first introduced in 1979. All foreign exchange earned through exports must be sold to the Bank of China at the official exchange rate, but the provincial government and the export enterprise are entitled to purchase a share of the foreign exchange at the official rate for later use on approved items that require the use of foreign exchange. It should be noted that the entitlement did not confer a secure right to use foreign exchange. In the 1985 crisis, enterprises seldom received approval to use their entitlements owing to the tight foreign exchange situation. Provincial governments sometimes requisition the entitlements of enterprises under their control without compensation (Zhao and Liu 1986: 28). With the improvement in the balance of payments since 1986, however, the right to foreign exchange entitlements has become more secure.

Before the 1988 trade reforms, provincial authorities and export enterprises gained from more exports owing to the foreign exchange retention scheme, but they did not assume financial responsibility, which remained with the central government. Provincial authorities thus did not hesitate to procure goods at high prices and dump them overseas at a loss (Xue 1986: 4), leading to a rapid rise in the COEFE.

The foreign exchange retention ratios were gradually raised, and the restrictions on the transfer of foreign exchange entitlements were gradually relaxed. Since 1980 enterprises have been allowed to swap their foreign exchange entitlements for *renminbi* with other enterprises through the Bank of China at negotiated rates that were allowed to rise a maximum of 10 percent above the official rate (Wu 1987: 9). The ceiling on the maximum rate was progressively raised. Restrictions on the trading of foreign exchange were further relaxed with the establishment of foreign exchange adjustment centers, where enterprises can trade foreign exchange at negotiated rates. The first center was established in Shenzhen in December 1985. By the late 1980s, such centers were established in most provinces of China, and a national market in foreign exchange began to emerge (*Ta Kung Pao,* May 12, 1988).

Before the 1988 trade reforms, the usual ratio of foreign exchange retention was 25 percent, with half going to the provincial and local governments and the other half going to the export enterprises. The Guangdong and Fujian provincial governments were allowed to retain an extra 5 percent, giving a total retention ratio of 30 percent. As mentioned before, in the 1988 trade reforms, the retention ratios were raised and the restrictions on the sale of foreign exchange entitlements were relaxed to enable FTCs to come close to financial independence. According to the 1991 trade reforms, 20 percent of the foreign exchange earnings from commodity exports were to be sold to Beijing at the official rate and the rest (80 percent) were to be distributed, with local governments claiming 10 percent, FTCs claiming 60 percent, and enterprises claiming 10 percent. Beijing, however, was entitled to purchase at the swap rate the retained earnings of enterprises and one-third of the retained earnings of FTCs; That is, Beijing was entitled to purchase at the swap rate 30 percent of the foreign exchange earnings from commodity exports.

In the foreign exchange adjustment centers, though the swap rate is not strictly controlled, restrictions are still imposed on the source and use of foreign exchange. The seller is required to specify that the foreign exchange is obtained from a legal source, and the buyer must specify a legitimate use of foreign exchange. Trading for speculation is strictly prohibited. Individuals are generally not allowed to participate in trade (*Wen Hui Pao,* August 18, 1988).

If China allowed exporters to retain 100 percent of their foreign exchange earnings and freely transfer such earnings to importers for imports, it would be equivalent to floating exchange rates for commodity trade with controls on the capital account. As it is, the retention ratio is slightly below 100 percent, and there are still controls on the use of foreign exchange, but China is not far from such a system of floating exchange rates.

Part of the financial loss on exports is misleading because of the heavy tariffs on imported inputs used in producing exports and also because of heavy indirect taxes. In the period 1981–1984, industry and commercial taxes accounted for 14 percent of China's national income. The significance of tariffs and other indirect taxes might also be substantial, but they cannot be quantified because of a lack of data. Tax rebates for exports have been proposed since the early 1980s, but provincial governments are unwilling to give tax rebates because of the adverse impact on provincial treasuries.[3] Many taxes in China are collected by provincial authorities and then shared between Beijing and the provinces. Manufacturing usually involves intermediate inputs produced in different regions, and the precise geographical incidence of indirect tax is difficult to determine. Tariff exemption for imported inputs used in producing exports involves only the central Treasury. From 1985 to 1987, the central government had rebated domestic taxes on the final stage of production, which was only one-third of the total taxes paid through all stages of production.[4]

The 1988 trade reform blueprint proposed a thorough rebate of indirect taxes through all stages of production. For products procured for export by FTCs, the rebates would be given to the FTCs. For products exported through the agency system, the rebates would be given to the production enterprises (*Ta Kung Pao,* December 3, 1987).

The Three-Tier Structure of Open Areas

China's open areas—coastal open areas, coastal open cities, and SEZs—form a three-tier structure in terms of increasing degrees of autonomy. The SEZs formerly had a tremendous competitive edge in terms of low taxes and high foreign exchange retention ratios, but the edge has been eroded by the opening of other cities and areas. In order to maintain their lead, the SEZs have been forced to grant more and more concessions to foreign investors. The competition among different open areas to grant concessions to foreign investors may not be in the national interest, but Beijing has not been able to prevent it as more and more economic power has been decentralized from Beijing to the provinces and municipalities.

The 15 percent profit tax for foreign investors in SEZs had been attractive in comparison with the 30 percent profit tax elsewhere in China. However, twelve coastal cities among the fourteen opened in 1984 established Economic and Technology Development Districts

---

3. Information obtained in interviews with Chinese trade officials.
4. Information obtained in interviews with Chinese trade officials.

(ETDDs) in which the 15 percent profit tax also applied. The 15 percent profit tax was then applied to special enterprises outside the SEZs and ETDDs, including technology-intensive enterprises; enterprises with foreign investment over US$30 million; investment with a lengthy payback period; or investment in energy, transportation, and harbor facilities. The 15 percent profit tax of Hong Kong, which was first adopted by Shenzhen, appears to be spreading throughout China. The coastal open areas also joined in the tax-reduction competition and offered a variety of tax cuts and tax holidays. For instance, the profit tax of the Liudong peninsula was fixed at 24 percent instead of the standard 30 percent.

In March 1988, after the central work conference on the opening of the coastal areas, Vice Premier Tian Jiyuan summed up the division of labor among the three different kinds of open areas (*Ta Kung Pao,* March 19, 1988): the coastal open areas are expected to export labor-intensive manufactures and agricultural products; the coastal open cities should rely on their strength in technology and industry to upgrade traditional exports, promoting the export of electrical machinery in particular; and the SEZs should be a model of an externally oriented economy with advanced technology. Tian's statement was little more than an after-the-fact rationalization of the confusion that emerged in the competitive drive of various open areas to grant preferential terms to foreign investors.

Since Tian's speech, various inland areas, including Hubei, Anhui, Kiangsi, Gansu, Honan, Shenshi, Beijing, and Sichuen, have also granted preferential terms to foreign investors (*Hong Kong Economic Times,* June 15, 1988). Chinese economists have started to talk about a four-tier structure of open areas, with inland open areas as the first tier. The distinction between each tier is not sharp. Many inland open areas granted preferential terms that are as attractive as those of the coastal open areas, or even more attractive. For instance, the Loyang ETDD in Honan exempts all profit tax for a period of three years. The four SEZs and the ETDDs in the fourteen coastal cities exempt profit tax for a period of only two years (*Hong Kong Economic Times,* June 15, 1988).

The SEZs initially tried to attract technologically advanced industries and turned away processing and assembling operations. They managed to attract very few high-tech ventures, however, and were forced to accept processing and assembling operations. Counties in the Pearl River delta (a coastal open area) such as Dongguan, Zhongshan, and Foshan have been able to attract foreign investment in industries that are as sophisticated as those in the SEZs. Though SEZs have a better infrastructure, they are less flexible in their policies because they have been pushed into the limelight and thus suffer from the attention and meddling of Beijing. The obscure counties mentioned above can afford to ignore central directives and pursue more flexible policies. The planned division of labor among the different types of open areas exists more on paper than in reality.

EVALUATION OF THE OPEN DOOR POLICY

Ten years have lapsed since the inauguration of the open door policy. Commodity trade, services trade, and foreign investment in China have increased by leaps and bounds, but problems remain. Macroeconomic imbalances have emerged in the liberalization phase of each of the four reform cycles, and reforms have suffered setbacks as administrative measures have been used to stabilize the economy. Symptoms of economic inefficiency abound in both trade and investment. Details of the achievements and deficiencies of the open door policy in the areas of trade and investment follow.

The Rapid Increase in Trade

The increase in exports and imports since 1979 has been extremely rapid. From 1978 to 1992, the value of China's exports grew at an average annual nominal rate of 17 percent in dollar terms, while imports grew 15 percent annually. Exports increased by a factor of eight and a half in the period.

The ratio of China's exports and imports to its GDP has also risen rapidly since 1978. Table 4.5 shows the ratio of exports and imports to GDP for both China and India. India is chosen for comparison because the ratio is usually lower for large economies and higher for more developed economies, and India is comparable to China in size and level of development. In the thirteen years of reform and open door policy from 1978 to 1991, China's ratio of exports to GDP rose sharply from 5 to 19 percent, while the same ratio for India hovered around 4 to 6 percent. China's export drive thus appears to have been remarkably successful.

Devaluation and Trade Response

Until the late 1980s, most of China's academics and trade officials believed that devaluation had failed to boost exports and constrained imports in China. This belief was a result of superficial statistical analysis.

Chinese academics usually measure both the exchange rate of the *renminbi* and the value of trade in terms of the U.S. dollar (Table 4.1). According to their analysis, the yuan was devalued by close to 50 percent at the beginning of 1981 with the adoption of the internal settlement rate that applied to commodity trade. From 1980 to 1983, however, China's exports grew by only 23 percent and imports contin-

TABLE 4.5 RATIO OF EXPORTS AND IMPORTS TO GDP IN
CHINA AND INDIA, 1978–1991 (PERCENTAGE)

Year	China		India	
	Exports	Imports	Exports	Imports
1978	4.7	5.2	5.6	6.6
1979	5.3	6.1	5.9	7.5
1980	6.1	6.7	5.3	9.2
1981	7.7	7.7	4.5	8.4
1982	8.0	6.9	5.0	7.5
1983	7.6	7.3	4.5	6.7
1984	8.4	8.9	4.9	6.2
1985	9.5	14.7	4.4	6.2
1986	11.2	15.5	4.1	6.8
1987	13.0	14.3	4.4	6.5
1988	12.6	14.6	4.7	6.7
1989	12.2	13.8	5.7	7.4
1990	16.7	14.4	5.9	7.8
1991	19.4	17.2	6.6	7.5

Source: China's exports, imports, and GDP from the State Statistical Bureau, *Statistical Yearbook of China* (Beijing, various issues); India's exports, imports, and GDP are from the International Monetary Fund (IMF), *International Financial Statistics* (Washington, D.C.: various issues).

ued to rise by 7 percent (Wang 1986: 45–46). In 1985 the yuan was further devalued by 14 percent, but exports grew only 5 percent and imports soared by 54 percent, giving rise to a huge trade deficit. Devaluation thus failed to achieve its objective (Wu and Zhang 1987). In 1987 the yuan was not devalued, but exports soared 28 percent and imports rose by less than 1 percent. This result appears to support the contention that administrative measures are more effective than devaluation in promoting exports and restraining imports.

The alleged ineffectiveness of devaluation, however, is only a statistical artifact, because the exchange rate of the yuan and the value of China's trade have not been measured correctly. Because of the sharp fluctuation of the U.S. dollar against major currencies since 1981, the exchange rate of the yuan should be measured against a basket of currencies rather than against the U.S. dollar. Moreover, because China's exports are heavily subsidized and its imports are heavily taxed, the relevant variable is not the nominal or official exchange rate, but the effective exchange rate (EER). The EER is defined as the number of units of local currency actually received by the exporter, or paid by the importer, per unit of foreign currency of goods traded. The real exchange rate can be calculated from the EER after adjusting for foreign and domestic rates of inflation.

The value of China's trade should not be measured in U.S. dollars. The correct procedure is to measure the value of exports or imports in local currency deflated by the export or import price deflator. This procedure cannot be used for China, however, because China has not released reliable export and import price deflators. Moreover, the official data on the *renminbi* value of exports and imports are biased downward to avoid charges of dumping. The data are obtained by converting the U.S. dollar value of exports at the official exchange rate, which is substantially lower than the true cost of exports and imports. In this chapter I will use export- and import-weighted baskets of currencies to measure the value of China's exports and imports.

A simple example shows the importance of measuring the value of trade and the exchange rate with a currency basket. Suppose all of China's exports go to Japan and the exchange rate of the *renminbi* against the yen is constant. Other things being equal, the value of exports of China in yen will also be constant. Suppose, however, the yen appreciates against the U.S. dollar by 100 percent. If the U.S. dollar is used to measure China's trade and exchange rate, we will arrive at the ridiculous conclusion that a 100 percent appreciation of the *renminbi* has led to a 100 percent increase in China's exports.

The results of this study are contrary to the conventional beliefs of China's academics and trade officials. The depreciation of the real exchange rate of the *renminbi* from 1981 to 1985 was moderate and the export response was appreciable. The real exchange rate depreciated rapidly in 1986, and exports and imports have responded rapidly to the devaluation.

This study therefore uses an export-weighted basket of currencies to measure the value of China's exports and the nominal export exchange rate of the *renminbi* and an imported-weighted basket of currencies to measure the value of imports and the nominal import exchange rate. I chose six major trading partners of China: namely Hong Kong, Japan, the United States, the United Kingdom, the former West Germany, and Singapore. Their shares in China's exports to these six economies were used as weights in the export-weighted index and their shares in China's imports were used as weights in the import-weighted index.

The base period is January 1980. The indexes belong to the Paasche type of index as weights are changed annually. The six economies chosen accounted for roughly 75 percent of China's exports and 65 percent of its imports and the remaining portions were mostly accounted for by countries of Comecon. Since trade with the Comecon bloc and the exchange rate of the *renminbi* against the currencies of the Comecon bloc are not mainly determined by market forces, the currencies of the Comecon bloc are not included in the currency basket. The six economies chosen in this study accounted for over 90 percent of China's trade with market economies.

Table 4.6 shows the indexes of the value of China's exports and imports in U.S. dollars and in the currency baskets. The nominal exchange rate indexes in U.S. dollars and in the currency baskets are also presented. Manufacturing exports are distinguished from total exports, because traditional exports are less sensitive to exchange rate changes. I will focus on China's manufacturing exports, not only because they are more price sensitive, but also because the value of traditional exports can be erratic owing to price fluctuations. For instance, in 1986, the price of oil dropped markedly and China's total exports (in terms of the currency basket) stagnated. Manufacturing exports, however, exhibited healthy growth.

Because of the sharp appreciation of the U.S. dollar against major currencies from 1981 to February 1985, measurements in terms of the U.S. dollar overstate the extent of the devaluation of the *renminbi* and understate the extent of export growth. After February 1985, the reverse is true.

The export-weighted exchange rate index of *renminbi* rose from 100 points to 179 points in 1981 owing to the adoption of the internal settlement rate. The index fell back to 150 points in 1984, however, because of the sharp appreciation of the U.S. dollar against other currencies. Thereafter, the index rose sharply to 217 points in 1987 as a result of (1) the devaluation of the *renminbi* against the U.S. dollar, and (2) the sharp depreciation of the U.S. dollar against major currencies. The movement of the imported-weighted index is broadly similar to that of the export-weighted index. The fall of the imported-weighted index from 1981 to 1984, however, was less substantial than that of the export-weighted index, and its rise thereafter was more dramatic since the weight of the Japanese yen was higher in the import-weighted index than the export-weighted index. The two indexes were stable from 1987 to 1989, when the U.S. dollar was stable against the other major currencies. The *renminbi* depreciated rapidly in 1990/91 because of the substantial devaluation of the *renminbi* against the U.S. dollar.

To gauge the response of trade to devaluation, we must estimate the real EER and the real value of trade in terms of a basket of currencies. The COEFE (Table 4.4) is used as a proxy for the export EER. It is not a perfect proxy, as the producer may earn a profit over and above cost, but it is difficult to find a better proxy given limited data. It should be noted that a rise in the EER represents depreciation of the *renminbi* and a fall represents an appreciation. The COEFE is redenominated in terms of the currency basket rather than the U.S. dollar.

It is difficult to estimate the import EER because there are few data on China's complicated system of import charges, indirect taxes, and subsidies. Because taxes and subsidies are usually levied on an *ad*

TABLE 4.6 INDEXES OF CHINA'S EXPORTS, IMPORTS, AND FOREIGN EXCHANGE RATES, 1980–1991

| | | Nominal exchange rate index | | Total exports | | Manufacturing exports | | Total imports | |
| | | Y/basket of currencies | | | | | | | |
Year	Y/ US$	Export-weighted	Import-weighted	US$	Basket of cur-rencies	US$	Basket of cur-rencies	US$	Basket of cur-rencies
1980	100	100	100	100	100 (100)	100	100 (100)	100	100 (100)
1981	187	179	182	122	127 (116)	132	137 (126)	110	115 (106)
1982	187	169	169	123	139 (119)	138	156 (134)	96	108 (95)
1983	187	153	164	123	150 (121)	141	172 (138)	107	130 (111)
1984	187	150	161	144	179 (137)	159	198 (152)	137	170 (139)
1985	196	159	168	151	185 (139)	151	185 (139)	211	259 (206)
1986	230	193	230	171	204 (145)	220	263 (186)	214	256 (198)
1987	247	217	248	218	248 (169)	294	334 (228)	216	245 (179)
1988	248	223	251	262	292 (187)	367	409 (262)	276	307 (212)
1989	251	216	242	290	337 (199)	415	482 (285)	295	342 (221)
1990	319	271	286	343	404 (227)	512	603 (338)	266	313 (184)
1991	355	303	337	397	465 (244)	618	724 (380)	319	374 (210)

Note: Figures in parentheses are real (price-level deflated) indexes.
Source: Values of exports and imports are from Economic Information Agency, *China Customs Statistics* (Hong Kong, various issues). In 1980 the breakdown of total exports between manufacturing and nonmanufacturing exports is not available from *China Customs Statistics,* though total exports are available. The 1980 share of manufacturing exports in total exports is taken from U.S. Central Intelligence Agency, National Foreign Assessment Center, *China: International Trade.*

valorem basis, however, the index of the official foreign exchange rate can be taken as a crude index of the import EER.

The real exchange rate, which is a measure of the exchange rate that is adjusted for changes in purchasing power between China and the rest of the world, can be computed from the EER. The export real EER, which is a proxy for the real exchange rate, is defined as follows:

$$\text{export real EER} = \text{export EER} \times \frac{PW}{PD}$$

**TABLE 4.7   CHINA'S EXPORT EFFECTIVE EXCHANGE RATE,
              1980–1990**

Year	Nominal exchange rate (Y/US$)	Cost of earning foreign exchange (Y/US$)	Effective exchange rate index		Export-weighted CPI of six countries	China's GDP deflator	Real EER index
			US$	Currency baskets			
1980	1.50	2.31	100.0	100.0	100.0	100.0	100.0
1981	2.80	2.48	107.4	103.2	109.4	102.2	110.5
1982	2.80	2.67	115.6	102.4	116.7	102.2	116.9
1983	2.80	3.07	132.9	109.2	124.1	103.7	130.6
1984	2.80	2.80	121.2	97.5	130.4	108.4	117.2
1985	2.94	3.19	138.1	112.5	133.1	118.3	125.5
1986	3.50	4.18	181.0	151.5	141.0	123.7	172.6
1987	3.73	4.70	203.5	179.1	146.8	129.9	202.5
1988	3.72	4.52	195.7	175.7	155.8	145.2	188.5
1989	3.72	5.06	219.0	188.8	168.8	158.6	201.0
1990	4.81	n.a.	n.a.	n.a.	178.3	167.4	n.a.

n.a. = not available.
Source: The nominal exchange rate and the cost of earning foreign exchange come from Table 4.4. The
consumer price indexes of the six importing countries are from the IMF, *International Financial
Statistics*. The GDP deflator is from the *Statistical Yearbook of China*. The estimation of the various
EER indexes has been described in the text.

and the import real EER is

$$\text{import real EER} = \text{import EER} \times \frac{PW}{PD}$$

where *PW* is the index of the world price level, and it is taken to be the
export- or import-weighted consumer price index of the six countries
in the currency basket; and *PD* is the index of the domestic price level,
and it is taken to be China's GDP deflator.

The export and import EER indexes are given in Tables 4.7 and 4.8.
The depreciation of the export real EER of *renminbi* was moderate
during 1980–1985 (an average of 4.4 percent per year) but depreciated
by 27 percent in 1986 and 15 percent in 1987. Rapid depreciation in
1986–1987 was attributable to the rapid rise in the COEFE and the
sharp depreciation of the U.S. dollar in the period. The rate of growth
of the real value of manufacturing exports was moderate from 1980 to
1985 (an average of 6.8 percent per year) but it grew by 34 percent and
23 percent respectively in 1986 and 1987 (Table 4.6). The real EER of
the *renminbi* stopped depreciating in 1988 and 1989 because of the
emergence of inflation in China, and the rate of growth of the real value
of manufacturing exports also slowed to 15 percent in 1988 and fell

TABLE 4.8   CHINA'S IMPORT EFFECTIVE EXCHANGE RATE, 1980–1991

	Effective exchange rate index		Import-weighted CPI of six	China's GDP	Import real EER
Year	US$	Currency basket	countries	deflator	index
1980	100	100	100.0	100.0	100.0
1981	187	182	107.8	102.2	192.4
1982	187	169	114.4	102.2	189.5
1983	187	164	117.9	103.7	185.4
1984	187	161	122.9	108.4	182.1
1985	199	171	125.6	118.3	180.9
1986	233	232	129.1	123.7	242.2
1987	249	251	137.1	129.9	264.6
1988	248	251	145.3	145.2	251.2
1989	248	239	154.9	158.6	233.8
1990	322	289	170.4	167.4	294.4
1991	355	337	178.3	172.5	348.4

Source: China's GDP deflator is from the *Statistical Yearbook of China*. The CPI of the six countries is from the IMF, *International Financial Statistics*. The computation of the various EER indexes has been described in the text.

further to 9 percent in 1989. It appeared that China's manufacturing exports were responsive to changes in the real exchange rate.

The import real EER depreciated sharply from 1980 to 1981 owing to the adoption of the internal settlement rate. It appreciated slightly from 1981 to 1985 because of the appreciation of the U.S. dollar. The depreciation of the import real EER was much more marked than the export real EER. This is partly because of the larger change in the nominal exchange rate (which is taken as proxy for the import EER) in comparison with the change in the COEFE, and partly because the weight of trade with Japan was higher in imports than in exports, and the depreciation of the U.S. dollar against the Japanese yen was particularly sharp. We do not expect a close relationship between movements in the import real EER and the real value of imports, since imports in China are determined mainly by administrative means. However, the sharp depreciations of the import real EER in 1981, 1986–1987, and 1990–1991 appeared to help to constrain imports in 1981–1982, 1986–1987, and 1990–1991 (Table 4.6). The appreciation of the import real EER from 1981 to 1985 and 1988–1989 appeared to encourage the import binges in 1983–1985 and 1988–1989.

It is clear that there have been significant depreciations in the import and export real EERs in the 1980s and that China came close to setting a realistic exchange rate in the late 1980s through the mechanisms of foreign exchange retention and foreign exchange adjustment centers. International studies indicate that setting a realistic exchange rate is a prerequisite to successful trade liberalization (Krueger 1978: Chapter 10). The depreciation of China's export EER since 1980 is an important factor behind the rapid expansion of China's exports.

Import Liberalization and Bias Reduction

Under exchange controls, imports are constrained by administrative means, and the nominal price of imports (price paid by users) is usually lower than their scarcity price, resulting in a premium for import licenses. Devaluation is usually not large enough to absorb the entire premium (otherwise, administrative controls of imports would be redundant). Devaluation would thus increase the nominal price but not the scarcity price of imports, absorbing part of the premium, leading to a "liberalization" of imports (Krueger 1978: 87). The benefits of liberalization or premium absorption include improved efficiency in the allocation of imports, a decrease in rent-seeking activities, and more equitable income distribution as the windfall gains of importers are partly wiped out.

Devaluation under foreign exchange controls usually does not affect the scarcity price of imports. As the international prices of exports are given in the world market (except for the few commodities in which China has monopoly power), devaluation would raise the domestic price of exports. The relative price of import-competing goods to exports, or the bias of trade, would thus decrease. Resources would then flow from import-competing industries into export industries.

There are not enough data to detail the change in liberalization and the bias of trade, but the crude data that are available indicate significant import liberalization and bias reduction. The depreciation of China's import EER since 1980 has been marked, indicating a substantial rise in the nominal price of imports and import liberalization. The rise in the import EER should curb import demand, implying that import controls and foreign exchange controls can be eased. We do observe a relaxation of foreign exchange controls with the institution of foreign exchange retention schemes and foreign exchange adjustment centers, and these developments are consistent with import liberalization.

As mentioned before, China's imports have grown rapidly. The ratio of imports to GDP stayed around 7 percent from 1980 to 1983, rose to 9 percent in 1984, and jumped to 15 percent in 1985 (Table 4.5). The ratio stayed around 15 percent from 1985 to 1988. The jump in imports and the relaxation of foreign exchange controls point to a decrease in the scarcity price of imports. This, together with the large rise in the export EER, implies a significant reduction in the bias of trade. The fall in the ratio of imports to GDP in 1989 was due to trade sanctions imposed on China after the Tiananmen incident. These sanctions turned out to be temporary, and the ratio jumped to 17 percent in 1991, indicating continual liberalization. International empirical studies indicate that bias reduction is a key variable in stimulating exports (Krueger 1978: 298).

Open Door Policy and Economic Decentralization

Since 1979 China has attempted to pursue an open door policy through the decentralization of the powers of trade and investment. Compared with Hua Guofeng's strategy, this policy represented a step in the right direction. Decentralization of the external sector, however, should not precede the economic reforms necessary to control and coordinate decentralized economic units. Such economic reforms include reforms to make enterprises sensitive to profit and loss and reforms in the system of economic coordination, replacing direct quantitative controls with indirect economic levers such as prices, taxes, and exchange rates. China has decentralized the power to trade without enacting the necessary economic reforms, and this lack of coordination lies at the heart of China's trade problems. For example, China started to decentralize the power to trade in 1979 but did not require foreign trade corporations to be financially independent until 1988. The result was the rapid rise of the COEFE as the system encouraged foreign trade corporations to procure goods at high prices for export to meet mandatory export targets. China has now decentralized the power to trade, but the exchange rate is still overvalued despite repeated devaluations. The result is a trade deficit, since imports are artificially cheap and exports are artificially expensive. China has decentralized the power to trade but has carried out few price reforms. The result is inefficient resource allocation, because China is exporting goods that appear to be cheap to produce but are really expensive and importing goods that appear to be expensive to produce but are really cheap.

Chinese enterprises, like most enterprises in command economies, are not sensitive to profit and loss, and the effectiveness of economic controls is limited. Moreover, China's price structure is highly irrational, and control through the present price mechanism would be inefficient. Because exchange rate reforms, price reforms, and enterprise reforms will take a long time to accomplish, import and export licenses, quotas, and foreign exchange controls are useful interim administrative levers while China moves from a centralized to a decentralized system. In the long term, China should replace import and export licenses and quotas with price instruments such as tariffs and subsidies.

Both politics and the technical difficulty of coordinating reform measures accounted for China's failure to institute adequate economic and administrative controls in conjunction with the decentralization of economic power. Efficient economic controls imply price reforms that are technically complicated and politically unpopular. Given the rapid and arbitrary price system in China, price reforms would involve massive income redistribution and would kindle fears of open inflation.

The use of administrative controls would appear to be easier than price reform in an economy such as China's. However, Chinese politics and administration have long been characterized by a highly personal style and ad hoc approach. The Chinese bureaucracy has been noted neither for its impartiality nor for its efficiency in administering sophisticated controls. The cost of administering such controls is high because China is a vast and diversified country. Central planners appear to have been overconfident of their ability to restrain and check subordinate units through traditional ad hoc methods.

Unlike economic and administrative controls, the decentralization of economic power to subordinate units is politically popular. Regionalism has always existed in China because of its size and geographical diversity, and decentralization of the external sectors enables provinces, ministries, and selected enterprises to break the state's monopoly on foreign trade and investment. It should also be noted that China launched its open door policy and reform drive immediately after the Cultural Revolution, at a time when the party and central government were politically weak and vulnerable to regional pressures. A Chinese trade official admitted:

> The management and regulating system of foreign trade are very much imperfect. We have inadequate experience and we have under-estimated the change in the external sector following the reforms. . . . The lift of rigid control of foreign trade has only contributed to a situation in which each does things in its own way without coordinating with others. At one time, Hong Kong and Macau were flooded with smuggled goods. The cause of this is that effective control and adequate management measures have not been introduced following the relaxation of control (Li 1987: 7).

Problems With China's Foreign Trade

The two main problems with China's foreign trade are (1) macroeconomic imbalance and (2) the ineffectiveness and inefficiency of trade instruments.

Macroeconomic imbalance has been a recurring problem, and China has undergone four stop-and-go cycles since 1979. The inflationary bias of the Chinese economy since 1979 can again be attributed to the lack of coordination in reform measures. While economic power has been decentralized, the interest rate remained centrally fixed and artificially low, leading to runaway credit expansion and inflation. The rate of inflation was over 20 percent in 1988, but deposit rates were a meager 9 percent in 1988, rising to only 12 percent in early 1989. The soft budget constraint of state enterprises also contributed to inflation. State enterprises are likely to overinvest because the state will bail them out of unprofitable investments.

The adverse impact of inflation on the trade balance can be softened to some extent with the adoption of floating exchange rates, but rampant inflation will inhibit trade liberalization. The exchange rate will depreciate rapidly under rampant inflation, and its rapid depreciation will heighten inflationary expectations, leading to expectations of further depreciation and capital flight. These developments will generate a vicious cycle of inflation and depreciation (World Bank 1985: 15). The government will be forced to adopt quantitative restrictions on imports to restore balance of trade, thus reversing the trend toward liberalization. In early 1993, double-digit inflation again emerged and the *renminbi* depreciated by over 40 percent in the foreign exchange adjustment centers. Inflation again threatens to derail China's trade reform. Good macroeconomic management is a prerequisite for the successful reform of the external sector.

Ineffectiveness and Inefficiency of Trade Controls

The ineffectiveness and inefficiency of China's trade controls is a vast subject that deserves detailed study. Trade decentralization under irrational prices, exchange rates, and inadequate controls gives rise to gross inefficiencies. For example, Chinese enterprises competed among themselves to export pig iron despite the fall in the export price from US$180 per ton in autumn 1981 to US$98 per ton in autumn 1982. Energy is the main input in the manufacture of pig iron and Chinese energy prices were artificially low because rent was not included in the cost of production (Du 1985: 65). It is very difficult to determine the rent without a market mechanism. The enterprises are in fact exporting cheap energy. Another obvious case of inefficiency is the overexpansion of native product exports in which China has a monopoly; prices have fallen so much that less foreign exchange has been earned for more exports. The prices of vegetables, meat, and fish in Hong Kong fell by 30 to 50 percent in early 1985 because of overexpansion of exports (*Economic Reporter,* April 22, 1985: 8). Even for manufactures in which China is a small exporter, earning more foreign exchange through selling more exports may be deceiving; the domestic resource cost of some exports is so high that China's national income may in fact be lowered by selling more exports. Controls are also circumvented through rampant smuggling, illicit trade, and false invoicing. Although the reimposition of centralized administrative controls in late 1988 suppressed some of the symptoms of poor economic management, it is only a stopgap measure, because recentralization increased effectiveness at the cost of efficiency. Cutting off direct contacts between producers and foreign buyers is detrimental to long-run export performance.

Ideally the result of careful planning, controls on China's foreign trade were implemented haphazardly in response to the confusion that emerged after the partial decentralization of China's foreign trade in 1979. Export licenses were instituted in 1981, two years after the first steps toward decentralization were taken, and largely in response to the overexpansion of those native products in which China had a monopoly. From 1981 to 1985, the system of export licenses was adjusted about twenty times (*Wen Hui Pao,* November 14, 1985) in response to particular circumstances. It was only in late 1985 that China held a national conference to discuss a comprehensive system of export licenses. Even after the conference, action to establish a comprehensive system of export licenses was slow. In late 1988 the MOFERT finally established a bureau to manage export and import licenses and increased the number of its local offices from five to thirty to prevent overissue of licenses. Provincial governments tended to license more than their allocated quota of exports, because they benefit from more exports under the foreign-exchange retention scheme (*Ta Kung Pao,* December 12, 1988).

This ad hoc approach to export licenses was evident in the notorious case of raw silk exports (*Wen Hui Pao,* November 15, 1985). Export licenses for raw silk were first granted by provincial authorities. This arrangement, however, did not stop parallel trade, that is, trade outside regular channels, including smuggling and obtaining licenses through corruption and influence. When the MOFERT centralized the granting of export licenses, it discovered that the total exports licensed by provincial authorities amounted to four times the annual raw silk production of China. There are numerous reports of corruption in the granting of export and import licenses, particularly to influential institutions such as the army (*The Nineties,* December 1985: 63–64). Centralization of export licenses under the MOFERT did not stop parallel trade. In the first half of 1988, parallel trade accounted for 48 percent of China's silk exports. The price of raw silk through parallel trade was only US$43–48 per kilo, whereas the price through regular channels was US$60–70 per kilo. China lost US$20 million in foreign exchange as a result of parallel trade in raw silk in the period (*Ta Kung Pao,* November 5, 1988).

Perhaps the best-known case of Chinese mismanagement of exports is the overshipment of textiles to the United States and the European Communities (EC). The overshipment was so serious that the United States embargoed thirteen Chinese quota categories by June 1987 (*South China Morning Post,* June 22, 1987). Many provincial authorities granted licenses in excess of their quotas, and the forging of false export licenses by Hong Kong businessmen exacerbated the situation. In 1988 China established direct links with the computer network in major ports in the United States, and the United States confirmed the validity of each textile export license with China before admitting the goods. Instances of overshipment of textiles to the United States decreased in that year (*Hong Kong Economic Times,* October 3, 1988).

The frequent changes in the export license system have been the object of bitter complaint among those who trade with China. For example, the MOFERT prohibited the export of selected nonferrous metals starting in January 1989 owing to domestic shortages, but in March 1989 the MOFERT released a new list of commodities for which export licenses were required, and the prohibited items were included in the list. In mid-1988 a MOFERT official pledged to Hong Kong traders that export licenses were only a temporary measure, and their use would decrease in 1989. The number of commodities for which export licenses were required, however, increased from 130 in 1987 to 140 in 1988, and then to 159 in January 1989 and to 166 in March 1989. Traders sometimes get caught in the frequent changes, and goods already licensed under the old system have been held at ports because they have to be relicensed under the new system (*Wen Hui Pao,* March 22, 1989).

On the import side, the lack of coordination and market information has led to excessive imports of assembly lines for popular consumer products, such as refrigerators, television sets, and washing machines, resulting in chronic excess capacity. Hainan Island alone imported more than twenty assembly lines for color televisions in 1984–1985, and the number of plants manufacturing refrigerators mushroomed to 116 by 1985. In mid-1985 the State Council ordered the closure of 76 refrigerator plants because of excess capacity (*The Nineties,* August 1985: 61–62). Strong administrative controls were imposed on imports in mid-1985, but banned items, including luxury consumer goods, continued to make their way into the Chinese market through irregular channels (*Ming Pao,* July 6, 1987).

Mistakes in planning also led to tremendous waste. For example, China imported about 20,000 Japanese trucks in 1985, but the trucks could not be sold because China's largest domestic truck producer was conducting a sales drive to get rid of its old models. The Japanese trucks were allowed to rust for two years in the open air before state agencies mounted a sales drive to sell them in October 1987 (*Ta Kung Pao,* November 29, 1987).

Regional Approach to Trade Decentralization

China's regional approach to trade decentralization complicates the task of trade controls. While export-processing zones with relatively liberalized trade regimes are common in developing countries, the regional approach to trade decentralization in China has been applied not only to the five SEZs, but also to provinces and cities that are not export-processing zones.

Because China is a vast country with substantial regional differentiation, there is an economic rationale for a regional approach to decentralization. The Chinese are not experienced in managing the administration of decentralization. It may therefore be wise to choose particular regions, such as Shenzhen and Xiamen, for decentralization experiments.

The regional approach can, however, create problems. In the event that the liberalized region enjoys special privileges in trade, such as tariff exemptions or higher foreign exchange retention ratios, the flow of goods between liberalized and nonliberalized regions must be regulated. The ensuing supervision costs can be extremely high if there are many liberalized regions. The presence of liberalized regions will make it easier to evade controls elsewhere in the country, with the result that such controls will become more complicated. The spreading of the developmental process from the cities to the hinterland will be hampered by regional barriers. The creation of liberalized regions also raises the question of regional inequality; the nonliberalized areas will press for similar special status.

Problems of Foreign Investment

China's problems in foreign investment are similar to but more complicated than those in foreign trade. China has decentralized the power to solicit foreign loans and investment without devising appropriate economic and administrative instruments of coordination. For instance, the overvaluation of the yuan means that the prices of China's resources are artificially expensive for the foreign investor. Low energy and raw material prices mean that investments in such sectors are unprofitable, though these sectors constitute the worst bottlenecks in China's economic growth. Investment is attracted instead to sectors where prices are artificially high, for example, to the manufacture of consumer durables protected by high tariffs. The regional approach to liberalization implies that different regions vie with each other to grant more concessions to the foreign investor.

China's difficulties in foreign investment are more complicated than those in foreign trade because investment represents a lengthy commitment whereas trade is a one-shot deal. Chinese traders must learn to live with lengthy negotiations and slow bureaucratic decision making, but there is light at the end of the tunnel once the deal is concluded. For investors, concluding the deal merely represents the beginning of their nightmares. Investors must learn to operate in a command economy where essential raw materials are rationed rather than sold in the market and delays and defects in raw material supplies are very common. The labor system in China also constrains the autonomy of foreign investors in hiring and firing workers.

Red tape, stringent foreign exchange controls, inadequate infrastructure, and arbitrary charges and fees imposed by local governments have been the chief complaints of investors. On three occasions in 1982–1983 Beijing ordered local authorities to stop levying arbitrary charges on foreign investors, but to little avail.

China's inadequate infrastructure is particularly severe in power and transportation. The power supply for factories is insufficient, and the transport of raw materials and products is difficult and unreliable. The twenty-two-point investment enticement package of October 1986 addressed the problem of red tape. The package stipulated that officials must process investment applications (a procedure that has been known to take a year or more) within three months. The package also marginally relaxed stringent foreign exchange controls: foreign enterprises were allowed to swap yuan for foreign currency among themselves in the foreign exchange adjustment centers. The restrictions on foreign exchange swapping were further relaxed in 1988, and foreign enterprises were permitted to trade foreign exchange with domestic enterprises.

Although the twenty-two-point package specified that foreign enterprises have the power to hire and fire employees, foreign investors often have to hire workers through local labor bureaus. Working for a foreign enterprise is lucrative; workers often have to bribe local officials before they can be recommended for recruitment. Local officials therefore frown upon dismissal of workers in foreign enterprises. Moreover, because the local labor bureau is responsible for finding a new job for dismissed workers, local officials do their best to prevent such dismissals (Qi 1986: 35).

In China, it must not be assumed that more foreign investment necessarily leads to improved welfare. Given China's arbitrary policies

and the import-substitution policy in particular, more foreign investment can make China worse off. This phenomenon is known in the
economic literature as immiserizing foreign investment. The paradox
occurs because an import-substitution policy distorts resource allocation and makes import-competing industries artificially profitable. Foreign investment will be attracted to such industries, exacerbating the
distortion in resource allocation, and the recipient of foreign investment ends up worse off (Bhagwati and Srinivasan 1983: 296). One way
to avoid immiserizing foreign investment is to insist that foreign investors export instead of catering to the highly protected domestic market.
This is in fact the Chinese policy, but it is not welcomed by foreign
investors, who are attracted to the vast Chinese market.

Foreign investors seem to have numerous ways of circumventing
the Chinese insistence on exporting. The contract of a camera-assem-
bling operation, for example, specified that 30 percent of the products
had to be exported, and the remainder could be sold in China. The
exported cameras, however, were taken apart in Hong Kong and
shipped back to China as components. Another case is the manufacture
of lounge suits that were exported to Hong Kong and sold by hawkers
at US$3 per suit; the price did not cover the cost of materials (Yuan
1985: 56). The firm's profits came mainly from internal sales and from
the illegal sale of raw materials (which were exempt from tariffs as they
were supposedly imported for use by the foreign enterprise). Many
compensation trade agreements have turned out to be mere shelters for
importing tariff-free raw materials. The foreign partner can avoid in-
vesting any money because the Chinese partner can overinvoice the
value of the imported equipment by around 20 to 30 percent; the foreign partner then supposedly contributes capital up to the overin-
voiced portion of the agreement (Yuan 1985: 56). The authority to approve foreign investment has often been decentralized to provincial
and local authorities, and local officials are ready targets for bribery.

Problems of Loans

China's problems in foreign loans are similar to those in foreign investment and foreign trade. China has decentralized the power to borrow
without devising appropriate economic and administrative instruments of coordination. By the end of 1986, over 1,700 agencies in China
were able to borrow from external sources (*Economist,* March 19, 1988).
Until 1988 China did not have comprehensive statistics on the loans of
subordinate units, and the data on foreign debt that China reported to
the International Monetary Fund (IMF) were several billion dollars
lower than foreign estimates. China's debt management was extremely

crude, and China did not have systematic projections of external loans (He 1988: 99–100).

The debt service ratio of China in 1987 was only 7 percent, much better than the average ratio of 22 percent in developing countries in 1986. China, however, has been paying only the interest on its loans. The repayment of principal is bunched together in 1991–1993 because of poor debt management. Moreover, yen debt accounted for 46 percent of China's foreign loans at the end of 1986, and China is paying heavily for the appreciation of the yen (*South China Morning Post,* March 16, 1988).

Enterprises and local governments tend to overborrow as they are subject to a soft budget constraint and the central government has to shoulder the financial responsibility if the investment projects of subordinate units go sour. As a result, loans may not be efficiently used, and some local enterprises have not been able to repay their external loans on schedule (*Hong Kong Economic Times,* December 5, 1988). The debt service ratio of Fukien province (calculated on the foreign exchange retention of the province) had already reached 39 percent in 1987 (He 1988: 102).

To strengthen control over its foreign loans, China severely recentralized the power to borrow external loans in February 1989. Only ten organizations were permitted to borrow foreign commercial loans. They include three banks (Bank of China, Communications Bank, and China Investment Bank), the CITIC, and six provincial/municipal international trust and investment corporations (Guangdong, Fujian, Hainan, Shanghai, Tianjin, and Dalian). All other agencies must apply for foreign commercial loans through the People's Bank of China, and all foreign loans must be registered with the SAFEC (*South China Morning Post,* February 27, 1989).

PROBLEMS AND PROSPECTS OF THE OPEN DOOR POLICY

Despite the many problems of China's open door policy, China was close to having effective controls on trade, foreign investment, and foreign loans in 1989. In late 1988 the MOFERT established a bureau to manage export and import licenses. In February 1989 the power to borrow foreign loans was greatly recentralized, and China set up a Debt Management Office under the Ministry of Finance to centralize debt management (*South China Morning Post,* March 16, 1989). China's investment environment has improved since 1987. Moreover, China has already achieved considerable success in its reform of commodity trade. The incentive to export has increased considerably with the rise of the export EER; import liberalization has occurred with the rise in import EER, and the bias of trade was reduced. The ratio of exports to GDP is high and increasing.

Effective controls, however, do not imply efficient controls. Recentralization achieves effectiveness at the expense of efficiency. Instituting efficient controls on foreign transactions will take a very long time. To achieve efficiency, China has to accomplish four tasks: exchange rate reform, price reform, enterprise reform, and financial reform.

China has already had considerable success with price reform and exchange rate reform. Most commodity prices in China have already been freed. The *renminbi* is close to convertible on the current account. China wants to enter the GATT and pledged in early 1993 to achieve a unified exchange rate and convertibility in five years.

Enterprise reform is more difficult, for it involves property rights and the likelihood of massive urban unemployment. China has had only partial success in enterprise reform with the contract responsibility system. Foreign trade enterprises also implemented the system in 1988 and have largely stopped exporting below cost, because the foreign trade corporations have become financially independent and must bear their own losses (*Wen Hui Pao,* May 11, 1988). The contract responsibility system, however, goes only partway to fully autonomous enterprises. The enterprises must renegotiate the relevant targets with the supervising agency every time the contract expires, giving the supervising agency an opportunity to meddle with the enterprise. Moreover, the problem of soft budget constraints is deeply ingrained in socialist economies and the hardening of budget constraints has to wait for long-term reform in property rights.

It is well known that financial reform is most difficult. It is also crucial. The Chinese economy is inflation prone precisely because of its cumbersome financial system, and inflation will hamper price, exchange rate, and enterprise reforms. After the Fourteenth Party Congress in 1992, the Communist party adopted the goal of building a "socialist market economy." China allowed foreign banks to enter the Chinese market and was planning to gradually free the interest rate. Beijing appeared to be determined to complete the difficult task of financial reforms.

China Joining the GATT

China's adoption of the goal of building a socialist market economy in 1992 removed a major hurdle in its application to rejoin the GATT. It appeared in late 1992 that China would join the GATT in due course.

Despite major reforms in 1992, joining the GATT would still pose major problems for China's import-competing industries. China has pledged to drastically reduce import licensing and slash its tariffs from the 1992 average of 22.5 percent to around 13 percent. However, China's restrictive import licensing and high tariffs overstated the extent of protection because of rampant smuggling and the gradual relaxation of controls on domestic sales by joint ventures. Though China's adjustment to the GATT will be difficult, GATT membership would enforce efficiency on Chinese enterprises and substantially strengthen the momentum of economic reform in China. GATT membership would also represent the logical conclusion and achievement of the open door policy.

The Open Door Policy in Historical Perspective

Despite the severe setback of the Tiananmen incident, economic reforms and the open door policy have survived and prospered, indicating that political support for the open door policy and economic reforms is very strong. The Fourteenth Party Congress held in 1992 pledged to continue the policies laid down in the historic Third Plenum of the Eleventh Party Central Committee in December 1978, which marked the inauguration of Deng's era of economic reform and open door policy. The approach adopted in 1978 involved focusing on economic construction, upholding political orthodoxy, carrying out economic reforms, and opening to the outside world.

The problem with Deng's policy is that it calls for both Communist orthodoxy and economic liberalization. In the long run, however, economic liberalization undermines Communist orthodoxy. Despite the tension between political repression and economic liberalization, they can coexist for a considerable length of time; examples of countries where successful economic development has occurred under repressive political regimes include Taiwan, the Republic of Korea, and Brazil.

The tension between Communist orthodoxy and economic liberalization has accounted for many of the twists and turns of Chinese politics since 1978. During the economic imbalances following the first and second reform drives in 1980–1982 and in 1985–1987, conservatives attacked the reformers and their policies (Sung and Chan 1987). Student unrest in December 1986 triggered a strong conservative backlash leading to the forced resignation of the liberal leader Hu Yaobang and a campaign against "bourgeois liberalization." The Tiananmen incident and the ousting of Zhao Ziyang in June 1989 can be regarded as the culmination of the tension between Communist orthodoxy and economic liberalization.

The twists and turns of Chinese politics since 1978 have surprised most observers, but the open door policy appears to be supported by all factions of the Party with the exception of the far left. China has remained committed to the open door policy despite setbacks in 1979–1980, 1984–1986, 1988, and 1989. With the exception of the far left, most Chinese leaders realized that access to foreign technology was essential to China's modernization. The Party old guard, however, also clung tenaciously to Communist orthodoxy, which serves their vested interest, and the tension between Communist orthodoxy and economic reform may continue until they pass away. In its relationship with other countries, China has explored a one-sided interaction with the socialist bloc and has tried self-reliance. Both policies failed, and China has had little choice but to open its doors to the world. Barring major wars and disasters, economic rationality is likely to triumph over ideology in the long run.

REFERENCES

Almanac of China's Foreign Economic Relations and Trade. 1985.
Bhagwati, J. N., and T. N. Srinivasan. 1983. *Lectures on International Trade.* Cambridge: MIT Press.
Du, W. 1985. "The Foreign Exchange Rate and Tariffs" (in Chinese). *International Trade Journal* (April):64–65.
He, X. 1988. "Will a Debt Crisis Explode in China?" (in Chinese). *Hong Kong Economic Journal Monthly* (September):99–102.
Ho, S. P. S., and R. W. Huenemann. 1984. *China's Open Door Policy: The Quest for Foreign Technology and Capital.* Vancouver: University of British Columbia Press.
Howe, Christopher. 1978. *China's Economy.* London: Paul Elek.
Krueger, A. O. 1978. *Liberalization Attempts and Consequences.* New York: National Bureau of Economic Research.
Kueh, Y. Y. 1987. "Economic Decentralization and Foreign Trade Expansion in China." In Joseph C. H. Chai and Leung Chi-keung, eds., *China's Economic Reforms.* Hong Kong: Centre of Asian Studies, University of Hong Kong.
Kueh, Y., and C. Howe. 1984. "China's International Trade: Policy and Organizational Change and Their Place in the Economic Readjustment." *China Quarterly* (December):813–48.
Li, W. 1987. "On Structural Reform of China's Foreign Trade and Functions of Foreign Trade Bodies." Speech at a seminar on China's foreign trade sponsored by the Hong Kong Trade Development Council in Hong Kong, May 29.
Qi, X. 1985. "From an Import Spree to a Sudden Damp-down" (in Chinese). *The Nineties* (June):47–52.
_____. 1986. "China Cheapens the Price while Foreign Investors Hesitate and Wait" (in Chinese). *The Nineties* (December):32–35.
Sung, Y. W. 1991. *The China-Hong Kong Connection: The Key to China's Open Door Policy.* Cambridge: Cambridge University Press.

Sung, Y. W., and T. M. H. Chan. 1987. "China's Economic Reform I: The Debates in China." *Asian Pacific Economic Literature* 2, no. 1 (May):1–25.

Tian, L., et al. 1986. "The Change in the Instruments of Macro-control on China's Foreign Trade" (in Chinese). *Caimao Jinji* (The Economics of Finance and Trade) (February):36–40.

Wang, Shenzhong. 1986. "Changes in the Exchange Rate and Economic Development in the External Sector" (in Chinese). *Jingji Yanjiu* (April):44–51.

World Bank. 1985. "Alternative International Economic Strategies and Their Relevance for China. Background Paper to *China: Long-Term Issues and Options,* Report no. 5206-CHA. Washington, D.C.: World Bank.

Wu, N. 1987. "A Discussion on the Decontrol of the Foreign Exchange Market in China" (in Chinese). *China's Foreign Trade* (May):9–10.

Wu, Nianlu, and Zhang Ying. 1987. "The Reform of the Exchange Rate of Renminbi: Effects, Impacts and Counter Measures" (in Chinese). *Wen Wei Po* (June 6).

Xue, M. 1986. "A Discussion of the Reform of the Foreign Trade Management System" (in Chinese). *Quoji Maoyi* (International Trade) (March):4–8.

Yuan, L. 1985. "The Distinction between Insiders and Outsiders in Import of Technology" (in Chinese). *The Nineties* (July):56–60.

Zhao, W., and J. Liu. 1986. "Formulation of Export-Promotion Policies to Increase the Vitality of Producer Enterprises" (in Chinese). *Jingying yu Guanli* (Enterprise and Management) (February):36–38.

Zheng, T. 1984. "Problems of Reform in Foreign Trade" (in Chinese). *Jinji Yanjiu* (Economic Research) (November):27–33.

5

Foreign Trade Policies and India's Development

T. N. Srinivasan

Indian economic development strategy, particularly relating to industrialization, has been driven by perceived foreign exchange scarcities and the desire to ensure that scarce foreign exchange is used only for purposes deemed "essential" from the perspective of development. Industrialization and self-sufficiency in essential commodities have been important objectives of policy, in no small part because of the fear that dependence on other, more powerful countries for imports of essential commodities would lead to political dependence on them as well. Nearly a decade before independence, in 1938, the National Planning Committee was set up by the Indian National Congress (the political party that led the struggle for independence) under the chairmanship of the future prime minister Jawaharlal Nehru. This committee viewed that

> in the context of the modern world, no country can be politically and
> economically independent, even within the framework of international
> interdependence, unless it is highly industrialized and has developed its

I have drawn extensively from my contribution to Subroto Roy and William E. James, eds., *Foundations of India's Political Economy* (New Delhi: Sage Publications, 1992), and from J. N. Bhagwati and T. N. Srinivasan, *Foreign Trade Regimes and Economic Development: India* (New York: Columbia University Press, 1975).

power resources to the utmost. Nor can it achieve or maintain high standards of living and liquidate poverty without the aid of modern technology in almost every sphere of life. An industrially backward country will continually upset the world equilibrium and encourage the aggressive tendencies of more developed countries. Even if it retains its political independence, this will be nominal only and economic control will tend to pass to others (Nehru 1946: 413).

and

The objective for the country as a whole was the attainment, as far as possible, of national self-sufficiency. International trade was certainly not excluded, but we were anxious to avoid being drawn into the whirlpool of economic imperialism (p. 403).

Later the First Five-Year Plan went further:

Control and regulation of exports and imports, and in the case of certain select commodities state trading, are necessary not only from the point of view of utilising to the best advantage the limited foreign exchange resources available but also for securing an allocation of the productive resources of the country in line with the targets defined in the Plan (Planning Commission 1950: 42).

Indeed, an elaborate system of government control over production, investment, technology and locational choice, prices and foreign trade was instituted in the mid-1950s. In what follows, I argue that the development strategy based on import-substituting industrialization and the system of controls that were implemented failed to produce rapid growth, self-reliance, and eradication of poverty, but instead led to lackluster growth, an internationally uncompetitive industrial structure, a perpetually precarious balance of payments, and, above all, rampant rent seeking and the corruption of social, economic, and political systems.

FIVE-YEAR PLANS: OBJECTIVES AND POLICY INSTRUMENTS OF IMPLEMENTATION

India gained its independence on August 15, 1947. After extensive debate in the constituent assembly, a constitution was adopted, and India became a republic on January 26, 1950. Not entirely coincidentally, the Planning Commission was established almost immediately, in March 1950, as an advisory body with no executive functions. There had been a broad consensus on the need for planning for national development even during the struggle for independence from Britain. Indeed, soon after the National Planning Committee was established in 1938, a group of private businessmen produced the so-called Bombay Plan. Even the colonial government had put together development plans for postwar India. The adoption of the constitution, however, gave a particular impetus to planning.

The constitution enunciated a set of guiding principles for the formulation of government policy, called the Directive Principles for State Policy. They enjoined the state to strive to secure "a social order in which justice—social, economic and political—shall inform all the institutions of national life" and "to minimize inequality in income, status, facilities and opportunities, amongst individuals and groups." Further, the state was required to ensure "that the ownership and control of the material resources of the community are so distributed as best to subscribe to the common good; that the operation of the economic system does not result in the concentration of wealth and means of production to the common detriment" (Basu 1983). The constitution also protected rights to work, to education, and to public assistance in case of unemployment, disability, or sickness. It is evident that these principles envisaged a dominant role for the state in achieving an egalitarian society through state intervention in economic activity.

Besides the overarching goal of poverty alleviation, the three broad objectives of the Indian development strategy are economic growth, self-reliance, and social justice. Even though the state was assigned a dominant role in developing the economy, leaders across the political spectrum recognized to varying degrees that India had a mixed economy with a significant private sector, and more important, that the private sector had a vital political role in ensuring social stability and in the functioning of the democratic framework of the constitution.

Indian planning was influenced by Soviet planning, with which Prime Minister Nehru and Professor P. C. Mahalanobis (the author of the Second Plan) were familiar. Although Soviet planning operated with totalitarian political control of the society and state ownership of the means of production, India's mixed economy and democratic polity ruled out planning by command. Instead, the policy framework had to create incentives for the private sector to conform to the priorities of the plan. In designing such a framework, the Indian policy makers opted in most cases for direct, discretionary, nonmarket, quantitative controls over indirect, rule-based, market-mediated controls operating through the price mechanism. Unfortunately this choice adversely affected economic growth, efficiency, and equity. Above all, it corrupted the political system.

Agriculture dominated the economy, accounting for nearly 60 percent of gross domestic product (GDP) and providing employment to over 70 percent of the labor force when the first plan was initiated in 1950.[1] Its share in GDP drastically declined to less than 30 percent by 1990/91. Yet over 60 percent of the labor force still depends on agriculture for employment. This fact, more than anything else, demonstrates that the Indian industrialization strategy failed to generate significant productive employment opportunities outside of agriculture for a growing labor force. No significant redistribution of land emerged from the land reform legislation of the 1950s. Concentration of land ownership, however, has not meant that a large proportion of farms are operated on a large scale. In 1982, the year of the most recent sample survey of land holdings, only 20 percent of the farm area was operated in holdings exceeding ten hectares. Early planners showed some enthusiasm for cooperative farming. The National Commission on Agriculture, reporting in 1976, concluded that under Indian conditions, small peasant-owned farms cultivated mainly with family labor should be the preferred mode of organization of production rather than large Soviet-style collective farms or large capitalist farms cultivated with farm machinery and hired labor. This preference has not hindered mechanization in some regions and the emergence of large capitalist farms, particularly in the fast-growing agricultural regions of Punjab and western Uttar Pradesh. Small owner-operated farms, however, continue to be the dominant mode of operation.

State intervention in agriculture, while significant, has been different in nature from state intervention in industry. In agriculture the state has made substantial investments in irrigation, fertilizer production, and infrastructure. Other state interventions affected the prices that farmers paid for their inputs and received for their outputs. Irrigation, water from public reservoirs, and electricity for private irrigation pumps were subsidized. Prices paid for the part of output that was purchased by the government for its subsidized public distribution system were regulated. There were some quantitative restrictions, such as the ban on interstate movement of foodgrains on private account, but these were abandoned early on. Policies that placed quantitative restrictions on millions of individual producers were obviously infeasible, although access to subsidized credit is an exception. Remarkably, India has maintained a constant trend growth in agricultural output of

---

1. Agricultural development is discussed in Chapter 3 of this book.

about 3 percent per year over nearly four decades despite slow growth in cultivated area. This trend reflects the superiority of the largely market-mediated interventions in agriculture, unlike the discretionary interventions in industry.

The government's industrial policy resolution of 1948 (amended and elaborated in 1956) divided industries into three broad groups: those to be developed exclusively by the public sector, those reserved for the private sector, and those open to development by either or both sectors. The development of key industries, such as railways, telecommunications, and electricity generation, was assigned to the public sector. In addition, industries producing key industrial raw materials and equipment, such as steel, petroleum, and heavy machinery, including electric generators, were also in the public sector. The philosophy behind the resolution was that by controlling the "commanding heights" of the industrial landscape—that is, the infrastructure and industries supplying key raw materials—the state could cause the development of all industries, in the private and public sectors, to follow socially desirable directions. Goods and services produced and supplied by the public sector could be priced appropriately for generating surpluses to be used for investment in the public sector and to finance other public expenditures. Also, the state hoped to promote the development of backward regions through the location of public sector projects. Finally, the public sector was to be a model for the private sector to follow with respect to the wages and working conditions of workers.

The public sector did not evolve as planned. A major share of investment in the five-year plan was appropriated by the public sector. Yet the enterprises created by the investment and others acquired through nationalization (such as major commercial banks) performed poorly in supplying key services and inputs at a reasonable cost, in appropriate amounts, and at the time and place where demands arose. The public sector therefore acted as a brake on private sector development rather than promoting and channeling it in socially desired directions. Policy making with respect to location, technology, employment, and pricing in the public sector became politicized. Inefficiency and waste in resource use, overmanning, and mounting losses were the results. Far from generating resources, the public sector became an albatross around the neck of the taxpayers.

The system of industrial licensing and exchange controls was the favored tool for making the private sector conform to the plans. Its broad features remained essentially unchanged from the late 1950s until the 1991 reforms, though its severity waxed and waned. The system was meant to achieve several goals. First, capacity created in the private sector had to be made consistent with plan targets. Second, the location of private sector plants had to be such that they did not overload the infrastructure, particularly in cities and other areas to which they would naturally gravitate. The system induced plant owners to move to backward regions with a potential for development. Third, the objective of self-reliance had to be promoted; that is, domestically available technology, equipment, and raw materials were to be used rather than imports. Fourth, concentration of economic power was to be prevented. Given the perennial shortage of foreign exchange, the state looked at every investment proposal from the point of view of its demand for foreign exchange for imports of equipment at the time of investment and for imports of raw materials and spares during the lifetime of the plant.

An industrial license was required to invest in capacity creation if the quantity of investment or the value of equipment imports exceeded specified limits. For importation of equipment, a capital-goods license was needed. If foreign collaboration was involved, a separate clearance was required. In particular, foreign equity participation was limited to under 50 percent, with some exceptions. If foreign technology imports involving royalty payments were to be undertaken, yet another clearance was mandated. If part of the equity was to be obtained by selling shares in the domestic capital market, permission had to be obtained from the controller of capital issues. Even the investment projects of public enterprises required many of these permits, in addition to clearances from the ministry or department in charge of the enterprise and from other relevant ministries (such as finance). In sum, several hurdles had to be crossed before a single rupee was spent on any project in the private or public sector. Even though success in obtaining all the required clearances was by no means assured, entrepreneurs had to expend considerable time and resources pursuing them.

The licensing mechanism was designed to approve (often with many modifications) or deny an application for license. The criteria for evaluation of applications were sufficiently broad that the licensing authorities had substantial discretion in granting or denying a license. The licensing bureaucrats and their political bosses were under constant pressure from interested parties. It should cause no surprise that the exercise of their discretionary power led to their corruption and the politicization of decisions.

Obviously a private entrepreneur would apply for a license to invest in a project only if he expected it to be profitable. The license could be denied, of course, if the project was deemed socially unworthy. But licensing authorities could not induce a private sector entrepreneur to apply for a license and invest in a socially worthy project if he did not find it privately profitable. The grant of a license did not necessarily mean that the capacity licensed came on stream, and even if it did, that it came on stream at the time specified in the application. Since the processing of a license application often took so long and restrictive conditions were often attached to accepted applications, it was possible that the project for which a license was granted would no longer be profitable from the applicant's perspective and hence he would choose not to implement it. Further, given that licenses were granted only to the extent of capacity expansion called for in the relevant five-year plan, firms had a built-in incentive to take out a license and then fail to invest, essentially to foreclose competition by preventing other firms from getting it. An information system to keep track of the licenses granted and their implementation did not exist, so the link between capacity increases targeted in the plan and their actual realization through licensing was tenuous. In the final analysis, the procedure for license granting became ad hoc and followed rules of thumb rather than any economic rationale. It degenerated into an exercise in dispensing political and other kinds of patronage and a source of rents for personal and political use rather than a guidance mechanism for directing the private sector to conform to the plans.

Table 5.1 compares some performance indicators of the Indian economy under planning with those of other developing countries. It is clear that Indian performance is relatively poor. India's average annual rate of growth of per capita GNP from 1965 to 1990 is the lowest of the five countries and would have been even lower had the data for the 1980s been excluded. In 1965 India's manufacturing industry was more than five times the size of Korea's in terms of value added at current U.S. dollars. But by 1990 Korea's manufacturing industry had grown to exceed India's in size and its manufactured exports were nearly five times that of India. Only China, which also followed an inward-oriented development strategy until recently, had a greater share of the labor force in agriculture than India.

THE FOREIGN TRADE REGIME: ANALYTICAL PHASES AND CHANGES OVER TIME

J. Bhagwati and A. Krueger, in their comparative analysis of the impact of foreign trade regimes and economic development in a number of countries, defined a set of analytical phases in which an exchange control regime may be found (Bhagwati and Srinivasan 1975: 248). A country does not necessarily pass through all the phases, and the num-

TABLE 5.1 SELECTED INDICATORS FOR INDIA AND OTHER
DEVELOPING COUNTRIES

	India	China[a]	Brazil	Mexico[a]	Korea[a]
Population, mid-1990 (millions)	850	1,134	150	86	43
GNP per capita, 1990 (US$)	350	370	2,680	2,490	5,400
Average annual GNP per capita growth rate, 1965–1990 (%)	1.9	5.8	3.3	2.8	7.1
Inflation rate, 1980–1990 (%)	7.9	5.8	284.3	70.3	5.1
Share in GDP, 1990 (%)					
Agriculture	31	27	10	9	9
Industry	29	42	39	30	45
Value added in manufacturing, 1989 (billions of US$)	44	146	121	51	66
Gross domestic investment/GDP, 1990 (%)	23	39	22	20	37
Gross domestic saving/GDP, 1990 (%)	20	43	23	19	37
Life expectancy at birth, 1990 (years)	59	70	66	70	71
Total fertility rate, 1990	4.0	2.5	3.2	3.3	1.8
Labor force in agriculture, 1986–1989 (%)	63	74	29	23	18
Merchandise exports, 1990 (billions of US$)	18	62	31	27	65
Manufactured exports, 1990 (billions of US$)	13	45	16	12	61
Merchandise imports, 1990 (billions of US$)	24	53	22	28	70
Aggregate net resource flow, 1990 (billions of US$)	3.6	10.1	1.2	8.4	−0.2
Total outstanding external debt, 1990 (billions of US$)	70.1	52.6	116.2	96.8	34.0
Total debt service/exports, 1986 (%)	29	10	21	28	11
Overall central government deficit, 1990 (% of GNP)	−7.3	—	−16.6	0.8	−0.7

[a]GDP, GNP, and related ratios are at purchaser's prices.
Source: For labor force in industry and agriculture, United Nations Development Programme, *Human Development Report 1992* (New York: Oxford University Press, 1992). For all other data, World Bank, *World Development Report 1991* (New York: Oxford University Press, 1992).

bering of the phases does not indicate a chronological sequence. These phases were

1. *Phase I:* During this phase, quantitative restrictions (QRs) on international transactions are imposed, generally in response to an unsustainable balance of payments deficit, and then, after a period, are intensified. The period during which reliance upon QRs for containing the balance of payment deficit is increasing is Phase I.

2. *Phase II:* While QRs continue to be intense, various measures are undertaken to offset some of the undesired results of the system. Heightened tariffs, surcharges on imports, rebates for exports, special tourist exchange rates, and other price interventions are used. However, QRs continue to be relied upon as the primary means for controlling the balance of payments deficit.

3. *Phase III:* An attempt is made to systematize the changes introduced during Phase II. This phase often starts with a formal exchange rate change and may be accompanied by removal of some of the surcharges and other special measures imposed during Phase II and by reduced reliance upon QRs. Phase III may end up being little more than a tidying-up operation, in which case the chances are high that the country will re-enter Phase II. The country may also move beyond tidying and signal the beginning of withdrawal from reliance upon QRs, in which case it enters Phase IV.

4. *Phase IV:* If the response to changes introduced in Phase III are encouraging enough for the continuation and extension of liberalization, the country is said to enter Phase IV. A favorable response in the form of increased foreign exchange earnings would encourage a gradual relaxation of QRs. The relaxation may take the form of either changes in the nature of QRs or increased foreign exchange allocations, and thus reduced premiums, under the same administrative system.

5. *Phase V:* The exchange regime is fully liberalized. There is full convertibility on current account, and QRs are no longer employed as a means of regulating the ex ante balance of payments.

Bhagwati and Srinivasan (1975) provide a phase chronology of the

Indian foreign trade regime for the period 1950–1970. An unpublished Oxford doctoral thesis of Narahari Rao (1985) and private communication from an ongoing study by Gary Pursell at the World Bank have helped me extend it beyond 1970. The following phase chronology covers the entire period 1950–1992.

1950–1956 (Phase IV)

The period 1950–1956 included the First Five-Year Plan. It was a period of good harvests and a rough equilibrium in the balance of payments, with import demand more or less equaling export earnings that were stagnant once the Korean War boom was over. The machinery of import control inherited from the World War II period was not used in any systematic way to impose QRs.

1956–1962 (Phase I)

The ambitious, heavy industry–oriented Second Five-Year Plan was initiated in 1956, and promptly led to a severe balance of payments crisis in 1957. Instead of adopting appropriate macroeconomic policies including making exchange rate adjustments, the government imposed a regime of QRs on imports. The QRs and the industrial licensing system were both selective rather than across-the-board. Besides containing the demand for foreign exchange, the selectivity of QRs served the objective of the development of particular industries through import substitution. The QR regime was used to provide automatic and custom-made protection to any domestic activity that substituted imports. Foreign aid flows increased substantially from less than 0.5 percent of net national product in the pre-1956 period to over 3 percent in 1960/61.

1962–1966 (Phase II)

While the QR regime for imports initiated in 1957 continued, export subsidization was introduced in 1962 primarily to offset the penalties that the QR regime was in effect imposing on exports. Two exogenous events in this period had major economic consequences: the Indo-Pakistan War in late 1965 and the consequent suspension of foreign aid; and a major drought in the agricultural year 1965/66, which affected traditional exports adversely and increased the need for food imports.

Increasing use was made of import duties, in part to mop up the premia on imports that license receivers were realizing. Export subsidization and increasing import duties could be viewed as a *de facto* devaluation of the exchange rate, although unlike in a *de jure* devaluation, the impact was selective. Some efforts to loosen up the industrial licensing system were made toward the end of the period.

By early 1966 the combined effects of the drought and suspension of aid caused import premia to rise to unprecedented levels. The donors of bilateral and multilateral (the World Bank and the International Monetary Fund) external aid made resumption of large-scale aid and access to short-term credit conditional on the liberalization of the economy.

1966–1968 (Phase III)

The first step in the liberalization was the devaluation of the rupee by 57.5 percent (from Rs. 4.76 to Rs. 7.50 per U.S. dollar) announced in June 1966. Since this was also accompanied by the elimination of export subsidies and reduction of import duties, the net devaluation after allowing for these changes was on average less than the gross devaluation of 57.5 percent and varied among commodities. According to Bhagwati and Srinivasan (1975), the total net devaluation on the trade account was 21.6 percent for exports and 42.3 percent for imports. On the current account, the total net devaluation was 22.3 percent for receipts and 44.8 percent for payments. In 1966/67 another disastrous drought followed that of 1965/66. The two severe droughts in succession resulted in price increases, adverse effects on traditional exports, and an industrial recession induced by shortage of agro-based raw materials. Economic liberalization, of which devaluation was a major component, was stalled in part for economic reasons related to the drought. More important, the economic difficulties were accentuated by political problems: the fact that devaluation was seen as capitulation to pressure from donors of external aid made liberalization politically suspect, not only among the opposition but also within the ruling Congress party led by the newly installed and politically insecure Prime Minister Indira Gandhi. The 1967 general elections saw considerable erosion of support for the Congress party. To compound this loss of support, the external aid promised at the time of devaluation, which was meant to ease the short-run costs of adjustment to a liberalized economy, did not materialize. Under the circumstances, it was not surprising that the hesitant steps toward liberalization introduced with devaluation were soon abandoned.

1968–1975 (Phase II)

With the abandonment of liberalization, import premia rose, though not as high as immediately before devaluation. Export subsidies were reinstated and augmented. Industrial licensing reverted to its severely restrictive mode.

The economy experienced several exogenous shocks during this period. First, the Bangladesh War in 1971 and the refugee inflow that preceded it created severe economic strains. Second, adverse weather conditions during the 1972–1975 period led to stagnant agricultural output and double-digit inflation for two years in a row in 1972/73 and 1973/74. Third, the Bretton Woods system of fixed exchange rate parities collapsed in 1971. Following the collapse, India linked the rupee initially to the floating British pound and in 1975 to a basket of currencies. Between 1971 and 1975 the pound depreciated against the U.S. dollar and other major currencies, leading to a gradual and modest depreciation of the rupee against the U.S. dollar in that period. This depreciation provided across-the-board incentives for exports and import substitution. But with the rupee linked to a basket of currencies, its "vicarious" devaluation was halted (Bhalla 1989). Fourth, in 1973 the first oil shock occurred.

In this period "import policy became increasingly restrictive and complex. Scarcity of foreign exchange became even more acute—a new set of restrictive measures was introduced every year. Import allocation criteria became more complex and subject to marginal conditions. Tariff rates were gradually escalated (to absorb partially the increasing import premia generated by the tighter QR's)" (Rao 1985).

1975–1985 (Phase III)

Foreign exchange availability improved dramatically during the early part of the 1975–1985 period. Net reserves of foreign exchange went up from a low of US$758 million in 1974/75 to a high of US$7579 million in 1979/80, fueled in part by the dramatic increase in remittances from Indians working in West Asia. The decline in public investment and the slowing of industrial growth after the mid-1960s also contributed to reducing the pressure in the balance of payments. With dramatic increases in the output of wheat, and to a smaller extent of rice, during the green revolution, the public stock of foodgrains mounted and foodgrain imports ceased. The net result was a relaxation in the severity of the QR regime. Rao (1985) points out that "import allocation rules were made simpler and most non-competing 'essential' imports were liberalized. Protective quotas, however, remained intact and domestic industry continued to be completely shielded from import competition."

Interestingly, the second oil shock in 1979 did not lead to a tightening of the QR regime, partly because of the substantial increase in worker remittances and partly because of the fortuitous discovery and development of significant offshore oil deposits (the Bombay High Field) in the Arabian Sea. Output of crude oil more than doubled, from 8.4 million tons in 1975/76 to 21.1 million tons in 1982/83.

1985 to Mid-1991 *(Phase III Continued)*

In April 1985, in a significant departure, the government announced that the import and export policy was to cover a period of three years (1985–1988) rather than six months or a year as in the past. This innovation was meant to bring some stability to the policy and thereby reduce the uncertainty about year-to-year changes that exporters and importers faced. Yet the government could not resist introducing changes almost every week to the statement issued in April 1985, and a revised statement had to be issued in October 1986. Until 1988, there were 250 public notices regarding changes in the policy. The subsequent policy statement for the period 1988–1991, announced in April 1988, candidly recognized that changes have to be announced within the three-year period and stated, "It is proposed to issue a revised version of the import and export policy at the beginning of each year." So much for stable policy!

Although the complexity of the scheme of QRs had not diminished substantially, the two three-year policies did represent some major simplifications. In particular the number of items in the category of open general license (OGL)—that is, a license to import but with no quantitative restrictions—for capital goods imports had increased from nil in 1975 to over 1,100 items in the 1988–1991 policy. Similarly, many intermediate goods were put in the OGL category. Lest this give the impression that QRs had largely been abandoned, it should be pointed out that many of the items put under the OGL were noncompetitive imports; that is, there was no substitute for them from domestic production. Therefore, lifting QRs on their import had little effect on import competition with domestic production. Also, the import of some items formally in the OGL category was restricted on other grounds. For example, the value of equipment imports had to conform with licensed investment capacity. Although tires had been in the OGL category since 1978, no imports took place, in part because of high tariffs, in part because the firms in the replacement market did not qualify as "actual users" to whom OGL applied, and in part because actual users such as car and truck manufacturing firms were under "phased manufacturing programs" through which they were under an obligation to replace imports by domestic substitutes over time in a progressive manner. The share of the value of imports covered by OGL in total imports appeared to be modest (perhaps less than a fifth), though no official information is available.

Mid-1991 to Present (Phase IV?)

In July 1991 the newly installed minority government of Prime Minister Narasimha Rao announced a set of major economic reforms. In announcing the reforms to the Indian Parliament, Finance Minister Manmohan Singh declared with some hyperbole that "Let the world hear it loud and clear. India is now wide awake. The emergence of India as a major economic power in the world . . . is an idea whose time has come." The proximate reason for these policy changes was a crisis in the economy that was both acute and different from anything experienced in the postindependence era: a drastic fall in the foreign exchange reserves to a level not even enough to pay for three weeks of imports, a near default in the colossal external debt of over US$71 billion, and a fiscal deficit of nearly 9 percent of GDP. But the deeper reason for the changes was the realization that India's economic development strategy since 1950 and the regulatory framework created to implement it had failed miserably. The policy reforms were further extended in scope and coverage in 1992.

The chief elements of Rao-Singh reforms of 1991/92 are devaluation of the rupee; abolition of import licensing; replacement of cash subsidies for exports, initially by the so-called exim scrips (freely salable rights to imports linked to exports) and later by partial convertibility of the rupee under which exporters could sell 60 percent of their foreign exchange receipts at a market-determined exchange rate; abolition of industrial licensing except for investment in eighteen industries and for locational reasons in cases of "polluting" industries; relaxation of restrictions on large industrial houses under the Monopolies and Restrictive Trade Practices Act; easing of entry requirements (including equity participation) for direct foreign investment; and allowance of private investment in some industries hitherto reserved for public sector investment. A National Renewal Fund for assisting workers employed in enterprises that will have to be scaled down or closed altogether has been established, although without the support of the political barons of the labor aristocracy in the organized sector such scaling down is unlikely. The government has contemplated reform of the financial sector but has not yet implemented it.

It is obvious that these reforms are systemic and go beyond liberalizing the more irksome controls at the margin that earlier economic liberalizations attempted. Besides, authorities apparently realize that the benefits from reforming one sector would be limited if other related sectors are not also reformed. The needed reforms are conceived as a package of mutually supporting and consistent elements that call for coordinated action in several areas.

The elimination of import licensing and the introduction of partial convertibility of the rupee are certainly indicative of Phase IV. Since the reforms have been in place only since July 1991, however, a period which saw a recession in the industrial countries as well as the collapse of the Soviet Union, with which India had barter trading arrangements, the favorable potential of the reforms is yet to be seen. But as significant growth resumes in the industrial world and as Eastern Europe and the states of the former Soviet Union complete their transition to market economies, Indian reforms may begin to pay rich dividends. If the full convertibility of the rupee for current account transactions in the not-too-distant future (a declared objective of the government) is in fact realized, there is a good chance that the economy will enter the nirvana of Phase V.

THE ANATOMY OF THE PRE-1991 EXCHANGE CONTROL SYSTEM

The pre-1991 exchange control system divided imports into three broad categories: consumer goods, capital goods, and intermediate goods (raw materials, components, spares, and supplies). Consumer goods imports, other than those canalized and imported by state agencies (such as foodgrains, edible oils, sugar, and certain drugs and medicines) were not permitted. Other imports were divided into the following licensing categories: nonpermissible, limited permissible, automatic permissible, and recently, OGL.

The allocation of permissible imports by sector of use (private and public), by type of good (consumer, capital, and intermediate), by industry, and by firm within industries was carried out by an elaborate administrative machinery. For example, Volume 1 of the 1988–1991 policy statement relating only to import policy consists of 387 pages, divided into twenty-three chapters and seventeen appendixes! Broadly speaking, the complex system described in Bhagwati and Srinivasan (1975) and reproduced in the Appendix to this chapter held sway during the 1957–1991 period, although some categories and authorities changed names, others ceased to exist (for example, the category of established importers), and some new categories of both import and export licenses appeared. OGL became an increasingly important category. Canalized imports also grew in importance: the 1988–1991 statement listed nearly sixty items, the import of which were canalized through public sector agencies, ranging from paraffin wax to steel, petroleum products, fertilizers, and fatty acids.

The import control regime inevitably led to a lower effective exchange rate for exports than for imports on the average and for each industry. The scheme of export subsidization, initiated in 1962 in an attempt to redress this bias against exports, was extremely complex, with little or no economic logic to support its complexity. Subsidies took essentially two major forms: (1) direct subsidies through fiscal measures and (2) indirect subsidies through import entitlement schemes that entitled exporters to scarce and restricted imports. Some other relatively minor promotional activities included budgetary allocations for market development.

Before turning to the specific subsidy schemes, it is worth mentioning that analogous to the category of nonpermissible and restricted imports, there were also nonpermissible and restricted exports. As of 1988, there were 172 such products, 67 of which could simply not be exported. An important difference, however, was that exports of items not on this list could be made without a license, while a license was required for the import of any item other than personal baggage.

Turning to export assistance, the major fiscal measures were tax drawback schemes (that is, refunds of indirect taxes including import duties on inputs used in exports), exemptions from sales taxes, cash compensation schemes, and rail freight concessions. Import replenishment licenses, previously called import entitlement certificates, allowed the exporter to import certain restricted raw materials and components. Whereas under the import entitlement certificate scheme the value of the entitlement equaled twice the import content, under the import replenishment license scheme the value of the license was supposed to equal the actual import content of exports. Between July 1991 and February 1992 such licenses were called exim (export-import) scrips.

Import entitlements as a proportion of the f.o.b. values varied widely across different products. Since it was virtually impossible to assess the actual import content, such variation was more a reflection of arbitrary assignment by policy makers than of variation of actual import contents. There were fifty-eight pages in Appendix 17 and its annexes to the 1988–1991 policy statement on import replenishment licenses! The rates varied from a low of 3 percent to a high of 80 percent. For example, wheat bran exporters were given import replenishment licenses at the rate of 3 percent and permitted to import under those licenses only silk and nylon bolting cloth! Unlike actual user licenses, import replenishment licenses could be sold and transferred subject to certain conditions. Exporters were registered and classified under various categories such as manufacturer exporter, merchant exporter, export house, and "deemed" exporter (the last category refers to those domestic producers of intermediates who sell part of their output to exporters). Figures 5.1 and 5.2, taken from Rao (1985), illustrate the complexity of the import control mechanism and the transfer restrictions on import replenishment licenses as of 1975/76. The exim scrips of 1991/92 were however freely salable.

It is easily shown that it was not economically efficient to assist exporters through the import replenishment scheme. There was no compelling economic logic either for confining the scheme, at least in the early years, to certain categories of exports such as engineering goods or for the enormous variation across commodities in import replenishment rates.

The compensatory cash support scheme was initially introduced to compensate for taxes not refunded under the duty drawback scheme and for any excess of short-run marginal cost of production over f.o.b. realization. It was later extended to compensate for a whole host of factors, including losses incurred on exports when domestic demand was inadequate to use installed capacity fully. The rates of compensatory cash support also varied significantly across products with no apparent rationale.

The rationale for most of the export assistance schemes was that Indian exporters should be compensated for the excess costs they incurred compared with their competitors because of other distortions in the Indian economy. Since these excess costs were hard to quantify, there was no way to establish that the total assistance received under various incentive schemes to which a potential exporter was entitled was more or less than necessary to induce him to export. The bureaucratic requirements to be met in order to claim the assistance available under these schemes were complex, time consuming, and costly. Small-scale exporters often did not find it worthwhile to claim the incentives to which they were entitled. As is the case of import controls, export incentives schemes were made complex without any functional need for such complexity. By eliminating import licensing and introducing partial convertibility of the rupee, the 1992 reforms eliminated at one stroke the maze of complexity and variance in incentives across commodities of the import replenishment and compensatory cash support schemes.

THE POLITICAL ECONOMY OF THE FOREIGN EXCHANGE REGIMES

The political economy of India's foreign trade and exchange control regime before reforms were initiated in 1991 can be understood from

FIGURE 5.1. INDIA'S IMPORT CONTROL MECHANISM, 1975–1976

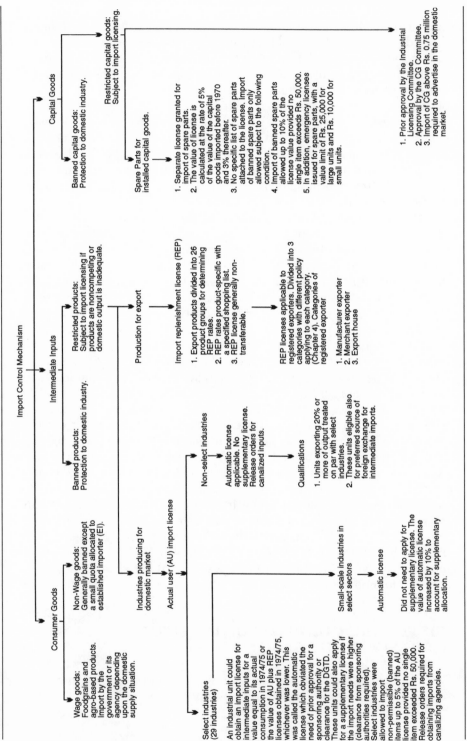

Source: Narahari Rao. "Exchange Rate and Commercial Policy in a Controlled Trade Regime: A Case Study of India." Ph.D. dissertation, Oxford University, 1985, Chapter 2.

FIGURE 5.2.   TRANSFER RESTRICTIONS ON INDIA'S REPLENISHMENT LICENSES, 1975–1976

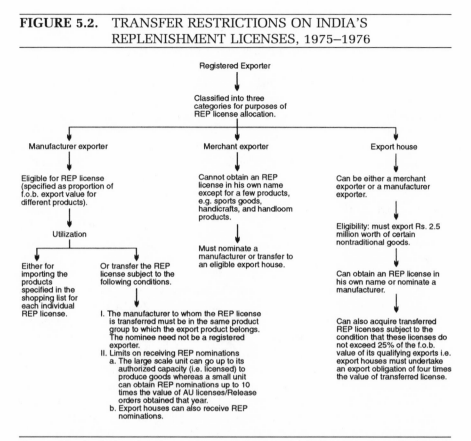

Source: Narahari, Rao. "Exchange Rate and Commercial Policy in a Controlled Trade Regime: A Case Study of India." Ph.D. dissertation, Oxford University, 1985, Chapter 2.

the implications of its selective, discretionary, and non-market-oriented character. First, macroeconomic instruments, including most importantly the exchange rate of the rupee, were never used to address balance of payments problems except for the rupee devaluation of 1966. Given that QRs on imports were substantially below market demand, the domestic price of an imported commodity far exceeded its landed cost inclusive of tariff duties and other taxes. As such there were rents associated with a license to import. Thus the power to grant a license meant power to confer the right to the rent involved. Since the domestic price of an imported commodity, and hence the rent to be earned per unit of import, would depend on the total quantity of imports allowed in, the licensing authority not only conferred the right to the rent but also determined its amount.

It hardly requires much imagination to realize that if rents could be created and allocated, individuals and groups would spend resources in influencing their creation and allocation in their favor. The analytics of lobbying for trade policies that create rents and for the allocation of rents once created have attracted the attention of trade theorists. Bhagwati, Brecher, and Srinivasan (1984) surveyed this literature, and it is still growing. More recent analysis appears in Meier (1991). Without delving into this literature, I will note some of the manifestations of rent seeking and their political and economic implications in the Indian context.

It should be evident even to a casual observer of the Indian scene that a significant amount of scarce talents and material resources that could have been used for producing goods and services were spent instead on seeking and dispensing rents. Senior bureaucrats who wielded power spent much of their time in meetings that decided individual cases rather than set broad policies. In a large country with an abysmal telephone system, businessmen from far corners of the country frequently flew to the seat of power at Delhi to influence decisions. Larger enterprises that had continuing business with the government maintained "embassies" in Delhi. Even if there had been no corruption, resources spent on such activities would have resulted in significant deadweight losses since those resources generated no material output. But there was certainly alleged to be corruption! Indeed, the point has been made that with a ban on corporate contributions to political parties, politicians gained resources for electoral campaigns through kickbacks from rents conferred. Of course, if adoption of favorable decisions and the prevention of unfavorable decisions had to be bought, so to speak, only those who could afford to pay the price would enter the market. Clearly entrepreneurs with relatively few material resources and contacts at crucial decision-making agencies were unlikely to enter the market.

Bardhan (1984) has suggested that there are essentially three proprietary classes in India: the industrial capitalists, the rich farmers, and the public sector professionals. He argues, "In the context of economic growth it is rather the capacity of the system to insulate economic management from political processes of distributive demands, rent-seeking and patronage disbursement that makes the crucial difference—a lack of political insulation from conflicting interests, coupled with the strong power base of the white-collar workers in public bureaucracy that keeps the Indian state, in spite of its pervasive economic presence, largely confined to regulatory functions, avoiding the hard choices and politically unpleasant decisions involved in more active developmental functions" (Bardhan 1984: 72–73). Indeed one could go further and argue that any effort to reform the system (or more accurately, to revolutionize the system) by "making a bon-fire of controls," as Dr. I. G. Patel, a distinguished ex-bureaucrat and controller, called for long after leaving office, would be stymied by the same constellation of forces. It would clearly not be in the interest of the members of the industrial capitalist class, who enjoy an oligopolistic if not monopolistic position in domestic markets by virtue of the QR regime, to support its dismantling. On the one hand, the rich farmers, who receive subsidies doled out by the system, would be interested in the demand stimulus for agriculture that more rapid growth would generate and in the availability of a larger range of less-costly and better-quality industrial goods that reform might bring. On the other hand, they might fear that the dismantling of industrial protection would soon be followed by the dismantling of various agricultural subsidies. They are likely to perceive the certain loss of subsidies more clearly and concretely than the uncertain potential benefit of more rapid growth and better-quality goods. The professionals in the public sector certainly have a vested interest in the continued expansion of the public sector, which a market-oriented reform might threaten. Thus, the three proprietary classes would collude, implicitly or explicitly, in stalling, if not preventing altogether, any reform. Of course, the usually unthinking leftist intellectuals in India have always identified controls and regulation with socialism and a market economy with imperialism. Unsurprisingly, they would fulminate against any liberalization. The interesting and vital question is whether the Rao-Singh reforms will be thwarted by these forces.

FOREIGN TRADE PERFORMANCE

Surjit Bhalla (1989) presents a simple econometric analysis of the determinants of India's aggregate exports and imports as well as some of their components. A satisfactory structural model of India's exports and imports, taking into account the full direct impact of the selective system of import controls and export incentives, the indirect impact of the industrial licensing system, restrictions on foreign collaboration and investment, and the performance of the public sector in the supply of key inputs and infrastructure for export supply and import demand is next to impossible to construct given the complexity of the systems involved and the paucity of available data. Bhalla's analysis, while insightful, must be viewed with caution. Instead of summarizing his analysis, this section is devoted to an analytical description of foreign trade performance.

Since the purpose of the import control regime was to confine imports to essential consumer goods, raw materials, and investment goods needed for domestic production and exports, it is not surprising that changes in the commodity composition of India's imports (Tables 5.2 and 5.3) reflected this. For example, foodgrains and edible oils

TABLE 5.2 INDIA'S MERCHANDISE IMPORTS, 1950/51–1978/79 (US$ MILLIONS AT CURRENT PRICES)

	1950/51	1955/56	1960/61	1965/66	1966/67	1968/69	1970/71	1973/74	1974/75	1975/76	1976/77	1977/78	1978/79
Foodgrains	n.a.	n.a.	378.4	670.3	854.0	443.0	271.8	597.0	951.3	1,537.3	958.7	121.2	114.4
Petroleum, oils, and lubricants	116.4	116.7	144.0	143.2	84.1	177.1	181.2	719.1	1,450.5	1,416.5	1,581.1	1,811.2	2,043.4
Fertilizers	25.9[a]	4.7[a]	22.3	82.1	132.2	228.7	100.9	242.8	617.6	609.5	214.4	301.4	451.8
Fertilizer raw materials[b]	n.a.	n.a.	10.8	26.8	34.6	40.5	32.4	52.0	134.2	102.2	101.1	139.5	144.7
Iron and steel	42.0	118.8	257.3	205.7	130.4	114.9	196.1	320.2	531.2	360.4	245.5	306.9	572.1
Nonferrous metals	59.4	51.6	99.4	144.4	114.2	118.7	159.2	180.1	224.0	116.0	175.7	224.4	301.6
Metal ores and scrap	0.9	1.0	7.0	4.3	7.2	8.2	14.6	17.1	7.5	23.3	34.8	52.7	82.2
Edible oils	n.a.	n.a.	7.4	14.8	14.9	12.9	30.6	72.8	15.0	15.8	111.7	829.0	649.3
Nonedible oils	n.a.	n.a.	2.7	13.7	4.7	12.9	20.7	10.5	28.4	3.5	20.0	31.5	5.2
Oilseeds	4.8	16.8	24.4	18.5	6.4	4.7	8.5	9.5	12.6	9.1	3.7	15.6	54.9
Cotton (raw)	211.6	120.4	171.7	97.0	75.3	120.3	131.8	66.8	34.4	32.6	144.9	232.2	35.4
Other fibers	n.a.	n.a.	18.8	65.1	91.4	42.3	37.2	52.4	49.7	51.8	80.6	270.8	294.5
Cashew nuts (raw)	6.0	10.2	20.2	31.6	26.1	41.8	39.2	37.0	45.9	38.8	20.5	21.0	11.2
Diamonds	n.a.	n.a.	0.7	0.2	1.9	30.0	25.2	84.7	59.9	90.5	193.1	375.3	557.8
Pulp and paper	22.2	38.4	39.5	40.7	41.9	38.3	49.8	49.4	87.0	85.2	76.4	120.4	178.8
Chemicals	n.a.	n.a.	157.7	138.4	140.9	149.3	155.5	212.3	285.6	240.8	250.6	405.9	514.2
Precision equipment	14.0	24.2	22.9	29.4	22.9	23.0	32.5	38.9	43.1	46.9	62.3	105.2	145.3
Machinery	192.0	273.2	547.3	885.4	685.2	596.8	437.5	714.4	707.7	898.4	980.9	1,033.6	1,166.6
Transport equipment	73.4	133.4	152.0	148.1	83.0	88.4	88.7	121.9	164.5	181.6	191.0	263.1	329.6
Other imports	n.a.	n.a.	306.9	198.1	219.6	253.0	165.5	194.3	215.4	224.1	229.0	369.6	616.0
Total imports	1,365.4	1,425.6	2,393.4	2,957.9	2,771.1	2,544.8	2,178.9	3,793.2	5,665.5	6,084.3	5,676.0	7,030.5	8,269.5
Revised total													4,272.8

n.a. = not available.
[a]Includes crude fertilizers.
[b]Rock phosphate, sulphur and unroasted iron pyrites, phosphoric acid, and ammonia.
Source: World Bank (private communication).

TABLE 5.3 INDIA'S MERCHANDISE IMPORTS, 1980/81–1991/92

	Value (US$ millions at current prices)											Growth rate (percentage)		
	1980/ 81	1981/ 82	1982/ 83	1983/ 84	1984/ 85	1985/ 86	1986/ 87	1987/ 88	1988/ 89	1989/ 90	1990/ 91	1985– 1990[a]	1990/ 91	1991/ 92[b]
Food	1,348	1,474	1,065	1,716	1,394	1,321	1,068	1,292	1,203	714	713	-11.6	-0.1	-53.6
Foodgrains	127	389	388	784	204	90	37	25	437	227	84	-1.4	-63.0	-27.5
Edible oils	865	700	399	705	775	600	479	709	503	127	180	-21.4	41.9	-54.3
Other	356	385	278	227	415	631	552	557	263	361	450	-6.5	24.7	-61.8
Other consumer goods	378	354	306	385	315	452	594	600	700	800	853	13.5	6.6	n.a.
Petroleum, oils, and lubricants	6,669	5,591	4,734	3,492	3,236	4,054	2,187	3,148	2,938	3,766	5,726	7.1	52.0	-13.5
Crude petroleum[c]	4,243	3,964	3,095	2,240	1,571	3,013	1,672	2,395	1,891	2,455	3,238	1.4	31.9	n.a.
Petroleum products	2,426	1,627	1,639	1,252	1,665	1,041	515	753	1,047	1,311	2,488	19.0	89.8	n.a.
Capital goods	2,307	2,219	2,672	3,078	2,546	3,337	4,910	4,732	3,656	4,189	4,292	5.2	2.5	-26.9
Intermediate: primary	1,277	1,460	1,620	2,058	1,886	2,156	2,474	2,997	3,800	4,488	4,184	14.2	-6.8	-10.4
Fertilizer raw materials	210	212	170	213	286	313	218	243	301	329	338	1.5	2.7	-10.9
Gems	528	445	757	1,065	868	899	1,170	1,538	1,984	2,546	2,079	18.3	-18.3	1.8
Other	539	803	693	780	732	944	1,087	1,217	1,515	1,613	1,766	13.4	9.5	-26.0
Intermediate: manufactures	3,920	3,923	3,343	3,430	3,722	4,744	4,564	4,504	7,167	7,295	7,790	10.4	6.8	n.a.
Fertilizer manufactures	826	571	212	199	847	860	387	132	341	737	608	-6.7	-17.5	5.6
Iron and steel	1,080	1,348	1,217	1,017	792	1,140	1,134	982	1,341	1,383	1,231	1.5	-11.0	-32.4
Nonferrous metals	605	445	358	379	346	443	324	444	544	752	618	6.9	-17.9	-48.5
Other	1,409	1,559	1,556	1,835	1,737	2,301	2,719	2,946	4,941	4,423	5,333	18.3	20.6	n.a.
Total[c]	15,899	15,020	13,741	14,159	13,100	16,064	15,798	17,273	19,464	21,252	23,557	8.0	10.8	-20.5
Statistical discrepancy	-7	532	646	623	2,324	1,231	1,930	2,539	3,875	3,162	2,870	18.4	-9.2	n.a.
Total[c]	15,892	15,552	14,387	14,782	15,424	17,295	17,728	19,812	23,339	24,414	26,427	8.8	8.2	n.a.

n.a. = not available.
[a]Compound growth rate between 1985/86 and 1990/91.
[b]Based on April–February data for aggregate imports, and April–January data for components.
[c]Net of crude oil exports.
Source: Ministry of Commerce, Directorate General of Commercial Intelligence and Statistics; Reserve Bank of India; World Bank staff estimates.

TABLE 5.4   INDIA'S SHARE IN WORLD
EXPORTS, 1950–1990
(PERCENTAGE)

Year	Bhagwati and Desai	Economic Survey	GATT
1950	2.0		
1955	1.5		
1960	1.2		
1965	1.0		
1966	0.9		
1967			
1970		0.6	
1973		0.5	
1975		0.5	
1977		0.6	
1978		0.5	
1979		0.5	
1980		0.4	
1981		0.4	
1982		0.5	
1983		0.5	
1984		0.5	
1985		0.5	
1986		0.4	
1988			0.5
1989			0.5
1990			0.5

Source: J. N. Bhagwati and P. Desai, *India: Planning for Indus-trialization* (London: Oxford University Press, 1970), Table 18.1, p. 370; India, *Economic Survey* (New Delhi: Government Printing Press, 1983 through 1992); GATT, *International Trade,* Vol. 2 (Geneva; GATT, 1985 through 1991).

accounted for about 16 percent of total imports in 1960/61 and about 1 percent in 1990/91. Imports of gems, which were negligible in 1960/61, accounted for US$2,079 million or nearly 8 percent of imports in 1990/91, reflecting the fact that gems and jewelry exports at $1,667 million comprised nearly a sixth of total exports. The share of crude petroleum, oils, and lubricants in total imports rose from about 6 percent in 1960/61 to a high of roughly 40 percent in 1980/81 only to fall to about 23 percent in 1990/91, reflecting in part the rise and fall of crude petroleum prices and in part the rapid growth of domestic crude output from the Bombay High Field.

Turning to exports, Table 5.4 shows that India's share of world exports has fallen steadily from about 2 percent in 1950 to less than 0.5 percent in 1990. Since world exports grew rapidly between 1950 and

1973 and somewhat more slowly thereafter, India's exports grew in absolute terms in spite of a declining share. But the dramatic fall in share reflects the fact that other countries were able to take greater advantage of growing world trade.

A crude index of terms of trade based on indexes of unit value of exports and imports shows no distinct trend but significant fluctuations (Tables 5.5 and 5.6). The volume of India's exports grew at an average annual rate of 3.0 percent during 1965–1980 and 6.5 percent during 1980–1990. During 1965–1980 the volume of world exports grew at an average annual rate of 6.6 percent and that of low-income developing countries grew at 5.1 percent per year during the same period. In the period 1980–1990 Indian export growth was faster than that of the world (4.3 percent per year) and that of low-income developing countries (5.4 percent per year).

The composition of India's exports (Tables 5.7 and 5.8) has, as expected, shifted moderately away from primary products to manufactured goods, whose share rose from about 45 percent in 1950/51 to 79 percent in 1990/91. In recent years, however, primary exports have been virtually stagnant, and manufactured products have accounted for almost the entire growth in total exports (Table 5.9). Among manufactured products, just four items—leather, gems, garments, and textiles—account for most of the growth in recent years. In contrast, the export of engineering goods, which rose by over 20 percent per year in value terms between 1950/51 and 1975/76 and between 1970/71 and 1978/79, declined between 1980/81 and 1985/86. From the low point of US$780 million in 1985/86, the value of engineering goods exports grew at an average annual rate of 20.5 percent during the period 1985–1990. Chemical exports show a similar pattern.

The export of gems has grown rapidly since the early 1970s. This export is heavily dependent, however, on the import of uncut small gems, the cost of which is determined in large part by the South African monopoly De Beers. The exports of garments and textiles are governed by India's quotas under the multifiber arrangement (MFA). Bhalla (1989) points out that until the 1980s India did not fully use its quotas, and India's competitors did better in quota, as well as nonquota, countries. It is possible that the recent spurt in India's garment and textile exports reflects better use of quotas and higher prices realized on the average. Whether India will be able to compete in the textile and apparel market in the absence of the MFA is debatable, particularly in view of the fact that the Indian textile industry has fallen behind technologically in the past four decades primarily because of the government's textile policy. A recent study by Trela and Whalley (1989) suggests that the general equilibrium welfare effects of removing bilateral

TABLE 5.5   UNIT VALUE AND VOLUME INDEXES OF EXPORTS
AND IMPORTS AND INDIA'S TERMS OF TRADE,
1950/51–1980/81

| Year (April–March) | Exports | | Imports | | Terms of trade |
	Volume index	Unit value index (in US$)	Volume index	Unit value index (in US$)	
1950/51	73	99	50	187	53
1951/52	58	145	63	123	118
1952/53	65	102	47	121	84
1953/54	65	93	44	112	83
1954/55	68	99	52	109	91
1955/56	75	91	55	106	86
1956/57	71	96	65	110	87
1957/58	77	96	74	120	80
1958/59	70	94	66	112	84
1959/60	75	94	73	104	90
1960/61	70	104	85	107	97
1961/62	74	104	80	110	95
1962/63	79	101	87	106	95
1963/64	89	99	89	109	91
1964/65	93	101	97	110	92
1965/66	87	107	102	117	91
1966/67[a]	84	102	99	106	96
1967/68	86	102	110	96	106
1968/69	100	100	100	100	100
1969/70	100	104	84	100	104
1970/71	106	106	87	100	106
1971/72	107	109	105	94	116
1972/73	120	117	99	94	124
1973/74	125	141	114	133	106
1974/75	133	172	100	225	76
1975/76	147	171	99	243	70
1976/77	174	176	97	233	76
1977/78	168	207	130	218	95
1978/79	180	214	140	238	90
1979/80	199	219	135	334	66
1980/81	194	241	199	322	75
Average compound growth rate (% per year)					
1950/51–1976/77	3.4	2.2	2.6	0.8[b]	
1970/71–1980/81	6.2	8.6	8.6	12.4	
1979/80	10.6	2.3	−3.6	40.3	
1980/81	−2.5	10.0	47.4	−3.6	

Note: The indexes available on four different base periods have been converted to the base 1968/69 by the chain base method.
[a]Relates to the period June–March.
[b]Note that for the base year 1950/51, the unit value index for imports was exceptionally high.
Source: World Bank (private communication).

TABLE 5.6 UNIT VALUE AND VOLUME INDEXES OF EXPORTS
AND IMPORTS AND INDIA'S TERMS OF TRADE,
1981/82–1990/91 (1980/81 = 100)

Year (April–March)	Exports		Imports		Terms of trade
	Volume index	Unit value index (in US$)	Volume index	Unit value index (in US$)	
1981/82	101	100.0	101	93.3	107.6
1982/83	97	98.0	94	92.3	106.2
1983/84	97	101.1	101	88.1	114.8
1984/85	103	98.5	95	87.1	113.1
1985/86	106	97.7	119	85.2	115.0
1986/87	118	97.1	124	80.3	121.0
1987/88	135	106.0	116	93.6	114.0
1988/89	154	107.8	130	93.8	115.0
1989/90	178	110.3	135	99.2	111.0
1990/91	186	115.2	140	106.0	100.0

Source: World Bank (private communication).

MFA quotas and tariffs on textiles and clothing for all countries are on
the order of a modest US$15.5 billion in 1986 U.S. dollars, of which
US$7.97 billion accrue to the developing countries. India gains an ex-
tremely modest US$0.08 billion. China (US$1.72 billion), Korea
(US$1.62 billion), Brazil (US$0.92 billion), and Taiwan (US$0.89 bil-
lion) account for most of the gains to developing countries. The Trela
and Whalley simulation, however, is a static exercise and assumes that
all countries have the same technology but differing labor productivity
and product quality. It is not clear whether the results will stand up if
changes are made in these assumptions. The fact that a relatively narrow range of product groups accounted for the recent growth in India's
exports and that their growth may not be sustained in the future if the
external environment changes is disturbing.

CONCLUSION

India's growth performance in the four decades since planning for national development was initiated in 1950 has been unspectacular. In the
1950s, 1960s, and 1970s the average annual growth rate of real GDP was
3.7 percent, 3.3 percent, and 3.4 percent. The 1980s saw some modest
improvement in the growth rate to 5.3 percent. India's development
strategy was inward oriented, and self-reliance was an important objective. The pursuit of this objective has resulted in a diversified industrial structure. Most of India's industries, however, are not internationally competitive in terms of either cost per unit or product quality.

TABLE 5.7 INDIA'S MERCHANDISE EXPORTS, 1950/51–1978/79

Commodity	Value (US$ millions at current prices)											Annual compound growth rate (percentage)			
	1950/ 51	1955/ 56	1960/ 61	1965/ 66	1968/ 69	1970/ 71	1973/ 74	1975/ 76	1976/ 77	1977/ 78	1978/ 79	1950/ 51– 1975/ 76	1970/ 71– 1978/ 79	1977/ 78	1978/ 79
Agricultural products	328.8	380.9	420.7	497.0	478.5	519.3	858.6	1,393.3	1,362.5	1,639.5	1,471.7	5.9	13.9	20.5	−10.2
Tea	168.9	229.2	259.6	241.2	208.6	197.7	187.4	273.8	327.9	665.3	414.9	2.0	9.7	102.9	−37.6
Oil cakes	0.1	11.1	30.0	72.8	66.0	73.9	228.7	111.5	262.2	155.6	141.1	32.4	8.4	−40.7	−9.3
Coffee	2.8	3.2	15.2	27.2	24.0	35.5	59.1	77.0	141.0	227.0	175.6	14.2	23.0	61.0	−22.6
Sugar	0.8	2.0	5.1	22.0	13.5	56.8	55.0	545.9	165.7	22.7	160.8	29.8	20.2	−86.3	608.4
Spices	53.4	22.4	34.9	48.5	33.5	51.8	70.7	82.7	85.9	160.1	180.4	1.8	16.9	90.8	12.7
Fish	5.2	7.9	9.7	14.3	30.3	41.7	114.5	147.0	202.0	203.6	278.2	14.3	26.8	0.8	36.6
Cashew	18.0	27.3	39.7	57.5	81.2	69.4	95.5	111.1	118.7	174.6	97.8	7.6	4.4	47.1	−44.0
Vegetable oils[a]	53.0	72.1	17.9	8.6	15.6	9.4	39.6	39.8	56.4	24.2	16.5	−1.1	7.3	−57.1	−31.8
Essential oils	26.6	5.7	8.6	4.9	5.8	5.1	8.1	4.5	4.7	6.4	6.4	−6.9	2.9	36.2	—
Raw materials	78.3	138.0	135.4	196.8	217.2	252.7	335.8	641.1	637.2	539.0	595.2	8.8	11.3	−15.4	10.4
Raw cotton	10.4	62.3	18.2	20.4	14.8	18.6	41.6	47.7	30.2	0.8	19.5	6.3	0.6	−97.4	2337.5
Unmanufactured tobacco	29.6	22.4	30.7	41.1	44.2	41.9	87.8	107.6	108.3	132.2	134.9	5.3	15.7	22.1	2.0
Iron ore	0.5	13.2	35.8	88.4	117.8	152.9	170.5	247.1	266.8	281.3	283.8	28.2	8.0	5.4	0.9
Mica	21.0	17.6	21.2	23.7	18.0	20.7	16.7	16.9	19.4	20.2	23.1	−0.9	1.4	4.1	14.4
Manganese	16.8	22.5	29.5	23.2	18.0	18.6	12.1	20.2	21.4	12.7	18.8	0.7	0.1	−40.7	48.0
Silver	n.a.	n.a.	n.a.	n.a.	4.4	n.a.	7.1	201.6	191.1	91.8	115.1	n.a.		−52.0	25.4

Manufactured items															
Manufactured items	568.8	457.3	571.7	782.4	977.2	976.3	1,543.7	1,992.4	2,848.6	3,300.1	3,801.7	5.1	18.5	15.8	15.2
Jute manufactures	239.0	248.3	283.8	384.0	290.6	253.9	292.0	290.0	225.0	285.9	203.0	0.8	-2.8	27.1	-29.0
Cotton textile															
Millmade	225.4	101.2	110.8	98.5	87.3	90.0	208.8	140.5	238.4	167.4	169.4	-1.9	8.2	-29.8	1.2
Handloom	22.8	17.8	10.0	17.5	6.7	10.4	41.6	45.8	60.6	95.0	74.4	2.8	27.9	56.8	-21.7
Coir manufactures	22.8	20.2	18.2	22.5	18.4	17.3	19.7	22.0	26.8	27.9	32.1	-0.1	8.0	4.1	15.1
Clothing	0.8[b]	n.a.	1.8	13.4	19.6	40.3	127.9	234.6	372.7	386.8	518.5	25.5[c]	37.6	3.8	34.0
Cotton yarn and thread	4.2	9.5	9.3	14.6	19.1	29.6	14.6	7.4	31.5	35.3	18.9[d]	2.3	n.a.	12.1	n.a.
Leather and leather manufactures	54.5[e]	48.3	56.6	72.6	206.5	108.8	239.5	263.6	264.4	317.6	430.4	6.5	18.8	20.1	35.5
Gems	n.a.	n.a.	0.3	31.0	59.7	55.8	137.2	171.6	321.1	637.4	865.9	n.a.	40.9	98.5	35.8
Other															
handicrafts	n.a.	n.a.	n.a.	21.4	32.4	37.3	85.6	119.6	188.7	240.5	294.6	n.a.	29.5	27.5	22.5
Iron and steel[f]	3.3[b]	n.a.	20.3	26.5	105.2	121.6	33.6	78.6	325.0	216.5	140.2	13.5[c]	1.8	-33.4	-35.2
Engineering goods[f]	1.2[b]	n.a.	37.8	41.6	89.8	155.3	258.9	477.3	633.5	721.0	852.3	27.1[c]	23.7	13.8	18.2
Chemicals[g]	17.9	12.0	7.2	19.2	25.8	39.2	64.6	98.6	124.0	136.3	178.3	7.1	20.8	9.9	30.8
Mineral fuels	n.a.	15.6	15.6	19.6	16.1	16.8	19.7	42.8	36.9	32.5	23.7	n.a.	4.4	-11.9	-27.1
Other	285.4[h]	302.7[h]	258.7	215.6	137.6	298.6	500.8	645.3	904.8	836.8	1,107.6	3.3	17.8	-7.5	32.4
Total	1,261.3	1,278.9	1,386.5	1,691.8	1,810.5	2,046.9[i]	3,238.9	4,672.1	5,753.1	6,315.4	6,976.2	5.4	16.6	9.8	10.5

n.a. = not available.
[a]Edible oils excluding vanaspati.
[b]Relates to 1951/52.
[c]Relates to the period 1951/52 to 1975/76.
[d]Excluding cotton thread.
[e]Excludes footwear.
[f]In accordance with the classification followed by the Ministry of Commerce. In 1972 several manufactured items formerly included under iron and steel were reclassified as engineering goods. Data from 1973/74 onward follow the new classification and hence are not comparable with data for earlier years.
[g]Excluding essential oils and plastics.
[h]Includes items listed above for which data are not available.
[i]Unadjusted total. Because of a change in recording technique, the data from the Directorate General of Commercial Intelligence and Statistics probably overstate exports by about 5% in 1970/71.
Source: World Bank (private communication).

TABLE 5.8 INDIA'S MERCHANDISE EXPORTS, 1980/81–1991/92

	Value (US$ millions at current prices)											Growth rate (percentage)		
	1980/ 81	1981/ 82	1982/ 83	1983/ 84	1984/ 85	1985/ 86	1986/ 87	1987/ 88	1988/ 89	1989/ 90	1990/ 91	1985– 1990[a]	1990/ 91	1991/ 92[b]
Primary exports	3,400	3,308	3,110	3,093	3,102	3,108	3,237	3,125	2,905	3,428	3,740	3.8	9.1	2.0
Fish	270	314	378	353	321	334	421	405	437	412	535	9.9	29.8	3.2
Rice	284	412	226	110	142	160	154	250	230	256	245	8.9	-4.3	22.5
Cashews	178	203	141	146	151	184	256	236	192	221	249	6.2	12.8	7.1
Coffee	271	164	194	176	177	216	232	203	193	206	141	-8.2	-31.4	-6.3
Tea	539	443	384	500	645	512	451	457	414	543	599	3.2	10.3	-25.5
Spices	141	111	98	113	174	227	218	238	173	148	130	-10.6	-12.2	14.2
Iron ore	384	394	395	389	387	473	427	419	464	557	585	4.3	5.1	5.7
Other primary	1,333	1,267	1,294	1,306	1,105	1,002	1,078	917	803	1,086	1,257	4.6	15.7	9.4
Manufactured exports	5,067	5,214	4,931	5,187	5,462	5,684	6,501	9,013	11,105	13,185	14,383	20.4	9.1	-4.2
Chemicals	298	420	362	317	406	406	456	635	1,058	1,759	1,781	34.4	1.2	7.6
Leather and leather goods	478	454	408	449	568	629	721	886	1,028	1,171	1,423	17.7	21.5	-10.8
Textiles	1,292	1,155	988	921	1,171	1,026	1,079	1,483	1,044	1,214	1,705	10.7	40.5	-1.3
Garments	717	737	628	719	827	872	1,040	1,382	1,449	1,935	2,252	20.9	16.4	-4.2
Gems and jewelry	783	909	1,054	1,255	1,040	1,228	1,622	2,016	3,038	3,178	2,903	18.8	-8.7	-3.6
Engineering goods	1,010	1,043	892	782	803	780	886	1,105	1,630	1,993	1,978	20.5	-0.8	-7.2
Petroleum products	10	28	178	346	215	425	327	488	349	418	523	4.2	25.1	-29.8
Other manufactures	479	468	421	-398	432	318	370	1,018	1,509	1,517	1,819	41.7	19.9	n.a.
Total[c]	8,467	8,522	8,041	8,280	8,564	8,792	9,738	12,138	14,010	16,613	18,123	15.6	9.1	-1.9
Statistical discrepancy	-135	175	348	810	1,205	669	722	506	252	237	362			
Total[c]	8,332	8,697	8,389	9,090	9,769	9,461	10,460	12,644	14,262	16,850	18,485	14.3	9.7	n.a.

n.a. = not available.

[a]Compound growth rate between 1985/86 and 1990/91.

[b]Based on April–February data for aggregate exports, and April–January data for components.

[c]Net of crude petroleum exports.

Source: Ministry of Commerce, Directorate General of Commercial Intelligence and Statistics; Reserve Bank of India.

TABLE 5.9   COMPOSITION OF RECENT EXPORT GROWTH IN INDIA, 1980/81–1990/91

	Average annual value (US$ millions at current prices)			Contribution to growth (%)
	1980/81– 1985/86	1986/87– 1990/91	Increase	
Manufactured exports	5,296	10,837	5,542	97
Consumption goods	3,408	6,514	3,106	55
Leather	502	1,046	544	10
Gems (gross)	1,097	2,551	1,454	26
Garments	757	1,612	855	15
Textiles	1,052	1,305	253	4
Investment goods[a]	860	1,518	658	12
Intermediate goods	1,028	2,805	1,777	31
Chemicals	382	1,138	756	13
Petroleum products	238	421	183	3
Other[b]	407	1,247	839	15
Primary exports	3,144	3,287	143	3
Fish	340	442	102	2
Rice	210	227	17	0
Cashews	165	231	66	1
Coffee	185	195	9	0
Tea	497	493	−4	0
Spices	145	181	37	1
Iron ore	408	490	83	1
Other primary exports	1,195	1,028	−167	−3
Total exports (Customs)[c]	8,440	14,124	5,685	100
Discrepancy	641	416	−226	
Total exports (BOP)[c]	9,081	14,540	5,459	
Memo				
Gems (net)[d]	290	688	398	

[a]Refers to engineering goods.
[b]Including unclassified exports.
[c]Total exports, f.o.b., net of crude oil.
[d]Exports less imports of gems and jewelry.
Source: Ministry of Commerce, Directorate General of Commercial Intelligence and Statistics; Reserve Bank of India.

Far from viewing foreign trade as an engine of growth, Indian planners sought to minimize import demand and viewed exports more or less as a necessary evil mainly to generate the foreign exchange earnings to meet that part of the import bill not covered by external assistance. They created an elaborate administrative regulatory machinery in an attempt to control investment and resource allocation in the economy and ensure their consistency with five-year plan targets. Controls over imports and exports were also part of this regulatory system. The system was exceedingly complex, and its rules of operation had no discernible economic rationale. Above all, it was selective and discretionary and relied on quantitative restrictions rather than on policy instruments that affected market prices. The integrity of the administrative and political structure was increasingly eroded by the enormous opportunities for rent seeking and the corruption this spawned.

India's share in world trade declined steadily from 2 percent in the 1950s to 0.5 percent in 1990. Most of the growth in exports in the 1980s was accounted for by just four product groups: leather, gems and jewelry, textiles, and garments. Exports of engineering goods and chemicals, which were once dynamic, suffered a decline in the first half of the 1980s and recovered somewhat in the second half. A diversified and dynamic export sector has yet to emerge.

It is clear that to achieve sustained, rapid, equitable, and efficient growth, India must abandon its inward-oriented, capital-intensive, and inefficient development strategy implemented through an administrative allocation system based on QRs. In its stead a system of economic management must be put in place that relies largely on market forces and that confines state intervention in the economy to investment in some infrastructure sectors such as transport, communication, and major irrigation and to those areas where there are no efficient private sector alternatives, including services such as primary education, primary health care, and agricultural extension and research. The Rao-Singh reforms are vital initial steps in these directions. They must be consolidated and extended. Above all, the credibility of the government's commitment to the reforms must be firmly established.

Because the reforms are solidly based on an understanding of what went wrong with the Indian development strategy that delivered neither rapid growth nor appreciably greater equity and because they constitute a package of mutually supporting and consistent elements, they are not as easily opposed on analytical grounds as earlier piecemeal efforts at economic liberalization. The collapse of the socialist economies of Eastern Europe and the realization that India has been left behind in development by other Asian economies have generated widespread support for reforms in the national press. The coherence of the reform package and support of the press, however, are not enough to convince producers in India and abroad that the government is committed to carrying out the package and that the short-run economic, social, and political costs of adjustment to a liberalized economy are manageable. Although the prime minister and the finance minister continue to stand by the reforms and proclaim that they are irreversible, concrete actions have been slow in coming. *The New York Times* (August 15, 1992) reports that "a year after the new policies were announced by Prime Minister P. V. Narasimha Rao, far less has been accomplished than promised, bureaucratic red tape still hamstrings new investment, both foreign and domestic, and not a single one of India's huge, bankrupt state controlled industries has been shut." It adds that Motorola, "which intended to invest $14 billion in India over the next decade has decided to move some of those investments to China. In the first three months of this year, China received $6.5 billion in foreign investment in contrast to [India's] $300 million."

To be fair to Rao and Singh, it should be pointed out that four decades of dirigisme is not easily replaced by market-friendly economic management in one year. Moreover, the government does not have an absolute majority in Parliament, though the divisions within the opposition and its reluctance to face another general election soon after the last one in 1991 give the government some room to maneuver. If India uses this narrow window of political opportunity effectively, with the support of expanded aid from the donor community abroad to ease the short-run costs of adjustment, the reforms would indeed become irreversible and their fruits would be realized.

Some actions, if taken promptly, could enhance credibility. For instance, the government could announce a phased program to reduce excessively high tariffs and their variance across commodities. If the announced reductions are bound with the General Agreement on Tariffs and Trade (GATT) so that they acquire the force of an international agreement, their credibility would be enhanced considerably. Another step would be successful negotiations with the labor unions in the public and organized private sectors to persuade them to change their focus from seeking protection of their existing jobs in inefficient industries that have to be scaled down or closed altogether to seeking better jobs in a liberalized economy in which employment opportunities would be rapidly growing and plentiful. With the National Renewal Fund (established in 1991) financing voluntary retirement opportunities for older workers and retraining opportunities for younger workers laid off from enterprises that are to be scaled down, adjustment costs should be manageable as long as productive employment grows more rapidly than in the past. For rural workers, a more efficient version of the existing employment creation programs could serve well. And a limited but better-targeted and -managed public distribution system for essential commodities would provide a social safety net for the poor.

Full convertibility of the rupee for current account transactions should be instituted as soon as possible. This step should enable the government to considerably scale down export subsidies, if not eliminate them altogether. With a better-functioning infrastructure and freer availability of imported inputs, industrial efficiency should improve, thereby reducing unit costs of production. In particular, reduced production costs for fertilizers should allow for the phasing out of fertilizer subsidies. With the exit of inefficient public sector units dependent on budgetary support, yet another source of the public sector deficit would disappear. With improvements in the revenue side of the budget (in particular, a wider tax base, reduced tax rates, and more efficient tax administration), the fiscal deficit would be brought within safe limits. With the reforms credibly enforced and extended, it should not take India as long as it took other such formerly inward-oriented economies, such as Mexico, to climb out of the unavoidable adjustment phase and move onto a path of sustainable, rapid, efficient, and equitable growth.

APPENDIX

The administrative allocation . . . took place essentially at three points: (1) an allocation was earmarked for the different public sector undertakings, for both raw materials and equipment, and was assigned to the ministries within whose domain they lay; (2) the iron and steel controller received a bulk allocation; and (3) the economic adviser in the Ministry of Commerce received a bulk allocation for the private sector's imports of raw materials, spares, and components (excluding, among other things, iron and steel; newsprint; and petroleum, oils, and lubricants).

The licensing procedures, through which each unit had to process all imports, involved three license-issuing authorities: (1) the chief controller of imports and exports (CCI&E), (2) the iron and steel controller (I&SC), and (3) the development officer (DO), Tools, Development Wing of the Ministry of Commerce and Industry. Except for iron and steel (cleared by the I&SC) and certain types of machine tools (licensed by the DO), the CCI&E controlled the issuance of all licenses.

The licenses issued by the CCI&E, which constituted the majority, were divided into the following categories: (1) established importers (EI); (2) actual users (AU); (3) newcomers (not covered by EI and AU); (4) ad hoc (covering items such as State Trading Corporation imports); (5) capital goods (CG); (6) heavy electrical plant (HEP); (7) export promotion, given as import entitlements to exporters in specific schemes;

The text of this Appendix is adapted from J. N. Bhagwati and T. N. Srinivasan, *Foreign Trade Regimes and Economic Development: India* (New York: Columbia University Press, 1975), pp. 36–46.

(8) miscellaneous categories: such as railway contracts (relating to orders placed by the railways), replacement licenses (to replace defective or unsuitable imports), and blanket licenses (mainly for petroleum, oils, and lubricants).

The procedures followed for each category of licenses, and the authorities involved in the process, reflected two major criteria: (1) the principle of "essentiality" and (2) the principle of "indigenous nonavailability." Thus imports, in terms of both magnitude and composition, were to be permitted under each category only if some designated agency of the government had certified that they were essential (such as inputs or equipment for production). At the same time, some agency had to clear the imports from the viewpoint of indigenous availability: if it could be shown that there was domestic production of the imports demanded, then the imports were not permitted (regardless of cost and quality considerations). Thus, in addition to the license-issuing authority, there was a sponsoring agency to certify essentiality and a clearing agency to certify indigenous clearance.

For public sector applications, the procedures were similar. Paradoxically, at times the procedures were even more complex, as when the sanction of the Department of Economic Affairs had to be obtained, in addition to indigenous clearance and essentiality certification, for many applications for raw material imports. Besides, in certain cases, the project authorities themselves had the authority to grant indigenous clearance and essentiality certificates. But these and others were, by and large, differences of detail.

Principles and Criteria of Allocation

The allocation of foreign exchange among alternative claimants and uses in a direct control system such as that just described would presumably depend on a well-defined set of principles and criteria based on a system of priorities. In point of fact, however, few such criteria, if any, were followed in practice. We shall examine, in particular, the allocations arising from AU licensing.

Two questions of economic significance arise: (1) how were allocations by industry decided and (2) how were these allocations further divided among the constituent firms or units? We shall examine each of these questions in turn.

Allocations by industry.   As far as the allocations by industry were concerned, it is clear that the sheer weight of numbers made any meaningful listing of priorities extremely difficult. The problem was Orwellian: all industries had priority; how was each sponsoring authority to argue that some industries had more priority than others?

It is not surprising, therefore, that the agencies involved in determining allocations by industry fell back on vague notions of fairness, implying pro rata allocations with reference to capacity installed or employment, or shares defined by past import allocations or similar other rules of thumb.

Allocations by unit.   The principles and criteria for subdividing industrial allocations among constituent firms or units were likewise without any rationale other than the even spreading out of a scarce resource on a "fair" and "equitable" basis. A great variety of norms were used, with significant opportunities for and occasional exercise of discretion. But the overwhelming bias of the system was toward some form of "equitable" allocation and cuts therein. This conclusion holds, not merely for the Directorate General of Technical Development (DGTD), but also for small-scale sector allocations, the scheduled industries not on the books of the DGTD, and the other classes of import applicants.

Quality of Information for Assigning Priorities

As we have already noted, numerous authorities were involved in the licensing procedure: sponsoring bodies, authorities granting indigenous clearance, and license-issuing authorities. Each such authority presumed to act on some set of priorities, in principle, and therefore had to have reasonable information to enable it to exercise its functions meaningfully. Although it was impossible to have a meaningful, well-defined set of priorities at any level in this bureaucratic machine, except in relation to overriding matters such as defense, no allocations were ever made without intensive scrutiny and examination of individual applications at each stage in the bureaucracy. The quality of the information on which these examinations and ensuing decisions were presumably based can be inferred from what is known about (1) the small-scale sector applications and (2) the working of the DGTD concerning imports.

Small-scale sector.   The State Directorates of Industries were the authorities that were supposed to process the import applications in the first instance and to attach essentiality certificates (ECs). While considerable time was indeed taken in granting these ECs, the quality of the information on which the relevant decisions were made was poor.

DGTD.   The case of the DGTD was hardly any better, despite its obvious advantages over the directorates in charge of the small-scale sector. It is well known, for example, that capacity and capacity use data, both of which ostensibly were taken into account in making unit allocations, are bad. Similarly, with respect to those units that must seek indigenous clearance from the DGTD, the DGTD directorates frequently maintained incomplete records of the indigenous suppliers, did not have sufficient information in adequate detail on what these suppliers could produce and of what quality, did not distinguish adequately between the mere fact of the existence of an indigenous supplier and the availability of the supply to an individual purchaser, and thus ended up occasionally withholding sanction even for critical imports.

The DGTD not only tried to secure indigenous clearance before permitting imports but even seemed to determine the quantitative mix of permissible imports in many cases. Clearly the DGTD had no capacity to form reasonable judgments on this issue in the absence of very detailed information on plant conditions—something that was automatically ruled out when we see that the DGTD carried on its 1965 book over 5,000 units.

Priority in Favor of the Small-Scale Sector

Although clear criteria for the allocation of imports among alternative uses were generally conspicuous by their absence and the informational basis for decision making was exceptionally weak, it might be contended that the authorities pursued certain broad priorities. A typical defense of the import control system was that it was the only way of ensuring that supplies were allocated on a "fair and equitable" basis to "small" entrepreneurs. This is not an argument for economic efficiency, but it is a valid argument for income redistribution if alternative ways of subsidizing smaller entrepreneurs are not feasible.

It is difficult to take this defense of the import control system seriously. In point of fact, there is reason to conclude that the control system discriminated against the small-scale sector, as when import cuts in face of a sudden accentuation of the foreign exchange shortage fell relatively heavily on the small-scale sector and much less on the well-connected larger firms. It does not follow, of course, that the small-scale sector would have either secured greater allocations or been more competitive if it had to purchase imports in a free market. This situation, however, does cast doubt on the usual claim that the import control system made the small-scale sector better off than under the alternative import regimes.

Foreign Exchange Saved From Being Spent On Consumption

It might be contended that the import policy regime was directed at preventing scarce foreign exchange from being frittered away on consumer goods and that this general priority was strictly maintained by the import-licensing authorities. It is certainly true that, over the period of our study, direct imports of consumer goods were slashed. This was reflected in the steady reduction of EI licenses and the growth of AU licenses granted to producers. We must make, however, two important points concerning this question:

1. While imports of manufactured consumer goods indeed fell, these declines were frequently offset by growth in domestic production of the same and other consumer manufactures.

2. The maintenance imports (that is, imports of raw materials and intermediates) necessary to support current production of domestic consumer goods industries were not negligible. Estimates of the direct and indirect import requirements of consumption in India show that for the years 1961/62 and 1963/64 the shares of total imports that went to support the consumption of luxuries were 7.6 and 8.5 percent, and the shares that went to support the consumption of necessities were 28.7 and 32.9 percent, respectively.

In any event, irrational as it may be to seek to prohibit imports of nonessential consumer goods while permitting their production domestically, this objective could have been as readily achieved, with none of the other detrimental effects of a full-fledged control system embracing all transactions, by a selective set of prohibitive tariffs or quotas on specific items to be excluded from imports.

Corruption and Frustration of Apparent Priorities

We have noted that the import control system was based on incomplete and unsystematic criteria and lacked any discernible economic rationale. Further, whatever limited allocational aims it may have had were frustrated, in varying degrees, by the corruption that inevitably arose from the large premiums on imports under the control system.

The control system generated two kinds of illegality: (1) since imports were remunerative in general, there were innumerable bogus claims to import license entitlement under the existing rules of allocation; and (2) since numerous restrictions applied to the transferability of imports and import licenses, black markets arose to transact such illegal traffic. It has not been possible for us to quantify any of these illegal transactions in a meaningful manner, but there is little doubt that they existed widely. We should also note that these illegal transfers of imports often must have served to increase economic efficiency by reducing the irrational inflexibility that the legal restrictions on transferability entailed.

Economic Effects of Import Controls

What were the economic consequences of these methods of allocating foreign exchange in India's QR regime? While the consequences for resource allocation and capacity use and the growth effects on savings, research and development, quality of production, inducement to invest, and other aspects of India's economic performance have been significant, we note here several other, mainly adverse, effects. In particular, we will consider (1) delays; (2) administrative and other costs; (3) inflexibility; (4) lack of coordination among agencies; (5) absence of competition; (6) inherent bias in favor of industries using imported, rather than domestically produced, inputs; and (7) anticipatory and automatic protection afforded to industries regardless of costs.

Delays.   The working of any system of allocation will take a certain amount of time. Even in a free foreign exchange market, the participants must expend time, for example, acquiring information about the availability of different kinds of foreign exchange. In principle, an administrative system of allocations need not result in a significant increase in time, and hence delays, over a price system in which scarce foreign exchange is rationed out in the market. The introduction of priorities would, in principle, be equally time consuming in both cases, though the procedure would be different, since the price system would involve administrative decisions about tax and subsidy incentives whereas the control system would involve administrative decisions about quotas.

In practice, however, the exchange control system seems to degenerate into an inordinately time-consuming allocational device. There are essentially three reasons for this. First, in a situation of general scarcity of foreign exchange, the definition of priorities becomes exceptionally difficult, and the system ends up having to accommodate all conceivable demands on some "equitable" basis, while making a pretense of administering priorities. This pretense frequently takes the form of collection of yet more information from applicants and time taken in "scrutinizing" it and "arriving at an informed decision." Delays become, sociologically, the conspicuous substitute for the exercise of priorities by the bureaucracy. Second, and equally important, the multiplication of the bureaucratic apparatus leads inevitably to slower decision making because procedures are inefficient. For example, when the DGTD has to obtain indigenous clearance from two or more other directorates, it seeks these clearances sequentially rather than simultaneously. Third, in explaining delays under the Indian allocation system, some significance must be attached to the fact that files often fail to move up in the system until appropriate graft is paid to the lower-level clerks. If all graft were paid promptly, this custom would cause no delay, but newcomers and honest applicants are unlikely to conform readily to this widespread practice. Hence delays occur on this account as well.

Administrative and other costs.   The elaborate bureaucratic machinery for operating the licensing mechanisms undoubtedly involved both direct costs and the costs resulting from the necessity for entrepreneurs to maintain elaborate and frequent contacts with the licensing authorities. Admittedly, alternative allocation mechanisms also necessitate administrative and information-gathering costs. But the specific type of command mechanism involved in the Indian QR and industrial-licensing regimes added to these costs by making necessary expenditures to ensure "file-pushing" by bribe-seeking bureaucrats at lower levels. For example, the considerable growth of Indian Airlines traffic into Delhi from major industrial cities such as Calcutta and Bombay could be attributed in large part to flights by industrialists and their representatives to Delhi to expedite and influence the allocation of licenses. Costs incurred in such flights as well as those of a growing license-allocating bureaucracy are net costs attributable to the regime. And if we could only disentangle (as we cannot) the job expansion in the bureaucracy that has resulted from the licensing machinery, much of the enormous expansion of current governmental expenditures during the 1956–1971 period may turn out to be a net cost of the licensing regime.

Inflexibility.   The twin principles of essentiality and indigenous nonavailability also introduced considerable inflexibility to the pattern of import use. This inflexibility came about through a rigid itemization of permissible imports, frequently by specified value for different items, both for AU and EI licenses.

At the same time, the theoretical premise that AU allocations were being made on the basis of well-defined priorities at the detailed industry level led the authorities to rule out legal transferability of the licenses among industries. Bureaucratic logic took the inevitable next step and eliminated transferability even among units within the same industry, thus making the transfer of AU licenses by the licensee units altogether illegal. Needless to say, none of the imports under the AU licenses were allowed to be legally resold either (but were occasionally sold in the black market, of course).

The rigid pattern of permissible imports (only occasionally adjusted through changing the contents of the lists by discretionary action) and the nontransferability of the AU licenses and imports were bound to create inflexibility leading to economic inefficiency for several reasons:

1. The total AU allocations to individual units were neither made by well-defined priorities nor based on assessment of reasonably accurate and analyzed information, but were mostly based on notions of "fair sharing" with occasional injection of "pragmatism" and "judgment of cases on merits."

2. The itemized breakdowns were based on (a) indigenous nonavailability, which, as we have noted, was assessed inaccurately by the responsible bodies such as the DGTD, and (b) these bodies' assessment of the optimal mix of imported inputs, which again was made on an administrative and ad hoc basis rather than on any recognizable criterion of economic efficiency.

3. There is considerable uncertainty about the availability of foreign exchange, leaving aside the general unpredictability of the entire economic situation, so that no "optimal mix" of inputs laid down in advance (even if worked out on the basis of well-defined criteria, accurately gathered available information, and explicitly assumed future developments) can hope to be optimal ex post, thus requiring flexibility in the matter of the input-mix and transfers of inputs from one set of users to another.

Yet another implication of the inflexibility arising from the nontransferability of import licenses might have been an excessive holding of inventories by Indian firms. Indian inventories, especially the raw materials and intermediates held, compare unfavorably with those of firms in similar industries elsewhere. However, other factors on the Indian scene probably explain these large inventories. For example, interest rates in the organized industrial sector are quite low, making inventory holding relatively inexpensive; on the other hand, it is not clear that the relevant Indian interest rates (real or nominal) have been significantly lower than those abroad. Lower efficiency in transport (and shortage thereof) would also make inventory holding more valuable. Furthermore, inventory holdings, including raw materials and intermediates, appear to have generally declined as a proportion of output through the period of our study for many industries. Hence, while it makes a priori sense to argue that, other things being equal, an import control regime of the Indian type would tend to inflate inventory holdings, it would not be correct to argue that the empirical analyses currently available support this hypothesis.

Lack of coordination among agencies.   The multiplicity of agencies dispensing imports further accentuated the applicants' difficulty in procuring desired imports. For example, the typical unit under DGTD jurisdiction would receive its share of the bulk allocations from the economic adviser to the DGTD, allocations of iron and steel from the I&SC's office, and nonferrous metals allocations from decisions made by the corresponding department (which in turn, received bulk allocations for this purpose). Unfortunately, the agencies do not appear to have routinely coordinated either the initial allocations or the cuts therein.

Absence of competition.   The import allocation system in force had virtually eliminated the possibility of competition, either foreign or domestic. Foreign competition was ruled out because of the principle of "indigenous availability": every item of indigenous production, no matter how much its cost of production exceeded the landed c.i.f. price, was automatically shielded from competition through imports. Indeed, the onus was put on the buyer to show conclusively that he could not procure the item from indigenous producers.

At the same time, the possibility of domestic competition was minimized by the combination of CG licensing (concomitantly with other industrial licensing provisions) and the method of AU licensing on a "fair-share" basis among rival firms in an industry. Strict CG and industrial licensing eliminated free entry by new firms as well as efficiency-induced expansion by existing firms. And the fact that each firm was entitled to its "share" of AU licenses, and no more, ensured that the efficient firms could not even (legally) enlarge output from existing capacity by competing away the scarce imports from less efficient firms.

Thus, all forms of effective competition, potential and actual, were virtually eliminated from the industrial system. The effects were (1) to eliminate incentives to reduce costs per unit of output (as the penalty for sloppy operations was no longer incapacity to survive against more efficient rivals) and (2) to prevent production from being concentrated in the most efficient units (and industries).

Inherent bias in favor of industries using imported inputs.   Under the actual-user system of allocation of imports, combined with the principle of indigenous nonavailability, it may be expected that the quantity of import allocations would, other things being equal, tend to be inversely related to the availability of indigenously produced inputs.

But this, in turn, would lead to a bias in the effective incentive provided to the industries using relatively more imported inputs: they would be able to obtain relatively greater allocations of imports under AU licenses and hence obtain these inputs at import-premium-exclusive prices (which would include only the explicit tariff duty) whereas the other industries would have to buy import-substitute, indigenous items at premium-inclusive prices (since these items would fetch a price equal to the c.i.f. prices plus the import premium). The effective incentive given to the former industries or processes would thus be greater, other things being equal. And, while it may fortuitously be the case that some of these industries may require relative subsidization on economic grounds, there is no gainsaying the fact that the import system in India gave rise to these differential incentives purely as an incidental side effect.

Anticipatory and automatic protection to industries.   Another significant impact of the Indian import policy, under which the principle of indigenous availability was used to exclude or restrict imports in favor of domestic import-substitutes, was that protection was automatically extended to all industries regardless of cost, efficiency, and comparative advantage. This automatic protection was further fully to be anticipated by every producer, merely as long as he was willing to make his capacity and production known to the relevant agencies (for example, the DGTD) in charge of "indigenous clearance."

REFERENCES

Bardhan, P. K. 1984. *The Political Economy of Development in India.* Oxford: Basil Blackwell.

Basu, D. C. 1983. *Introduction to the Constitution of India.* 10th edition. New Delhi: Prentice-Hall.

Bhagwati, J. N., and P. Desai. 1970. *India: Planning for Industrialization.* London: Oxford University Press.

Bhagwati, J. N., and T. N. Srinivasan. 1975. *Foreign Trade Regimes and Economic Development: India.* New York: Columbia University Press.

Bhagwati, J. N., R. Brecher, and T. N. Srinivasan. 1984. "DUP Activities and Economic Theory." In D. C. Colander, ed., *Neo-classical Political Economy.* Cambridge: Ballinger.

Bhalla, S. 1989. "Indian Exports, Imports and Exchange Rates: A Comparative Quantitative Analysis." (processed).

General Agreement on Tariffs and Trade (GATT). *International Trade.* Vol. 2. Geneva: GATT.

India. 1986. *Economic Survey 1985–86.* New Delhi: Government Printing Press.

_____. 1988. *Import and Export Policy.* Vol. 1. New Delhi: Government Printing Press.

Meier, Gerald M., ed. 1991. *Politics and Policy Making in Developing Countries.* San Francisco: ICS Press for the International Center for Economic Growth.

Nehru, Jawaharlal. 1946. *The Discovery of India.* New York: John Day Company.

Planning Commission. 1951. *The First Five Year Plan.* New Delhi: Government Printing Office.

Rao, Narahari. 1985. "Exchange Rate and Commercial Policy in a Controlled Trade Regime: A Case Study of India." Ph.D. dissertation, Oxford University.

Srinivasan, T. N. 1992. "Planning and Foreign Trade Reconsidered." In Subroto Roy and William E. James, eds., *Foundations of India's Political Economy.* New Delhi: Sage Publications.

Trela, I., and J. Whalley. 1989. "Unraveling the Threads of the MFA." Centre for the Study of International Economic Relations, University of Western Ontario, London, Ontario. Processed.

United Nations Development Programme. 1992. *Human Development Report 1992.* New York: Oxford University Press.

World Bank. 1991. *World Development Report 1991.* New York: Oxford University Press.

6

Economic Liberalization
and Future Prospects

T. N. Srinivasan

Earlier chapters evaluated India and China's broad development strategies, their specific policies with respect to agriculture and foreign trade, and their achievements and failures. It was argued that although both economies succeeded in building a diversified industrial structure, few of the industries could be deemed internationally competitive in cost or product quality. Both economies apparently experienced comparable, but modest, aggregate growth if the World Bank's income estimates for the early 1950s and late 1980s are to be believed, although the similarity of performance in the aggregate conceals substantial differences in sectoral performance. China's achievements in social sectors and in the growth of the manufacturing sector surpassed India's by a significant margin. Whatever their achievements and failures, it was becoming increasingly evident in both economies that their heavy-industry-oriented import-substituting industrialization strategy, pursued for more than three decades since the early 1950s, was unsustainable, and that a shift toward economic liberalization was essential if rapid improvements in their standards of living were to be achieved. China initiated economic reforms in 1978. India began a set of piecemeal

I have drawn on T. N. Srinivasan, "Indian Economic Reforms: Background, Rationale and Next Steps" (Yale University, 1993) in discussing Indian economic reform in this chapter.

reforms in the 1980s and was forced into a more comprehensive and far-reaching set of reforms following a major balance of payments crisis in 1991. This chapter compares and evaluates the future prospects of economic liberalization in the two economies.

THE STATUS OF ECONOMIC LIBERALIZATION

After the fall from power of the Gang of Four and the ascendancy of Deng Xiaoping as the paramount leader, China embarked on a program of economic liberalization in 1978. In India, although the late Prime Minister Indira Gandhi initiated piecemeal reforms in the 1980s, comprehensive reforms were introduced only in July 1991 by the newly elected Prime Minister Narasimha Rao. The origins, style, and content of economic reforms in China and India are quite different (Rosen 1992). Unlike other socialist economies, and unlike India to a significant extent, China was not forced to undertake reforms by any economic, political, or social crisis. Rather, China's leaders realized that in spite of significant achievements in the prereform era, such as elimination of mass poverty and substantial gains in the health, education, and quality of life of the people, the heavy industry-oriented development strategy was becoming increasingly costly in terms of personal consumption and they would therefore have difficulty sustaining the strategy indefinitely. Even though the post-Mao leaders have not abandoned the ideology of socialism and the supremacy of the Communist party, they realized that the Great Leap Forward and the Cultural Revolution were disastrously expensive, both economically and socially. By avoiding such adventurism and radically reforming the economy to allow material incentives rather than ideology to motivate workers, they hoped to modernize the economy and set it along a path of rapid and efficient growth.

In its highly adulatory, if not altogether uncritical, evaluation of the Chinese reforms, the World Bank (1992) correctly draws attention to the massive physical investment of the prereform period and makes the plausible point that the incentive (or more precisely, the disincentive) structure of that period prevented efficient use of the investment. With that investment in place, and the reforms providing the appropriate incentives, output increased rapidly. There is some evidence, particularly from the rapid spread of the household responsibility system in agriculture from Anhui province to the rest of the country, that the central authorities, far from being initiators and leaders, had to accept reforms that originated at lower levels. The World Bank also points out that "in almost all areas of reform, implementation has been spread over time, often several years, and usually after experimentation. Typically, such experiments take place in designated 'reform areas,' and after the results of trials are observed, they then spread to other parts of the country" (World Bank 1992: 37). But whether the authorities deliberately used the vastness of China and the inadequacy of its transport and telecommunications system to conduct a vast number of "independent" trials as the World Bank report implies is debatable. For example, the World Bank claims to have found four consistent themes in the Chinese approach to reform: gradualism, partial reform, decentralization, and self-reinforcement of reforms, that is, reforms in one area create pressure for reforms in another. It asserts that

> the great advantages of (China's) gradual approach . . . are clear: severe shocks are avoided, trials permit mid-course correction, institutional development can occur in line with the new system, and economic agents can adjust slowly to the new conditions. China has thus been able to first bypass and later dismantle its administrative controls at the pace that market mechanisms capable of regulatory functions have emerged (World Bank 1992: 38).

One can argue that the apparent success of Chinese reforms has been due as much to China's being a closed dictatorship as it is to the factors applauded by the World Bank. Chinese leaders did not have to respond to pressure groups that stood to gain or lose from reforms and to a press that was free to be critical, even where criticism was not necessarily warranted. Members of the ruling coalition at the top were thus able to resolve their different views about the direction and pace of reforms by putting into practice each view and letting the performance of the economy determine which was most appropriate. The reforms therefore appeared to proceed in a two-step-forward-one-step-back manner. Further, the dominance of the coalition helped keep the bureaucratic apparatus intact and reasonably efficient while the pro-market ideology of its paramount leader Deng Xiaoping took hold. The authoritarian roots of Chinese success were noted by the former Russian Prime Minister Yegov Gaidar, who is reported to have said that he too would have found China's method of change easier but that it was possible only with a "powerful structure of authoritarian rule" (*New York Times,* October 7, 1992).

By starting with the introduction of the household responsibility system and the abolition of the communes in agriculture, Chinese authorities laid a firm foundation for reforming other sectors. Although agriculture was highly repressed before reform, the organization of production in the communes was not heavily centralized and mechanized as in the Soviet Union. Above all, members of communes were indeed peasants with husbandry skills and not wage laborers of giant mechanized state farms as in the Soviet Union. And fortunately Mao Zedong's disastrous communication policies (including allowing a major famine to occur between 1959 and 1961) did not kill off as large a share of the peasantry as Stalin's collectivization had done. Once they were given the right incentives, the Chinese peasants quickly and massively responded by increasing output and productivity. Of course lack of effective input and output markets that could replace the state-organized supply of inputs and acquisition of outputs inhibited agricultural reforms in the Soviet Union.

In the nonagricultural sector, the World Bank (1992) suggests that the Chinese emphasized marketization—that is, letting state-owned enterprises buy and sell an increasing proportion of their inputs and outputs on the "free" market—rather than privatization, presumably because it is politically and economically infeasible to privatize a dominant state sector. Increasing numbers of non-state-owned, township, and village enterprises that compete with state-owned enterprises were also an important element in the Chinese success. The share of state enterprises in the total value of industrial output fell from 78 percent in 1979 to 65.3 percent in 1991. The World Bank, however, might have been too quick to pronounce Chinese success in reorienting its bureaucracy "away from planning goals toward economic performance" and perhaps too trusting, if not naive, in its belief that the "Party . . . saw its political interests geared increasingly to the achievement of economic success" (World Bank 1992: 67).

The Chinese focused on expanding exports without significantly liberalizing imports. Even though the large size of the Chinese (and Indian) markets could in principle allow vigorous domestic competition without import liberalization, in practice, without competition from imports, domestic competition tends to be limited. Be that as it may, the establishment of special economic zones in coastal areas, the provision of incentives such as foreign exchange retention, tax rebates, direct subsidies on planned exports, and above all the effective use of the exchange rate led to the phenomenal growth in exports in the 1980s. Indeed, a parallel foreign exchange market introduced as part of the reforms accounted for about a third of all transactions in 1991. The real effective exchange rate depreciated by as much as 65 percent between 1980 and June 1991 (World Bank 1992: 59).

The World Bank again takes a benign view of China's failure to reform social sectors in suggesting that the reason for this "seems to be twofold: first, by keeping the enterprise-based social safety net in place, it has postponed, or possibly avoided, many potential social problems;

second, China continues to be concerned about growth of large urban areas, so has resisted major labor reforms" (World Bank 1992: 61). The report goes on: "By using the gradual approach, and by not subjecting the state sector to major shocks, China has succeeded in avoiding severe social costs during its transition. The Chinese effort has focused much less on changing old enterprises and more on generating new opportunities" (p. 67). Since the same report recognizes that "China's state-owned enterprises (SOEs) continue to display many characteristics of public enterprises throughout the world, not least in making losses, funded both via the budget, and, in a less open way, through the banking system" (p. 61), a less benign view of China's approach is appropriate. By keeping the SOEs dominant and attempting to make them competitive without liberalizing imports, China simply absorbed the cost of their inefficiencies. This option was not available to other developing countries undertaking reforms while in the midst of a macroeconomic and fiscal crisis. It would seem that China has not really avoided potential social problems but merely postponed them at a resource cost. Whether this cost is more or less than the cost of not postponing is arguable.

The post-1978 reforms appear to have been phenomenally successful. Without necessarily subscribing to the uncritical use of Chinese data as the World Bank (1992) does or accepting the assertion that "several of the studies cited have begun to provide reliable estimates of gains in total factor productivity (TFP) during the reform period, incorporating re-estimates of the value of China's capital stock" (p. 52), it is possible to view the figures of Table 6.1 as generally indicating the success of reforms. According to the World Bank, the productivity gains in the reform era are in stark contrast to an estimated decline in combined agricultural and industrial TFP at an average annual rate of -1.41 percent during the 1957–1965 period and a gain of only 0.62 percent during the 1965–1976 period.

In India there were several attempts to liberalize or reform the system of economic management: in June 1966, again in the final years of the prime ministership of Mrs. Indira Gandhi, and finally during the regime of Rajiv Gandhi. It is fair to say, however, that all of these attempts involved modifying some aspects of the system of bureaucratic and discretionary control over industry and foreign trade and payments without changing the system in a fundamental way. Besides, not all of the liberalized policies and procedures were sustained without reversals. For example, the import liberalization that took place with the June 1966 devaluation of the rupee was reversed within a year. Only the reforms announced since the assumption of power by Prime Minister Narasimha Rao in June 1991 can be viewed as attempts to

TABLE 6.1   ECONOMIC GAINS IN CHINA DURING THE REFORM
                ERA, 1980–1988 (PERCENTAGE GROWTH PER YEAR)

Productivity indicator	1980–1988	1980–1984	1984–1988
State sector			
Growth	8.49	6.77	10.22
TFP growth	2.40	1.80	3.01
Use of materials	4.31	3.72	4.90
Collective sector			
Growth	16.94	14.03	19.86
TFP growth	4.63	3.45	5.86
Use of materials	9.70	8.30	10.85
Agriculture			
Output growth	6.12	7.71	4.13
TFP growth	6.44	9.52	2.60
Land under cultivation	−0.13	−0.38	0.12
Use of fertilizers	6.75	8.20	5.33

Source: World Bank, *China: Reform and the Role of the Plan in the 1990s* (Washington, D.C., 1992), Table 2.3.

make fundamental changes in the system of economic management and, even more important, as a coherent and mutually consistent and reinforcing set of reforms in several areas.

In contrast to the case of China, the Indian reforms of 1991 were forced on the government by an acute crisis brought about by several factors. First was the lax fiscal management of the 1980s financed in part by external borrowing at hard commercial terms. Second was the Gulf War of 1990, which raised the cost of imported crude oil, substantially reduced exports to the Gulf area, and eliminated remittances from Indian workers in the Middle East, besides resulting in expenditures for bringing them home. Third were the political uncertainties associated with an unstable coalition government at the center. The confidence of external creditors (in particular of nonresident Indians who had sizable deposits in Indian banks) had been adversely affected. The rate of inflation rose to double digits. The outflow of deposits of nonresident Indians and the lengthening of the lag between exports and corresponding foreign exchange receipts (and the shortening of the lag between imports and foreign exchange payments) in anticipation of a devaluation resulted in a run on foreign exchange reserves. Even with assistance from multilateral lending agencies and bilateral donors, reserves fell to the equivalent of the cost of two weeks of imports, and the country came close to default on external debt service.

The government in power before June 26, 1991, had attempted to tackle the emerging foreign exchange crisis through a series of draconian measures: a cash margin on imports other than capital goods was imposed at the rate of 50 percent in October 1990, then raised to 133.3 percent in March 1991 and to a whopping 200 percent in April 1991. In May 1991, a 25 percent surcharge was imposed on bank credit for imports. Auxiliary customs duties were raised in December 1990. Although these measures compressed imports drastically at the cost of a fall in industrial production and brought the trade deficit down from US$781 million per month in October–December 1990 to US$172 million per month in April–June 1991, the outflow of deposits of non-resident Indians accelerated from US$59 million per month in October–December 1990 to US$310 million in April–June 1991. As the government's *Economic Survey 1991–92* put it, "By June 1991, the balance of payments crisis had become overwhelmingly a crisis of confidence in the Government's ability to manage the balance of payments. The loss of confidence had itself undermined the Government's capability to deal with the crisis by closing off all recourse to external credit. A default on payments, for the first time in our history, had become a serious possibility in June 1991" (India 1992: 10).

To the credit of the Rao government that came to power on June 21, 1991, although it took immediate policy measures to avoid defaulting on external debt, it recognized the long-term problems with India's economic management that underpinned the development strategy of the previous decades. As already noted, this strategy (and China's strategy in the prereform era) emphasized industrialization based on import substitution across the board and the development of heavy industry. Thus the Rao government's immediate policy measures aimed not only at containing the crisis but also at longer-term structural reform. The stabilization measures included an austerity budget that spelled out fiscal and monetary measures to reduce absorption so as to bring the fiscal deficit down from 9 percent to 6.5 percent of GDP and a devaluation of the rupee by 22 percent. While announcing the continuation of the draconian import compression measures introduced by the previous government until the foreign exchange situation improved, the government made clear its intention to address long-term structural problems through reform of the control mechanisms on foreign trade and private investment, taxation, the financial sector, and public enterprises.

The reforms announced in July 1991 replaced the cash subsidies for exports with a salable right to imports linked to exports called exim scrips. Some quantitative restrictions on imports were relaxed. A new industrial policy opened certain industries to the private sector, eliminated licensing requirements for private domestic and foreign investment in certain industries, and relaxed the restrictions under the

Monopolies and Restrictive Trade Practices Act on expansions, diversifications, mergers, and acquisitions by large firms and industrial houses.

The budget for 1992/93 presented to the Parliament on February 29, 1992, went much farther in reforming the foreign trade and payments system. Exim scrips were abolished. Partial convertibility of the rupee was announced under which exporters were allowed to exchange 60 percent of their foreign exchange earnings at a rate determined in an interbank market. Imports (other than crude oil, edible oil, fertilizers, and government purchases) were to be made at the interbank rate. The maximum import tariff rate was reduced from 150 percent to 110 percent, and quantitative restrictions on imports of most intermediate and capital goods were abolished. The many different categories of import regimes that had existed before were replaced by a single negative list containing a few intermediate and capital goods (that required a license to import and were subject to quantitative restrictions) and consumer goods whose imports were not allowed. All items not on the negative list were freely importable at the market exchange rate. Partial convertibility of the rupee also reduced the variance in, but did not eliminate, the multiple exchange rate system. Full convertibility of the rupee, however, which would have eliminated the distortions of the multiple rates, was announced as an objective to be achieved in the not-too-distant future.

In fact, in his next budget speech of February 27, 1993, the finance minister announced full convertibility of the rupee on the trade account. The number of tariff lines and rates were reduced, and the negative list was pared. Excise taxes on a number of commodities were reduced. During its two years in office, the Rao government announced several policy measures to deregulate the industrial sector. Foreign majority participation in enterprises was no longer precluded. The power sector, which had been a monopoly of the public sector, was opened to private domestic and foreign investors. Regulations on pricing and distribution of steel were lifted. Subsidies on potassic and phosphoric fertilizers were withdrawn. Domestic and foreign investors were invited to invest in the production, refining, and marketing of oil and gas and in certain segments of the coal industry. A National Renewal Fund was established to assist workers who might be laid off during the process of modernizing, restructuring, or closing uncompetitive firms in the public and private sectors. Privately owned and operated airlines were allowed to compete with the publicly owned Indian Airlines in some sectors. The committees appointed by the government to look into the functioning of the financial sector and of the tax system have reported. Some of their recommendations, though not many, have been implemented. Another committee formulated guidelines for the privatization of public enterprises. Only limited progress has been made in privatization.

Unlike in China where the leadership at the top of the dictatorial regime could, in principle, formulate and implement reforms with little or no concern for political opposition from those adversely affected by the reforms, the Indian government has to convince the opposition in Parliament and the press about the need for and the gains from reforms. What is more, the Rao government did not command an absolute majority in Parliament when it came to power in June 1991. After a year in office, it had managed to put together a slender majority with its regional allies through by-election victories and defections from the opposition, only to lose early in 1993 when one of the regional parties withdrew its support. The labor unions in the organized public and private manufacturing sector and in public sector enterprises continue to oppose modernization and restructuring because of their lack of confidence that a reformed economy will generate equally remunerative employment were they to lose their current positions. There are no labor unions in China.

There is another major difference between Chinese and Indian reforms. As noted earlier, in India agricultural land has always been in private hands and the organization of production consisted overwhelmingly of small owner-operated farms. Since Indian agriculture was never communized, it did not have to be decommunized. Further, the Rao government has proposed no significant agricultural reforms. Thus the spectacular growth in output and productivity that China has experienced since 1978 after the household contract responsibility system replaced the disastrous communes has no counterpart in India, where the growth in total factor productivity is more gradual, contributing roughly one quarter of output growth in the pre–green revolution period (1950–1967) and nearly three-quarters in the latter part (1980–1989) of the post–green revolution period (Dholakia and Dholakia 1992). To place China's spectacular post-1978 growth in perspective, however, one should compare India's performance with China's during the pre- and postcommune eras taken together. In such a comparison Chinese performance in agriculture does not appear to be superior to India's. For example, in China production of foodgrains rose from 163 million tons in 1952 to 435 million tons in 1991 (World Bank 1983: Table 6.3; 1992: Table 8.1). In India output of foodgrains was 51 million tons in 1950/51 and 177 million tons in 1992/93 (India 1993: Part II, S-1). The index of all agricultural production in India (with a base of the triennium ending in 1969/70) went from 58.5 in 1950/51 to a provisional value of 195.9 in 1992/93). In China real agricultural output in

1991 was 4.5 times that in 1952 (World Bank 1983: Table 2.3; 1992: Table 1.2b). Chinese data include, however, the output of animal husbandry, brigade enterprises that produce primarily nonagricultural goods and services, and forestry and fishery in agriculture, and the share of all of those activities in total agricultural output increased over time (for example from 16.9 percent in 1952 to 33.1 percent in 1979; World Bank 1983: Table 6.2). After adjusting for these factors, one is likely to find that the growth of the agricultural sector proper over the four decades since 1950 is roughly similar in India and China.

The major thrust of Indian reforms has been in foreign trade and industry. These reforms are too recent, however, to have had any significant impact. Of course the short-run measures to contain the acute foreign exchange crisis were successful in that foreign exchange reserves went up from a low of US$896 million on January 16, 1991, to over US$5.5 billion at the end of March 1992. They fluctuated around this level, subsequently reaching US$5.3 billion at the end of February 1993. This rise was not due to any permanent improvement in the fundamentals of balance of payments but was primarily a reflection of the return of confidence of the nonresident Indians in the Indian economy and support from multilateral donors. Indeed, with the collapse of the Soviet Union and the rupee trade with it, as well as the global recession, Indian exports declined during 1991/92. The import compression also led to a decline in industrial production, and with only a marginal increase in agricultural production, real GDP growth declined to 1.2 percent in 1991/92 compared with 5.6 percent in the previous year. Real GDP is expected to grow by over 4 percent in 1992/93. The inflation rate (in terms of the wholesale price index) in 1991/92 was 13.6 percent, which fortunately then declined (the index in the week ending February 20, 1993, was only 6.7 percent higher than its average during March 1992) (Table 6.2).

FUTURE PROSPECTS

It is one thing to devise a coherent reform package. It is an entirely different thing to convince producers and investors at home and abroad that the government is committed to carrying out the package and that the economic and political costs are manageable. If the government's commitment and ability to manage the short-run costs are not credible, there will be no movement of resources in "new directions." In the Indian economy, where the bureaucracy gains power in large part from its discretionary intervention in the resource allocation processes, it is natural that it would attempt to retain its power by slowing down, if not

TABLE 6.2 KEY ECONOMIC INDICATORS FOR INDIA, 1987/88–1992/93 (PERCENTAGE CHANGE OVER PREVIOUS YEAR)

	1987/88	1988/89	1989/90	1990/91[a]	1991/92[a]	1992/93[a]
Gross national product[b]						
At current prices	13.2	19.4	14.6	16.4	14.9[c]	14.0[d]
At 1980–81 prices	4.1	10.5	5.6	5.2	1.4[c]	4.2[e]
Gross domestic product						
At current prices	13.7	19.0	14.5	16.9	14.8	14.0[d]
At 1980–81 prices[b]	4.3	10.9	5.6	5.2	1.2[c]	4.2[e]
Index of agricultural production	−0.8	21.0	2.1	2.7	−2.8	5.0[d]
Foodgrain production	−2.1	21.0	0.6	3.2	−5.3	5.7[d]
Index of industrial production	7.3	8.7	8.6	8.3	−0.1	3.8[f]
Electricity generated (TWH)	7.7	9.5	10.8	7.8	8.4	4.6[g]
Wholesale price index	10.7	5.7	9.1	12.1	13.6	7.8[h]
Consumer price index for industrial workers	10.9	8.5	6.6	13.6	13.9	8.4[i]
Money supply (M3)	16.0	17.8	19.4	15.1	18.5	11.2[g]
Imports at current prices						
Rupees	10.7	26.9	25.4	22.0	10.8	38.7[g]
U.S. dollars	9.1	13.6	9.1	13.2	−19.4	16.5[g]
Exports at current prices						
Rupees	25.9	29.1	36.8	17.6	35.3	23.1[g]
U.S. dollars	24.1	15.6	19.0	9.1	−1.5	3.4[g]
Foreign currency assets						
Rupees	−4.7	−9.4	−12.4	−24.2	232.2	40.2[j]
U.S. dollars	−5.2	−24.8	−20.3	−33.6	151.8	38.8[j]
Exchange rate (Rs/US$)[k]	1.4	10.5	13.0	7.2	26.7	6.8[l]
Market rate (Rs/US$)[k]						20.3[l]

[a]Provisional.
[b]At factor cost.
[c]Quick estimate.
[d]Anticipated.
[e]Advance estimate.
[f]April–October 1992.
[g]April–December 1992.
[h]End of December 1992.
[i]November 1992.
[j]As of January 31, 1993, for 1992/93 and at the end of March for previous years.
[k]Percentage change indicates the rate of depreciation of the rupee.
[l]April–January 1993.
Source: India, *Economic Survey 1992–93* (New Delhi: Government of India Press, 1993).

sabotaging altogether, the implementation of the reform package announced by its political masters. There are already some disturbing signs that this might be happening.

Krishnaswamy (1992: 1471) points out that there have been "no significant reductions in the number and size of ministries and their staff, the delays, hassles" and adds that "gratifications associated with obtaining 'clearances' from government departments are no different today than they were a year or more ago. Tax laws are yet to be made 'transparent' and refunds from government being quicker. . . . No matter where you go the forms and procedures are unaltered, notwithstanding umpteen pronouncements by ministers." The *New York Times* (August 15, 1992) agrees: "A year after the new policies were announced by Prime Minister P. V. Narasimha Rao, far less has been accomplished than promised, bureaucratic red tape still hamstrings new investment, both foreign and domestic, and not a single one of India's huge, bankrupt state controlled industries has been shut." It reports that China is outpacing India in attracting foreign investment.

Fortunately the finance minister is fully aware of the bureaucratic and procedural problems. In his budget speech on February 27, 1993, he said:

> However, I am constantly told that despite liberalization at the policy level, our procedures in many areas remain archaic and cumbersome. Many of our laws also need a thorough review to bring them in line with the emerging economic environment. The government has therefore decided that a special review group will be constituted in each ministry to make a review of the existing laws and procedures to identify changes needed in the light of the new policies (*India Abroad,* March 5, 1993).

To be fair, four decades of dirigisme are not easily replaced by market-friendly economic management in a year or two. Fortunately, India is not in the same boat as the erstwhile Soviet Union, where more than seven decades of despotic rule destroyed all markets and financial institutions as well as knowledge among potential private producers about how to function in a market economy. India has a large, though protected, private sector that is accustomed to operating in a market economy. Financial institutions exist, though there are doubts about their solvency and the efficiency of their functioning. The legal system, for all its slowness, politicization, and corruption, still provides a framework essential for the functioning of markets. In other words, the basic institutional infrastructure exists and does not have to be created anew. What is needed of course is a vast improvement in the fairness and efficiency of its functioning. In particular, a thorough reform of the financial sector must be instituted forthwith, while ensuring that prudential regulations are not only maintained, but also enforced, so that manipulations on a massive scale such as the recent stock exchange scandal do not occur.[1]

Above all, the credibility of the government's commitment to reforms still must be firmly established. Several actions could enhance credibility. For instance, a phased program to reduce the excessively high tariffs to levels consistent with revenue objectives and the variance in the tariff structure in a period of, say, five years should be announced. By binding the announced tariffs with GATT, the credibility of the announced trade reform could be enhanced considerably. Second, the credibility of the government's capability to manage the short-run adjustment problems would be vastly improved if, first, the labor unions of government servants and employees of public sector enterprises, nationalized banks, and the organized industry in the private sector could be persuaded to shift from seeking protection of their jobs regardless of whether the enterprise is socially unprofitable to adopting a vision of a rapidly growing economy in which employment opportunities are plentiful. With the National Renewal Fund financing both voluntary retirement opportunities for older workers and retraining opportunities for younger workers laid off from enterprises that are to be scaled down, adjustment costs should be manageable as long as productive employment grows more rapidly than in the past. For rural workers, a more efficient version of the existing employment creation programs could serve well. Finally, a better targeted and managed public distribution system would provide a social safety net for the poor.

If the reforms already announced are not reversed and further reforms of the public enterprises and the financial sector are undertaken speedily, if the National Renewal Fund eases exit from unviable industries, and if needed investments in infrastructure are undertaken, it

---

1. The scandal arose from an illegal diversion of funds from foreign and state-owned domestic banks to an apparently booming stock market through collusion between bank officials and brokers. The banks who were required to invest much of their resources in low-yielding government securities and in risky loans at subsidized rates to sectors deemed priority sectors by the government saw an opportunity to make handsome returns by such diversions, although it was illegal. The diversion would have been detected had there been a computerized and efficient recording system for interbank transactions in government securities. Because such transactions were recorded manually with considerable delays, the funds realized from the purchasing bank were used in the stock market (in the period before the recording of the sale and receipt of sale proceeds by the seller) through the broker who arranged the transaction.

TABLE 6.3 EFFECTS OF THREE REFORM SCENARIOS FOR CHINA

	1990	Base reform scenario		Slow reform scenario		Accelerated reform scenario	
		1995	2000	1995	2000	1995	2000
Growth rates (%)							
GDP	5.6	7.5	7.5	5.0	8.2	8.5	8.5
Consumption	2.2	8.2	8.5	1.9	8.2	10.4	9.7
Imports	−12.8	8.8	8.5	0.7	8.2	9.7	9.4
Exports	12.6	7.8	9.4	7.1	7.5	8.1	9.8
Incremental capital-output ratio	7.10	4.80	4.40	9.70	6.10	4.10	3.60
Investment/GDP (%)	36.6	36.0	33.0	38.8	36.6	34.9	30.6
Current account balance/GDP (%)	3.2	−1.0	−1.0	−0.8	−1.5	−0.9	−0.9
Total debt (millions of US$)	52,554	82,221	112,902	80,856	116,323	77,576	99,713
Total debt/GDP (%)	14.2	14.4	11.4	14.0	12.0	13.2	9.4
Total debt service/GDP (%)	10.3	8.6	7.7	8.9	8.3	8.5	7.3

Source: World Bank, *China: Reform and the Role of the Plan in the 1990s* (Washington, D.C., 1992), Tables 6.1, 6.2, and 6.3.

should not take India as long as it took Mexico (a decade) to climb out of the unavoidable adjustment costs and move on to a path of sustainable, rapid, efficient, and equitable growth. Indian farmers, workers, and entrepreneurs will respond as well as their counterparts anywhere in the world given the same incentives. Visveswaraya noted this fact long ago: "No credence should be given to the theory that the Indian people would not be capable of rising to the level of their compeers in progressive countries in production, industry or trade. . . ." (Visveswaraya 1934: 212). But Indian politicians and bureaucrats could still fail them: the former by fanning communal and sectarian conflicts for short-term political gains as the tragic events following the wanton destruction of Babri Masjid on December 6, 1992, have shown, and the latter by sabotaging economic reforms. The donor community, including the World Bank, might once again fail, as it did in 1966, by reneging on commitments to ease the pain of adjustment in the short run through more generous balance of payments support. Since the human costs of conflicts, the economic costs of dirigisme, and the setback to the liberalization of 1966 should be apparent to all, there is no excuse for failure now.

Turning to China, the World Bank (1992) compares the effects of three alternative reform scenarios. The base reform scenario assumes progress on an accelerated schedule compared with the reform plan in China's Eighth Five-Year Plan (1991–1995) and the Ten-Year Development Program. The plan covers six areas: enterprise reform, price reform and market development, macroeconomic management, social sector, external sector, and rural sector. The slow reform scenario assumes slow progress in reforming state-owned enterprises and in building macroeconomic management capability. The accelerated reform scenario ensures a much more aggressive pursuit of reform in these and other areas. Table 6.3 reproduces the World Bank's projections. These projections underlie the World Bank's conclusion that "China's economic prospects are extremely bright if the government continues to pursue a strong program of economic reform and appropriate development policies. Many of the economic problems that China has encountered in recent years are considered to be the consequence of incomplete reforms. . . . These problems can be avoided or minimized in the future if the program of reform is widened and deepened across a broad policy spectrum" (World Bank 1992: xi).

REFERENCES

Dholakia, R., and B. Dholakia. 1992. "Growth of Total Factor Productivity in Indian Agriculture." Working Paper No. 1033. Ahmedabad: Indian Institute of Management.

India. 1992. *Economic Survey, 1991–92, Parts 1 and 2.* New Delhi: Government of India Press.

———. 1993. *Economic Survey, 1992–93.* New Delhi: Government of India Press.

Krishnaswamy, K. S. 1992. "The Economy: Which Direction and What Atmosphere?" *Economic and Political Weekly* 27, no. 28: 1471–72.

Rosen, G. 1992. *Contrasting Styles of Industrial Reforms: China and India in the 1980s.* Chicago: University of Chicago Press.

Srinivasan, T. N. 1993. "Indian Economic Reforms: Background, Rationale and Next Steps." Yale University, processed.

Visveswaraya, Sir M. 1934. *Planned Economy for India.* Bangalore: Bangalore Press.

World Bank. 1983. *China: Socialistic Economic Development.* Vol. 1. Washington, D.C.: World Bank.

———. 1992. *China: Reform and the Role of the Plan in the 1990s.* Washington, D.C.: World Bank.

ABOUT THE CONTRIBUTORS

Justin Yifu Lin is deputy director of the Department of Rural Economy at the Development Research Center of the State Council, China; associate professor of economics at Peking University; adjunct professor at the Australian National University; and visiting associate professor at the University of California, Los Angeles. He has been actively involved in policy research in China and has published widely in Western academic journals on institutions and technology. He has been a consultant to the World Bank and the International Rice Research Institute and an associate editor of *Agricultural Economics.*

T. N. Srinivasan is Samuel C. Park, Jr. Professor of Economics at Yale University. He was a professor, and later research professor, at the Indian Statistical Institute, Delhi (1964–1977). He has taught at numerous universities, including the University of Minnesota, the Massachusetts Institute of Technology, Johns Hopkins University, and Stanford University. In addition, Professor Srinivasan has worked extensively with the World Bank (1977–1980), as a member of the Editorial Board of the *World Bank Economic Review* (1986–1991), and as a short-term consultant. He has published widely in the areas of development economics and international trade. His most recent books include *Agricultural Growth and Redistribution of Income* (coauthor), *Applied General Equilibrium Analysis and Economic Development* (coeditor), *Population, Food, and Rural Development* (coeditor), the *Handbook of Development Economics* (coeditor), and *Rural Poverty in South Asia* (coeditor). Professor Srinivasan is a Fellow of the Econometric Society and the American Academy of Arts and Sciences and holds a Ph.D. in economics from Yale University.

Yun-Wing Sung is currently a reader in economics and codirector of the Hong Kong and Asia Pacific Economies Research Program at the Chinese University of Hong Kong. He is also correspondent editor of *Asia Pacific Economic Literature.* Dr. Sung obtained his B.Soc.Sci. from the University of Hong Kong in 1970 and his Ph.D. in economics from the University of Minnesota in 1979. He was a researcher for the National Development Research Center at the Australian National University, the Asian Productivity Organization, the International

Development Research Centre of Canada, and the Hong Kong Tourist Association. He was a visiting scholar at the University of Chicago in 1985 and at the Harvard-Yenching Institute at Harvard University in 1989/90. His research interests include international trade, economic development, the Hong Kong economy, and the Chinese economy.

Index